The

Lost

Gospel

of the

Earth

Tom Hayden

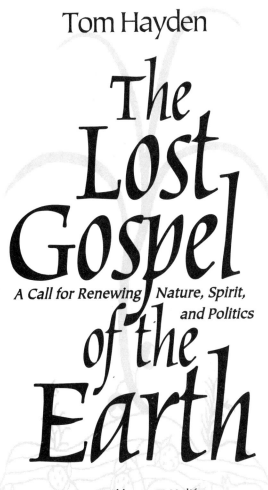

The Lost Gospel of the Earth

A Call for Renewing Nature, Spirit, and Politics

Foreword by Joan Halifax
Introduction by Thomas Berry
Afterword by Rabbi Daniel Swartz

SIERRA CLUB BOOKS
San Francisco

The publisher gratefully acknowledges permission to reprint the following: "On the Pulse of Morning" by Maya Angelou. Copyright © 1993 by Maya Angelou. Reprinted by permission of the author and Random House, Inc. From *Stone, Paper, Knife* by Marge Piercy. Copyright © 1983 by Marge Piercy. Reprinted by permission of Alfred A. Knopf, Inc.

Library of Congress Cataloging-in-Publication Data
Hayden, Tom.
    The lost gospel of the earth : a call for renewing nature, spirit & politics / by Tom Hayden.
        p.   cm.
    ISBN 0-87156-888-8 (cloth : alk. paper)
    1. Spirituality. 2. Nature—Religious aspects. 3. Nature—Religious aspects—Christianity. I. Title.
BL624.H365 1996
291.1′78362—dc20   96-20150
                                                              CIP

Production by Robin Rockey · Jacket design by David Bullen
Book design by David Bullen · Typeset by Wilsted & Taylor
Printed in the United States on acid-free paper
containing a minimum of 50% recovered waste paper,
of which at least 10% of the fiber content is post-consumer waste

10 9 8 7 6 5 4 3 2 1

Contents

Foreword

This is a book by a man whose voice has called to the conscience of the West for more than thirty years. Through the beginnings and endings of wars, institutions, and political careers, his voice is still calling to be heard. Now, at the end of the twentieth century, it is calling us to bring us down to earth: the Earth, a living organism worthy of respect and care, the very source of life.

Tom Hayden's impassioned call is for us to understand where we are in the cosmos. In the millions of galaxies and numberless solar systems that abound in the sky around us, Earth, this blue-green planet, is a gospel, a text of revelation and truth that cannot be ignored. In *The Lost Gospel*, Hayden brings to light the religious origins of an environmental understanding.

Not only does our postmodern society suffer from existential alienation and the habits of contemporary consumption that have created environmental abuses unparalleled in history, but other cultures and religions have turned their back on nature as well. The Garden of Eden (the wilderness, if you will) has been destroyed by need and greed, hatred and ignorance in our time and before.

Where is redemption in this story? Hayden sees it through the practical eyes of a political reformer. He knows you cannot legislate values. Values emerge through the cultural ground of experience. This experience is not in business, politics, or entertainment. It is in the intimacy of what we hesitatingly call the spiritual.

Tom Hayden's book is not simply about an ecology that is based in the spiritual. It is a call for an engagement in the transformative. Engaged spirituality, a way for us to bring our practice into service for others, is a path that is familiar to Westerners. The Judeo-Christian tradition has a long history of altruism. But Hayden is not writing here about a sectarian altruism. He asks us to look honestly and deeply at the suffering caused by consumerism and the desire to dominate. He calls us to a "politics of truth" that is rooted in spiritual integrity and essential democracy. *The Lost Gospel* reminds us to look where the feet are for the gospel truth about this earth and how we can redeem culture, society, and self through the greater self that is this precious planet.

Joan Halifax

Introduction

Tom Hayden belongs among the more fascinating public personalities of these times. An activist, he is intensely engaged in the authentic shaping of late twentieth-century America. He thinks in a comprehensive manner attained by few political personalities of the present. So too as a college professor he gives courses in life-meaning that, in their comprehensive insight and practical wisdom, are probably superior to most of such courses presently available in the academic establishment.

His understanding of the basic religious issues involved in human-earth relations is clearly better than that of many theologians that I am acquainted with. Most important he understands the urgency of rethinking the entire human project within the integral functioning of the planet earth, which he refers to as the lost gospel of the earth. He understands the tragedy of so emphasizing the transcendence of the divine that the earth becomes desacralized, the tragedy also of so emphasizing the spiritual dimension of the human that the earth becomes only a resource base for whatever humans choose to do with the earth. Few writers have stated so clearly that what happens to the earth happens to every being on the earth—including us humans, both individually and in community.

In its every aspect the human is a subsystem of the earth system, which is in turn integral with the great universe itself. We have no interior life, no soul life, no imaginative, emotional, or intellectual life except what is awakened in us from the outer world of nature. So in our community life. We can only understand our human community within the larger community of the earth and of the universe itself. All the basic rituals of human communities from the beginning were ways by which humans fulfill their role within the great celebration, the great liturgy of the universe. The earth, within the universe, is the immediate sacred community whence the human derives its own sacred dimension.

Tom Hayden understands that human societies in their earliest tribal forms as well as in their original urban civilizational forms have consciously shaped themselves within the seasonal renewal of the earth. To preserve the integrity of the planet was their primary concern, even though they did not always understand just how this was to be carried out.

Among the impressive aspects of this text is the weaving of the author's personal story into the narrative of the American continent. This is not an abstract text. It is a lived story. As with us all, the story of the times is our own story. We are supported by the larger cultural context of our lives even while we are threatened by the distortions carried within this cultural context. How to discern the one from the other? That is the genius of our lives. That is the genius of this book.

The author perceives quite clearly the pathos in our human situation at this historical moment. It is a time of foreboding. While we never know the precise form of the unfolding future, we do have some certainty as regards the general pattern of what is happening and the tragic course that the present is taking into the future. Indeed the future already exists in the present. Even now we witness the oceans of petroleum draining away in an ever-accelerating demand. Another fifty years and the oil resources of the planet will be mostly gone, leaving only a toxic residue in the air, the water, and the soil.

Already we witness a disturbance of the chemical balance of the planet worked out over some billions of years. The consequences will fall heavily on the next generations, since at present our food, energy, transportation, clothing, and plastics are all extensively based on chemicals derived from petroleum. This is only one of many referents that could be made to the future. The basic question before our American world is, How did this happen and what can be done to mitigate its threatening aspect? Also how can we assist coming generations into a new creative period?

This situation does not have a single cause or a single remedy. There are, however, some causes that are more basic and more pervasive than others. These have resulted in a deep cultural pathology. The most comprehensive shaping forces of our civilization are involved here. This is not a consequence merely of events or attitudes of these past few centuries. It cannot be explained simply through the empirical-based sciences of the post-Cartesian period or even of the eighteenth-century Enlightenment. Our difficulty goes back to our earliest scriptural and humanist traditions. For this situation did not arise out of a Buddhist or Hindu or Chinese or Islamic context. This situation arose out of a civilization with a biblical religious and Greek humanist matrix.

That the religious and educational establishments that sustain these traditions should be so unresponsive to the present devastation is evidence of a radical inability to understand just what is happening. Especially difficult for our educational and religious institutions is any realization that, in their lack of integral explanation of their own traditions, they are themselves largely responsible for our present situation.

It's in this context that the work of Tom Hayden needs to be read. He shows a rare insight into the issue with the stunning title: The Lost Gospel of the Earth. The title alone gives evidence that he has both the intellectual competence and the writing skill needed for his subject. He sustains the essential endowment of our Western civilization even while he shows how little insight we now have into the most basic and most valuable part of our traditions. The discernment he shows is one of the primary values of this book. Few of the writers that I have read can critique so deeply without rejecting or present the values of a tradition so well while showing the full extent of its deficiencies. To value without critique or to critique without appreciation is the more usual thing in such situations.

We begin from where we are. Since we are extensively shaped by our scriptural traditions we need to accept the true values that are already there. Then we need to ally these Mediterranean-

and European-derived traditions with the indigenous traditions of this continent. There is a hope and a guidance available out of these sources that can be restored and that can supply, at least in part, that vast psychic energy needed to realign our Western thinking with the well-being of the entire planet.

The most difficult change needed just now is to accept the planet and the universe itself, our Lost Gospel, as the primary revelatory experience guiding us toward our historical destiny. Yet while there is the need to deal with the more spiritual forces brought to our American society from the European world, there is even greater need to think profoundly of the revelatory import of this continent itself, a revelatory communication already articulated by the indigenous peoples of this continent before we arrived here. These earlier peoples had an intimacy with the continent that we have never attained. We brought our sacred traditions with us in a book. We never thought that this continent, its mountains and rivers and deserts, its forests and wildlife, its birds and butterflies, had anything to teach us concerning the deeper meaning of our existence. We never even thought that by coming here we must, by the urgencies of survival, take our place within the already existing society that includes every living being on this continent.

Through native peoples we are able to discover the meaning of what it is to live on this continent. During all these years when they were driven from their lands and taken from their own traditions, the indigenous peoples here have kept their psychic identity, their land relatedness, and their understanding of the mystique of this continent. If we had not lost our original gospel of the earth before we came here, we might have become integral with the peoples and with the land of this continent. But as it was, our cultural traditions without this basic gospel of the land caused us to bring about inestimable ruin, both upon the peoples and the land.

Still, the deeper heritage of the European world was partially available to us through Emerson and Thoreau and Emily Dickinson, through Walt Whitman, John Muir, and Aldo Leopold, all of whom were influenced by the Romantic movement from England, by Wordsworth, Coleridge, and Shelley, writers who gave expression in their writings to the mystical qualities of the natural world. While this seems to have been a passing mood, it is from these sources that the modern ecological traditions in America have evolved. For these traditions, however they were thought of at the time as being somewhat pagan in their structure, were in reality restoring an important segment of the primordial meaning of our lives.

The basic purpose of this book is to insist that no aspect of life, certainly no aspect of the public life of a society, can function effectively outside this deeper world of meaning. In this Tom Hayden aligns his own thought with that expressed by Václav Havel, also by Vice-President Al Gore in his book entitled *Earth in the Balance*. Public life deals with questions of life and death, justice and injustice, war and peace, education of the young, defense of the poor; these are all questions of ultimacy in human life, questions that demand the total energies and total dedication of a citizenry, questions also that are related to the manner in which humans integrate their own existence with the sun and the soil and the great complex of spirit powers in the world around them. Because these have always been sacred concerns, those in charge of governments have been required to take oaths to fulfill their role as something infinitely superior to the role of director of some commercial establishment.

For these past two centuries now among the greatest failures of governments in the Western world has been their inability to protect the life systems of the planet from the rapacious drive of the industrial enterprise. Not only is this a failure of the political establishment, it is also a failure of the religious tradition, for it too has failed to proclaim the gospel of the earth in its full expression. While there has also been a failure of governments to protect the impoverished, this failure to protect the life systems of the planet must bring about a special foreboding, for if the beauty of the land is disfigured, if the fertility of the soil is lost, if the rivers are polluted, if living species begin to disappear, then the integral life of humans is endangered. The human soul begins to shrivel. The imagination becomes either desiccated or distorted. Deep psychic needs are unfulfilled. Violence begins to erupt across the land and all the Machiavellian politics of the centuries can offer no remedy.

Thomas Berry

Thanks

To Thomas Berry, whom I consider the most profound voice of ecological theology, for his advice and encouragement. To Matthew Fox, for his inspiration and support during my time at Holy Names College. To Rabbi Dan Swartz and Rabbi Allan Freehling, for sharing Jewish tradition. To Joanna Macy, Carolyn Merchant, and Charlene Spretnak, for feminist insight. To Joan Halifax, and Stephen Mitchell, for Buddhist understanding. To David Phillips, for first getting me to teach at Santa Monica College. To Peter Kreitler, first Episcopal minister to the environment. To Paul Gorman at the National Religious Partnership for the Environment, for all his assistance.

To all my friends who practice environmentalism of the spirit, from Clayoquot Sound, to the Black Hills, to the battered mountains and watershed of Los Angeles.

To my wonderful staff and colleagues in government who stand for an uncompromising politics of the spirit.

To Barbara Ras, my encouraging editor at Sierra Club Books; Sarah Lazin, my literary agent; Alan Rinzler and David Peattie, for their focus and editing.

To my wife, Barbara, born in a Canadian rainforest, whose ancestors are Sioux, who incarnates the lost gospel in her life.

To Joe David, medicine man.

To Troy and Vanessa, and Jane, too, for what we've been through.

To keepers of Irish spirituality and fire, wherever we are.

Thank you all for what you have given me.

Tom Hayden

Preface

They swim in circles in the holding tank, flashes of silver grace, these creatures whose purpose is to journey thousands of miles to sea before returning to die where they were born. They are 261 Chinook salmon, and they swim in the Steinhart Aquarium in San Francisco. A placard says the aquarium is attempting "to preserve the genetic material of this imperiled salmon. We are only buying time until the Sacramento River improves. Like the condor, the last of this race will disappear in captivity unless we save their habitat."

A world without salmon, whether in California or beyond, would be a diminished world for humans. Not only would thousands of jobs and millions of dollars be lost in California's oldest industry, but the loss of salmon would mean the disappearance of wild rivers and rich forests that salmon depend on for life.

The loss of the salmon in its natural habitat brings the loss of its brilliant genetic development that has allowed it to journey from its freshwater spawning grounds to distant oceans and back. A world without salmon would diminish the human capacity for inspiration, too. Long ago, many native people embraced a gospel of the earth in which the salmon were a sacred symbol. In the Irish tradition from which I descend, the salmon symbolize an intuitive intelligence beyond human understanding. The salmon was the god of wisdom. According to native tradition in British Columbia, dancing was taught by the leaping salmon, and the great canyons of the Frazer River were created for salmon by Coyote. The Yurok people here in California held rituals for the annual return of the salmon to the mingled waters of the Klamath and Trinity rivers, which they believed to be the center of the world.

In the Los Angeles River, now a cement drainage channel, the last salmon were seen in 1910. Now they are disappearing in the great Sacramento River delta of northern California, too. Salmon runs on the Sacramento and San Joaquin rivers once numbered in the millions before the dams came, the forests were slashed, and the erosion made their birthplaces into cemeteries of silt. Once there were seven hundred thousand spring-run Chinook; now less than 1 percent of that number are found in the Sacramento River. In 1969 there were one hundred thousand winter-run Chinook; as of the writing of this book, there has been a 97 percent decline in their population. Commercially the winter-run is extinct, and may soon disappear altogether. The coho salmon of northern California are even closer to extinction's door.

Beyond the borders of California, the salmon are declining at alarming rates on the Pacific and Atlantic coasts. In 1994 a *New York Times* headline declared U.S. FISHING FLEET TRAWLING COAST WATER WITHOUT FISH, and called the salmon decline "catastrophic, threatening to wipe out not only whole industries but culture and communities." In 1995 researchers concluded that wild salmon populations were becoming smaller in more than forty-five of forty-seven runs from California to Japan.

THE THREAT TO salmon is the reflection of a spiritual debate. Often consciously, and always unconsciously, we operate according to spiritual values that define what we consider sacred and what is merely a utilitarian resource until it is gone. Over the centuries, we have been offered three spiritual perspectives toward saving particular species like salmon and the natural world as a whole.

Lords of the Universe. In this view, we have the God-given right to treat salmon as disposable and, if necessary, to exterminate them in order to extract the maximum beneficial use out of nature. The Lords find comfort in an interpretation of the Bible that accords human beings a divine right to dominate and subdue. They have axed the forests and dammed the rivers for power, irrigation, and export, turning what they considered worthless trees, swamps, and deserts into prosperous subdivisions and fields. Their achievements are awesome; the great California Aquaduct can be seen in photos from outer space. They measure achievement by the Gross National Product, which places no value on the loss of species. Salmon can swim elsewhere, the Lords shrug.

Stewards of Nature. These kinder, gentler apostles of growth believe that, by the ingenuity of man, nature can be molded to multiple benefits, rather than be destroyed. For them the salmon are a resource to be caught and managed for sport or commercial purposes. They believe the Sacramento River delta can be dammed to channel enough water for crops, suburbs, and salmon. And when the wild salmon perish, they can simply engineer new ones in hatcheries. Henry David Thoreau argued that in wildness lies the preservation of the world. Stewards do not revere the wild. They turn Thoreau upside down: in engineering, not wildness, lies the preservation of the world. The sacraments of the Stewards are trade-offs and compromise.

But playing God with salmon has not succeeded. Hatchery fish lack the genetic diversity created over millions of years that allowed salmon to thrive. In addition, in the political struggle for resources, the Lords of growth ultimately prevail over the preservers of natural streams and native species. Never mind, the Stewards say, science will find a fix, a technological messiah will come. From salmon hatcheries, to tree farms, to growth hormones for cattle, to fertility experiments on humans, to genetic engineering, the Stewards embrace a divine right to remake nature.

Kinship with Nature. We have seen the devastation wrought by the Lords and the shortcomings of the Stewards' grand plans. It is time for a third alternative, a spiritual sense that the earth's creative processes, which spawned the miracle of salmon, deserve our reverence. A sense that we are kin to salmon.

We have reached a crossroads in our valuation of nature. Fifty years ago, in a speech not untypical for politicians of the time,

California Governor Earl Warren declared that Californians "should not relax" until they "put into operation a statewide program that will put *every drop of water to work*" (italics added). Any water that ran off to the sea, the water that sustained the salmon, was officially considered as "water to waste."

At the same 1945 gathering, there was a lone minister, Reverend Everett Pesonen, who voiced an alternative to the Lords and Stewards, a spirituality that would have been familiar to native people as well as Christians like St. Francis of Assisi.

Reverend Pesonen asked in vain that the assembled officials and engineering bureaucrats listen to "the voice of the salmon." These great fish would be destroyed if the developers saw water only as a "sterile, inanimate liquid," the minister warned. The existence of salmon, he said, showed that water was "a medium in which life occurs" and was therefore sacred. He urged that any planning for water use "must be expanded to include all the life-supporting values of water." This spiritual view was also the life-saving view, at least for salmon and their habitat.

The words of Reverend Pesonen were not heeded. The profane rarely yields to the sacred. But today we must ask, Which of these voices will we heed in the twenty-first century? Will we live in a world without salmon and thousands of other species? What will happen to their beauty, their intelligence? It will be gone. What will happen to their streambeds, their watersheds? Gone. What will inspire us as they did? Nothing again.

I have killed many salmon in my time. I have caught them in many rivers, fought them, bludgeoned them, gutted and mounted them as trophies on my wall. For sport, for pleasure, for dominance. For the assertion of power over wild nature. I was not raised to have spiritual regard for lower orders of life.

I have changed now, and wish that Reverend Pesonen had been my counselor when I was a young boy. I believe there are many people like me, in the midst of deep changes in their personal beliefs about nature and the spirit.

And still the salmon swim in their tank, awaiting our response.

What will we tell our children when they die?

What will we tell God when we pray?

To find answers to these questions, I have written this book.

Tom Hayden

1

Recovering the Lost Gospel

The Search for an Earth-Based Spirituality

No important change in ethics was ever accomplished without an internal change in our intellectual emphasis, loyalties, affections, and convictions.

The proof that conservation has not yet touched these foundations of conduct lies in the fact that philosophy and religion have not yet heard of it.

In our attempt to make conservation easy, we have made it trivial.

ALDO LEOPOLD, *The Land Ethic* (1949)

I N THE GREEK myth of Sisyphus, the hero tries to aid the god of the river, Asopus, whose daughter has been carried away by the patriarchal god of the sky, Zeus. But because he questions Zeus, Sisyphus is condemned to forever roll a stone uphill in Hell.

I have no desire to be an environmental Sisyphus, nor to wish that role on anyone else. But the modern Zeus must be challenged all the same. We have abandoned the rivergod, the sacred spirit of the natural world, for a skygod that is separate from the earth. Our covenant with God has been relocated outside of nature. Until we restore a spiritual covenant with the earth, we will forever roll the environmental stone up a mountain of frustration.

Our mainstream Judeo-Christian tradition has treated nature primarily as a storehouse of raw materials for our benefit, and as a bottomless container for our waste. The human condition is considered the primary focus of morality, while the tortured condition of nature serves only as background. Salvation has been promised to the individual, but not to other life forms on our planet. The Ten Commandments prohibit adultery but not pollution, demand that we honor our parents but not the earth.

The most influential creation myth of Western civilization is the Book of Genesis, in which a hierarchical universe is created with humans given dominion over all other living creatures. This mandate of Genesis can have a greener meaning, but instead it is more commonly understood as a license for humans to use and control the natural world as we see fit. We are miniature lords of the universe and the earth is our personal playground. We continually recycle this "mandate from Heaven" in the most important myths that shape our identity: the creation stories of the universe, of the world, of Western civilization. In each chapter of these stories, from the outer cosmos to our local community, we rediscover the possibilities of Eden, only to spoil them.

But we divide grace from nature and spirit from matter at our peril. When we worship God above, the earth withers from neglect below. We develop a society where everything from human habits to politics and economics exploits the environment with callous indifference. Unless the nature of the State is harmonized with the state of Nature, our greed and ignorance will eventually take us beyond the capacity of the very ecosystems that support human existence.

Preserving the Sacred Life of Earth

This book is an effort to heal the divide between the human spirit and the natural world. It attempts to retrieve and apply an older vision in which the earth is alive, and the sacred is present there too.

But in what sense is the earth alive? Some will object to the notion that the earth is a living organism—a superorganism—a host to a myriad of interconnected life forms. I do not claim that the earth is conscious of itself; it does not think and scheme, envy and lust, love and hate as we do. But the earth as a whole is the birthplace, the subject and object, and burial ground for the *elements* of consciousness. I cannot share the reductionist view that it is merely dead physical matter or a lifeless chemical ball. I believe that since the earth contains the elements of life, the earth is a living form as well. Ironically, this view is considered sentimental and subjective, yet science itself cannot agree on a definition of "life."*

*A recent book on the new biology refers to an academic paper titled "The Meaninglessness of the Terms Life and Living" (Robert Augros and George

As for the sacred presence in the earth, I mean a dimension that is both beyond human understanding and at the same time the source of our understanding. The sacred is the indescribable realm of creation that inspires our awe and reverence. It is what Muir called the "first fountain" of the universe. Respect for the sacred is the opposite of utilitarianism and pragmatism. The sacred precedes human existence, and contains an inherent value apart from human calculation.

As I mean it, the sacred is interchangeable with God. But since God has acquired the image of a bearded gentleman in so many minds, a term like sacred, which evokes no human shape, seems more appropriate, inviting a creative participation in its mystery.

To say that the sacred, or God, is present in the living earth is to say that the miracle of creation includes the earth as well as its human inhabitants. Humans have long sought a fixed address for the divine. Long ago, the sacred was believed to reside in the earth. Then came an era when God and the sacred were pro-

---

Stanciu, *The New Biology*, 19). James Lovelock also notes that the concept of life is not even listed in the *Dictionary of Biology* (Lovelock, *Healing Gaia*, 27). If life is hard to define, must we agree with Jacques Monod that "anything can be reduced to simple, obvious, mechanical interactions. The cell is a machine; the animal is a machine; man is a machine"? (*BBC Interview*, July 1970). I prefer Lovelock's empirical hypothesis that the earth is a living, self-regulating system, containing a flux of matter and energy, able to maintain its state intact in an ever-changing environment (Lovelock, op cit., 29). I would add to Lovelock that the forces of creativity and consciousness that we most deeply associate with life are also locked into the earth's processes and cannot be understood or imagined apart from them. For a lyric expression of this view, see Henry David Thoreau's vision of a "living earth," which begins chapter 2.

jected from earth to a glorious cloud, stranding humanity in a waiting line below. Next, according to Christianity, the divine was reincarnated briefly on earth to redeem the human. Many await a second coming to lift up the faithful from the earth.

I cannot predict the future. But I believe the earth has suffered from the perception that the sacred is no longer resident in its depths. This book prays for a kind of reverse second coming, in which we experience a redemptive return of the sacred to inhabit the earth before it is further abused. We need a sacred presence that is more than an absentee landlord before the whole earth becomes a polluted slum. Only when we believe the sacred is present in the living earth will we revere our world again.

The ancient awe of our sacred environment amounts to a lost gospel of the earth, which existed among indigenous people long before the rise of monotheism. It continues to exist in the myths of my Irish ancestors and the teachings of Native Americans. It was common to the early religions that were based on the Goddess and continue in feminist spirituality today. It was expressed in the nature mysticism of Francis of Assisi, Hildegard of Bingen, and Maimonides. An earth-based spirituality was also central to the birth of environmentalism in the time of Henry David Thoreau and John Muir.

In seeking to preserve these ancient insights, I am not calling for withdrawal from the sensibility or achievements of the whole modern world. But in repressing the past as primitive, the modern world has ushered in a reckless emptiness. We have modernized everything in our path at great moral and ecological expense. The time has come to retrieve the gospel of the earth.

Our return to this simple spiritual insight is crucial to resolving our environmental crisis. Technical fixes are inadequate—the earth is not a machine whose parts simply need occasional replacement or tuning. When our sense of what is sacred excludes the natural world, we diminish our capacity to imagine remedies for what we have done to that world.

A State of Denial

While managing the environment as though it is only machinery needing repair, we sink into a deep denial of the magnitude of the crisis.

Nowhere is this more obvious than the debate over global climactic change. There is no question that carbon dioxide in the earth's atmosphere from burning coal and oil has increased significantly since the industrial revolution, most of the buildup coming since the 1950s. We are playing God; the life-sustaining atmosphere of the earth is being altered by human intervention. We have pumped 6 billion tons of carbon dioxide into the twelve miles of the earth's inner atmosphere, causing an increased risk of melting the polar ice caps, rising sea levels, agricultural disruption, and higher levels of skin cancer and other diseases. Since 1988 many respected scientists have issued warnings; in September 1995, twenty-five hundred experts on the Intergovernmental Panel on Climate Change declared that the cause of global warming was the burning of fossil fuels, and called for a 60 percent reduction in fossil fuel use to prevent a worsening of the trend.

Industry representatives and government officials continue to deny the conclusion of the world's scientists. Paid lobbyists for the oil industry recently spent $1 million in an effort to cast "scientific doubt" on the threat. The fossil fuel industries showed that not even a proven threat to the world's climate could alter their behavior. During the decade that scientists were issuing their warnings, electricity use in the United States went up 22 percent.

Global warming is not the only specter we deny. While our consumption in the West increases, world population has risen in my lifetime from 3 billion to 6 billion people: more than the total growth of human population since the dawn of human history. The earth adds 90 million people yearly, equal to eight new Calcuttas. One out of every five people on earth lives in absolute destitution, and their number will double in the coming generation.

If nothing is done, tropical rainforests will disappear in this same lifetime, and millions of species and subspecies with them. Overgrazing is causing the pasture lands of the earth to shrink; 30 million acres of arable land are eroded and ruined each year. The equivalent of five Mississippi Rivers is diverted from lakes, rivers, and aquifers for multiplying growth projects (water diversions for farms, suburbs, etc.) every year.

We deny the direct effects of these losses on ourselves, most poignantly in the linkages between pollution, high cancer rates, and the spread of infectious diseases. Perhaps the least cost-effective war we have ever fought is the twenty-five-year "war on cancer," which has cost tens of billions of dollars without defeating the "enemy." It is true that progress has been made in the treatment of childhood leukemia. Better medical treatment like advances in surgery and blood transfusion has improved mortality rates, too. But when medical journals like *Lancet* and the *American Journal of Industrial Medicine* report an increased incidence of most cancers over the past thirty years, and so little is being done, the first symptom of illness we have to treat is denial itself.

If anything should get the attention of patriarchal politicians and corporate executives, it would be the decline of their own sperm count. Two years ago, I attended a U.S. congressional hearing on evidence of male infertility caused by exposure to certain chemical compounds. The combined evidence of sixty-one studies from around the world showed almost a 50 percent drop in sperm counts. Many scientists believe that this fertility crisis is related to chemicals that are disrupting the reproductive system. The hearing began slowly in an atmosphere of skepticism and disinterest. But when one public health expert testified bluntly that "this means you are not half the man your grandfather was," there was a perceptible awakening on the congressional panel. Instead of taking the evidence seriously, however, they poked at whether it was completely certain. When the scientific witnesses candidly acknowledged their lack of absoluteness, the politicians relaxed into proposing "more studies," the same path of delay and denial promoted by chemical and tobacco companies for years.

WHAT IS THE cause of so much procrastination, this indifference to evidence of preventable planetary and human crisis? Part of the answer is the power of vested interests to lobby for the status quo. There is also a blindness that comes from ideology; in the words of one group of pro-growth scientific researchers, "markets ceaselessly encourage the development of more efficient resource uses, making the limited supply of any physical commodity ultimately irrelevant." But there is also the human tendency to resist bad news and displace the blame toward a scapegoat. Even such admired thinkers as Susan Sontag (who has battled cancer) and Dr. Lewis Thomas (former president of Sloan Kettering Cancer Center) have denounced as "paranoid" the view that cancer has roots in the workplace or petrochemical causes. The belief runs strong that a scientific cure for cancer will be discovered. Dollars spent on research and treatment far exceed any budgets for prevention and public health. As cancer strikes more people, the constituency for treatment and cures grows in scale, reducing the priority on prevention still further. The war on cancer continues virtually without popular opposition, whereas any other $20 billion, thirty-year stalemate against a foreign enemy would be reassessed.

At the deepest level, this denial seems rooted in a faith that there must be a technological fix for everything. We think that if we have polluted our bodies and the earth through the rise of an industrial society dependent on petrochemicals, we can find a cure using the same tools. The leading treatment for cancer is chemotherapy (and/or radiation).

Instead of a strategy of public health and wellness aimed at preventing the environmental causes of cancer, employing chemotherapy as a last resort, the priorities are reversed; attacking cancer with cancer-causing agents is the top priority and prevention or a healthier relationship with nature is neglected. This arises from a belief that the technologies of modern medicine can shield us from a natural world where disease and death would prevail. Our empathy has been transferred from nature to anti-nature: technology.

The alternative to this ongoing denial is not the wholesale rejection of science and technology, nor the refusal of chemotherapy for those it may help, but a new set of priorities. Instead of treating the environment as storehouse and toxic dumping ground, we need to restore an empathy for the natural world and its processes. In the case of global warming, for example, we have ejected massive amounts of carbon dioxide and greenhouse gases into the atmosphere without regard for the effects on the earth and, ultimately, ourselves. An empathy for the earth would prevent us from acting in this reckless manner and serve as a protective, early-warning system for our own health as well.

There are instances where this profound empathy is beginning to emerge. I found particularly moving the case of a scientist at the sight of a melting polar ice cap caused by warming seas, as described in a 1995 headline:

SCIENTIST WEEPS AS ANTARCTIC ICE SHELF DRIPS AWAY

"The first thing I did was cry," said the Argentine scientist upon seeing the cracking, the first time the continental ice cap had been exposed for twenty thousand years. Reading this report, I saw a double image: tears of the human falling on tears of the ice. I felt the scientist having sentiment for the ancient ice shelf itself. There has been enough academic research and debate about global warming, I think, but not enough tears. When enough scientists weep, we may awaken to the evidence that our souls have been frozen.

CONNECTING TO THE NATURE WITHIN US

The only way to avert the catastrophe of neglect is through an evolutionary leap in the way we see and feel our context. We need to experience nature and the universe *within* ourselves, not as external scenery we view outside the window of real life. In religious terms, we need to be "born again" in nature. We were baptized after our first birth into a special religious sphere that promised eternal life beyond natural boundaries. Now we need a rebirth, a connection to the nature we lost in that baptism.

It took many generations to develop a universal ethical standard for the treatment of all human beings as inherently deserving respect because all are made by the same Creator. We violate that standard routinely, but it is nonetheless an ethical organizing principle of great importance. The next step is to extend the experience of a common Creator to the natural world, and build a system of ethics, economics, and politics accordingly.

We need to see and feel ourselves in nature, not in a privileged and separate sanctuary called society. As the ecologist Aldo Leopold wrote in 1949, ethics are not simply theoretical: they involve the "loyalties, affections, and convictions" that are the very foundations of conduct. The creation of a new "land ethic" could not occur, he felt, unless the ecological issue took on a religious and philosophical character. That time has come.

The Purpose of This Book

This book begins with a personal description of what I call the *Divide*, the process by which we divide ourselves from the rest of nature. This Divide rationalizes our denial and is perpetuated by psychiatry, education, and the media. I then go on to address the *Default*, the role of organized religion in perpetuating this hierarchical schism between human beings and nature. I turn next to the *lost gospel traditions* in Christianity, Judaism, native spirituality, Buddhism, and American environmentalism. These are indigenous traditions whose voices have been oppressed, marginalized, and erased in the long process of conquest, industrialism, and modernization.

The question the book ultimately addresses is how to carry out a spiritually grounded transformation of our political culture and institutions today. Finally what I believe is needed is the kind of passionate engagement in the environmental cause that the clergy of America gave to civil rights in the 1960s, or that priests in Latin America invested in liberation theology on behalf of the poor.

Unfortunately, what we are seeing today instead is the Religious Right vigorously condemning environmentalists as pagans while defending the property rights of polluters as somehow protected by the mandates of Genesis. Meanwhile the mainstream religious institutions have been largely silent and little engaged in the environmental debate of the past twenty-five years. The religious community has not defined the actions of corporate and government polluters as a mortal sin against God's creation, nor have the clerics defended the earth as sacred in the way they have vigorously defended the poor and victims of discrimination as God's children. Religious institutions are the source of guidance and teaching on questions of morality and justice, and their relative silence on the fate of the earth robs the environmental movement of the moral legitimacy it needs to change our behavior. There is hope that the religious default is beginning to end, a change that this book is meant to encourage.

Out of Despair

I am neither a theologian nor a religious scholar. But as an environmentalist for twenty-five years, and as a senator who has chaired the Natural Resources and Wildlife Committee in the California Senate, I am convinced that we cannot resolve the environmental crisis without rediscovering its lost spiritual significance.

The idea of this book first arose in 1990 from a despair I felt on the twentieth anniversary of Earth Day. I concluded (and still believe) that the planet's condition was worsening at a more rapid speed than the rate of the progress we were achieving. Like Aldo Leopold warned in 1949, we were only willing to accept those environmental reforms that could fit comfortably with our existing cultural, political, and economic assumptions.

I began a quest to understand the religious and cultural origins of our environmental attitudes. Profound social change, like the American Revolution or the civil rights movement, always begins within consciousness, in what sociologist Robert Bellah has called the "habits of the heart." When enough people feel they are all creatures of the same maker, the spirit of compassion and equality proves more powerful than greed or domination. Only when enough people awaken to a deep spiritual connection with nature will environmentalism become a global ethic. With a new "habit of the heart," institutional change will follow. Without such a heartfelt shift, partisans of the environmental movement will continue to feel like Sisyphus.

While piecemeal reform is helpful in the short run, such pragmatic politics are not enough to hasten the change that is necessary. But spiritual withdrawal from the temporal world of politics and action is not the answer either. I decided to be as engaged spiritually as I was politically. I taught college classes on ecology and religion by night, while serving as the chairman of the California Senate's Natural Resources Committee by day. I have tried to align spirituality and ecology in a new approach to politics. In my first decade in Sacramento policy debates, for example, no clergy had ever testified in support of environmental bills, not even when endangered species were at stake. In 1995 we formed a network called Clergy for All Creation, whose members began testifying to the spiritual significance of preserving the web of life.

During the same five years, I began to notice a modest awakening to the silent pathos of the earth in many of our faith traditions, along with a new interest in bringing a spiritual perspective to politics. For example, America's major religious groups have created a formal National Partnership on Religion and the Environment. They are united around an interpretation of the Genesis mandate as "stewardship," a responsibility to "till and tend" the Garden, rather than an anti-environmental license to subdue and pollute. Meanwhile, as this manuscript neared completion, the foremost liberation theologian of Latin America, Father Leonardo Boff of Brazil, issued a ground-breaking work, *Ecology and Liberation,* which proposed a theology defending the natural world as sacred. He calls for recognition of a new cosmology, in which "the human race is part of nature and the biosphere, not the center of the universe." Boff defends mysticism as the "secret motor of all commitment, . . . the interior fire arousing the individual in spite of the monotony of everyday tasks." These are very important departures from a tradition that has placed the human above nature, and which has expected believers to be inspired by the dogma of the hierarchy. Where Boff's liberation theology founds its "church" in the slums of the poor, its extension to nature will rediscover the cathedrals of the forests as well. The role of human beings, he writes, should be to serve as "guardian angels" of nature.

For the past several years, however, America has been in retreat even from its modest twenty-five-year commitment to better manage the environment. A backlash has been underway in the name of God; one that asserts the absolute rights of human beings to help themselves to nature's bounty. As the backlash proceeds, as more of our forests and wetlands disappear, as more of our rivers and estuaries are degraded, as more of our cities are congested and polluted, I envision an even stronger environmental outcry arising once again.

This next wave of environmentalism must include a passionate, spiritual alternative. Just as we humans are not expendable parts of a machine to be used and thrown away, neither are forests, soils, and rivers. In every political and economic act, we must treat the earth as an organic whole, recognizing and appreciating the interdependent diversity of people and nature.

We need a new gospel (or Torah) of the earth to make our religious traditions relevant to the environmental crisis, and to provide the philosophical and spiritual basis for the evolutionary leap we must make for our quality of life to survive.

2

Overcoming
the Divide
of Soul
from Nature

The earth is not a mere fragment of dead history, stratum upon stratum like the leaves of a book, to be studied by geologists and antiquarians chiefly, but living poetry like the leaves of a tree, which precede flowers and fruit—not a fossil earth, but a living earth.

HENRY DAVID THOREAU

I T H A S T A K E N me many years to learn the simple feeling of *being* nature, not a being separate from it. When I ask myself why this is, I am confronted with an unavoidable sensation of my conditioned separateness. I still experience the world everyday as an entity outside myself. My ego and mind seem to work overtime to keep it that way.

Daily life in our society today seems to require and promote being a Self. In politics, for example, I run for office as an individual, a task which requires projecting the Self and its various accomplishments in exaggerated ways. On a more basic level, I feel my physical and emotional Self as an autonomous entity. By contrast, it is difficult to feel aware of being in the universe. For many years I was never aware at all. In pursuing what I thought to be life, I forgot air, water, earth, and fire. I lived across the Divide from nature. Most of us do.

Air

For nearly all of my life, I was unconscious of the act of breathing, though I could not have lived five minutes without it. Achievement-oriented and racing along, I often felt out of breath, because of expending energy outwardly toward society. Consequently I thought of breathing air as the equivalent of pumping gas into my personal tank.

Even during several years when I studied the martial arts, my attitude was that the karate master's concentration on breathing was in preparation to explode outwardly. I never had time for meditation or, as Zen masters described it, "watching over the breath." I tended to assume that those who needed meditation were simply less capable of dealing with stress than I was.

To be honest, I am usually this way today. However, in recent years I have begun to achieve an inkling of wonder at breathing. We do not choose to breathe. Both its beginning and end are involuntary. We breathe until one day our breathing ends. These two moments mark the boundaries of our life as human beings, a time in which breath is our constant and dependable companion.

In the Bible, breath (in Hebrew) is *ruah,* which also means spirit and wind, and *neshama* means the soul-breath. In Greek, the same forces are meant in *pnevma.* In Chinese culture, *ch'i* means breath, air, life force, energy. In the native language of the Inuit people, "to breathe" also means "to make poetry."

We are all breathing the same air our ancestors did, the same air as those with whom we think we share nothing in common. We breathe through nature. The air we breathe is generated and maintained by trillions of active organisms, from bacteria and termites to flowers and redwoods. I breathe in oxygen and breathe out carbon dioxide; the trees in my yard give oxygen to us and receive the carbon dioxide. How long it has taken me to understand that I breathe in relationship with these trees!

Ours is the only planet in the known universe where breathing takes place. We all breathe individually, but there is only one breathing process going on. When I look at NASA photos of the thin cradle of atmosphere around the planet earth, I am seeing the breath of life.

When we pollute the air that is seemingly above us we poison the breath that is really inside us.

Water

I never paid much attention to water. It was there on demand, in the tap, when I wanted it. I dismissed as medical overkill the doctor's advice to drink twelve glasses of water each day. Instead

I drove my body to dizzying thirst, only then reaching for my water.

When I was a student, no one taught me that we are mostly water. When I first learned that we all once floated around as embryonic selves in the sea of our mothers' wombs, complete with traces of gills and fins, I took it simply as physical evidence of evolution. I did not receive this information as a revelation of the sacred gift of nature. I believed water, like air, was a resource to pump into myself when needed. So was gum, or pizza.

My kinship with water started from years of fishing. From Michigan lakes to Alaskan rivers to Australian barrier reefs, I killed hundreds of fish for sport, challenge, and conquest, without remorse. I dominated those fish with my boats and rods, my waders and lures, especially with treble-hooks. Sometimes I threw them back alive. But usually when I brought them to the boat, I killed them with a sharp blow to the head, often with a club. I frequently photographed my catch, and sometimes mounted them as trophies.

But there came a time when I couldn't do more than catch-and-release, if I fished at all. I had looked into the eyes of too many fish and experienced *feelings* there: fear, bravery, and the pathos of mothers laden with eggs.

I couldn't stop returning to the water, however. Through fishing, I had learned that water was more than a barrier between myself above and fish below. Water was an environment that supported life, and had a life and integrity of its own. I learned that I was in a relationship with this water and the fish it harbored and sustained.

In years of silent contemplation of lakes and streams, I became able to sense instinctively where the fish were and when they would rise. The water and the fish no longer were objects below me. They were a subjective presence in the moving depths, amidst the rock-laden bottom, the submerged forests, the layers of light and dark, warmth and cold. I was entranced by the water that embraced me when I waded streams.

One day I even felt the water inside me while being in the water outside me. The stream ran through me; I was buoyed by water within my body that swelled to join the river through the porous boundary of myself.

Like the breath of air, the water around us is the only such water in the known universe. Hundreds of millions of years have produced this gift to life. Nearly all water is seawater; about 3 percent is locked away in icecaps or in aquifers below us.

Fortunately, more water returns to the land as rain than is lost in evaporation. Most of that flows away. The natural process leaves us only a trickle that is available for human life. Without this trickle transferred from the oceans to the sky and back to the land, life on the continents never would have evolved. Water is a miracle.

Let me return to the experience of baptism. Many of our religious traditions baptize us in water, but the lesson of nature has been lost. The baptism ritual arose from a recognition that we floated in water at the time of our birth. Baptism meant a second birth, a birth in God's kingdom. The problem in this division of natural life from eternal life is the absence of thankfulness for the miracle of water, and the transfer of our thankful eyes to heaven. But as Rachel Carson has written, the sea carries us through an eternal cycle too: "For all at last return to the sea . . . [it is] the beginning and the end."

Soil

I grew up like the character in Marge Piercy's poem "The Common Living Dirt," who says:

> we have contempt for what we spring from.
> Dirt, we say, you're dirt
> as if we were not all your children.
> we have lost the simplest gratitude.

All flesh is grass, wrote Isaiah. But growing up, I took the biblical notion of arising from dust as only metaphor. The notion that we return to dust after death, however, tortured my curiosity at an early age. It was horrifying to imagine one's flesh slowly disintegrating, being devoured by worms. As a boy I asked a lot of questions about coffins. Would a metal casket protect your body from sinking into the land of the flesh-sucking worms? No one could give me assurances.

Yet those same worms gave hints of liveliness in the soil. Catching night crawlers in the dark dampness held fascination. While I didn't want them sucking on my corpse, and though I intended to put fish hooks mercilessly through their wriggling bodies, it entered my mind that they enjoyed a life of sorts in the Midwestern soil. They could do things we couldn't, like split in half and still stay alive.

I also knew that our food came from the soil, not just the supermarket. At supper prayers I heard "the good earth" spoken of for the first time. We thanked God for this food, as if He had designed it for us.

If we returned to the earth after death, I wondered, where did we come from? Not the earth certainly. I imagined the sexual act of my parents that conceived me as having happened *above* the earth, in a bed on the second floor of our house.

Through my experience with lakes and forests I began to change to a view of the body as earth. The streambeds, I knew, were surfaces of life. They spoke to me, as did the great mountains and towering trees that cycled and used the waters around me. From streams and forests and mountains I felt excitement, beauty, inspiration. Where did these feelings come from? I first assumed that such feelings arose inside myself, from a chamber somewhere in my heart or mind. On thinking about it, however, I came to realize that my imagination and feelings were aroused not by self-generation alone, but because the earth was somehow communicating with me. The soil—the earth as a whole—had presence.

The earth has its own myriad energies, colors, movements, and sounds, each with a unique subjectivity. When we say we are moved by the earth's beauty, it does not only mean that we have a relationship with the earth inside the boundaries of our heads. We are dreaming in reaction to the earth's presentation of itself. We are not photographing the earth with our minds. We are in communion.

With study, I came to appreciate soil, as Aldo Leopold once wrote of it:

> It is a fountain of energy flowing through a circuit . . . food chains are the living channels which conduct energy upward; death and decay return it to the soil.

Leopold's argument persuaded Justice William O. Douglas that trees should have legal standing. In his dissenting opinion in *Sierra Club v. Morton,* Douglas cited Leopold and wrote that "a teaspoon of *living earth* contains a million bacteria, 20 million fungi, 1 million protozoa, and 200,000 algae . . . a stupendous reservoir of genetic materials that have evolved continuously since the dawn of the earth" (italics added).

I felt the soil to be life related to my own life, a "common elementary fund" as Muir named it. I began to experience myself not only as a specific individual, but as part of the surface of the spinning earth. The injunction "from dust to dust" started to convey a basic truth.

What we call dirt or dust comes from the universe originally, binding itself to become the surface of the planet. A cubic centimeter of earth can contain billions of tiny organisms creating photosynthesis at the surface, busily fixing nitrogen in roots, and all the while burying the carbon that allows oxygen in the air. Billions of years ago the same carbon that is in our bodies today exploded from a supernova, became the stuff of stars, and helped give rise to this planet.

The gift of soil is not given to us by an external Creator. It has been prepared over billions of years by the tiniest of beings. Single-celled bacteria eventually formed plants through photosynthesis; chloroplasts in the cells of plants created oxygen and organic material; dancing mitochondria in our own cells today turn those same elements into energy necessary for human life; and long after we die, our age will be measured in the gravestone of carbon that remains.

Each inch of the good earth takes ten thousand years to evolve. The surface difference between the earth and the moon is about thirteen inches of topsoil. Like water and air, there is no other soil like ours, nor any other life like ours, in all the Milky Way.

Fire and Light

The sun had lost its cosmic meaning to the suburban culture where I grew up. We took light for granted. There was no more awe about the sun's rising for me than there was in flipping on the light switch in my room every morning. Modern electrical systems had long ago broken our dependency on the cycles of light and dark. The sun seemed like an unreliable electric utility. The power companies finally had given us the possibility of a permanent sun, the banishment of a darkness in which humans had lived for millions of years. I complained about the sun as if it was an undependable servant. I wanted the sun to shine so that I could play baseball. I wanted the sun to tan my skin. I wanted the sun to stop the rains.

I was a student of literature and journalism, not of physics or astronomy. The nature of the sun, the source of its fire, its chemical composition, the traveling of light, impressed me little, at least in the mechanical way it was taught in the schools. The sense given to me by books was that the sun was nothing more than a big furnace, a useful appliance in a cold universe.

The civilization of materialism, of cars and malls, created an eclipse of the sun. The sun became background for a neon world. In time, however, I was affected by the majesty of the sun rising and setting, a sight so overwhelming that I couldn't ignore its power. No cosmic or religious story interpreted this experience for me, but my deeper senses, my imagination, my sensuality, were aroused by the dawn's first light and the blood-red, expiring moment of sundown.

The light of the stars touched me, too. I began to feel the earth moving on its celestial path, the stars like lights of distant cities. One night looking at the stars the thought arose that I was "in heaven," that there was no above and no below, just patterns of light.

The mechanical view of the universe as taught in school diminished my ability to feel the miracle of light. We were asked to choose between two stories: either that a distant God created light through an announcement ("Let there be Light"); or that light began with a massive and accidental explosion called the "Big Bang." In both stories, light is reduced to a kind of background medium in which more important events, like the growth of civilization, could take place.

When I visited Newgrange on the Boyne River in Ireland, perhaps the most ancient site of human life still standing, I understood that humans, prior to this century, experienced and related to the sun's light in a radically different way from how we do now. These Irish sites and those of the Mayans, the Olmecs, the Navaho, and Sioux, were always oriented exactly to the patterns of the sun. They were the pathways of God, the map of the heavens, the guide to the seasons, the way of planting and harvesting.

At Newgrange, carefully constructed of huge rock slabs several thousand years ago, a small aperture was set above the entrance to the main chamber. Precisely at the dawn of winter solstice, the sun's first rays pierced the hole and illuminated the circular interior, lighting ancient drawings on the back wall, bringing warmth to the cold floor of earth. For me, such amazing sites prove that our ancestors, whatever their many deprivations, genuinely lived in the universe with a sense of cosmology that we have been denied.

The revelations of modern science, if we think of them as a vision and not dull formulas, could be just as overwhelming. A first fire ignited the cosmos and gave off light. That same light is expanding today, carried within inscrutable energy units called photons. The fire continues in the center of our earth, and starstuff is in our own beings. Like air, water, and soil, we need light for life itself, for our well-being, not only in a physical sense but in a spiritual one. As Thomas Berry and Brian Swimme note, while we ponder the Milky Way, we are also a dimension of the Milky Way pondering its own nature. What could be a more powerful sign that each of us is a participant in an ongoing creation?

Close Encounters with the Universe

In addition to gradually realizing that we are intimately connected to the miraculous elements of air, earth, water, and fire, I also have experienced what might be called close encounters with the universe—unexplainable moments when a barrier falls and a deep connection is revealed. Such encounters transform nature from a perceived object to an experienced subject. Something in nature "communicates" with us.

In Martin Buber's classic *I and Thou*, the philosopher considered whether there can be an I-Thou relationship with a tree, or whether the experience of dissolving a subject-object split into a relatedness was available only to humans. Buber wrote, "I have no experience" communing with a tree, but he offered a brief conclusion (italics added):

> It *can* come about, if I have both *will and grace*, that in considering the tree I become bound up in relation to it. The tree was now no longer "it."

What Buber found possible with a tree, through "will and grace," I have found true many times in encounters with nature. In such experiences lies the possibility of overcoming our separation and alienation from the universe that dictates so much of our behavior—our dread of death, our embrace of other-worldly religion.

I hope that two examples from my own experience may clarify what this "close encounter" with nature is all about.

ANCIENT CONSCIOUSNESS
IN THE WILDERNESS

In August 1993 my son and I were sleeping in a small tent just above the Arctic Circle, within the Alaskan National Wildlife Refuge. It is a place that humans seldom visit, and never stay—home to vast caribou herds and a target of oil industry lust. Quite by chance, U.S. Interior Secretary Bruce Babbitt was camping overnight with a party of officials and reporters in an old shelter a half-mile across the cold tundra from us.

At dawn something woke me, a presence. I crawled out of the sleeping bag onto a tundra dusted with light snow. Neither my eyes nor my mind could focus until I felt the presence again. There was no noise, no motion. But a 600-pound musk ox was standing before me.

A solitary bull, he seemed to wait until I was fully awake. Then he took a small agile step, stopped again, and started meandering along a glacier-fed stream bed, in a path straight toward the sleeping Secretary of the Interior. I pulled on my parka and started off after him. The animal was exploring the possibilities of the plateau for his herd. Or was he going to introduce himself to Babbitt? The secretary, after all, was investigating whether this place should be opened for oil drilling.

Musk ox look like a buffalo with the curled horns of a mountain sheep. A male can weigh up to 650 pounds and stand about six feet tall. The Eskimos call them *oomingmaq*, or "animal with skin like a beard." Their brown bodies are covered by a skirt of hair up to twenty-five inches long. If all the hair on one musk ox was braided in a single strand, the nature writer Barry Lopez says, it might stretch one hundred miles.

The animal is 3 million years old, and probably crossed a land bridge from Asia 125,000 years ago to occupy the modern American Midwest until the northward retreat of the glaciers. Lopez once wrote that the musk ox has a "pose of meditation" and takes the most deliberate step he's ever seen in a large animal.

The musk ox was taking one deliberate step after another toward the Babbitt party. When the musk ox arrived at a rocky point just above the Babbitt cabin, the animal stopped, just as he had by our tent. Then the cabin doors opened and the secretary and associates stepped out in the early morning light to stare at their ancient visitor.

The animal delivered a message, all witnesses later agreed. He did not need to speak. His presence alone communicated that this land was a necessary home for living beings that have evolved over millions of years, and we were no more than his guests.

Then the animal gently went back to his family business. He knew what he was doing. In comparison with his 3 million years' experience, did I?

The Gingrich Republicans are still trying to open the Arctic wilderness to drilling, and Babbitt is fighting them. The secretary apparently got the message.

SACRED PLACES IN THE EARTH

In December 1994 my wife, Barbara, and I rode horses along the green, lazy Macal River in western Belize and slowly climbed a steep trail into shaded jungle in the Vaca mountains, looking for an ancient Mayan cave that had been discovered only a few years before.

Here the term broadleaf jungle took on real meaning as palm fans stretched a hundred feet around us. Below was a steep drop into a green canopied canyon with a thousand-foot waterfall. At the top of the falls, a guide waited to take us still higher to the cave.

Known as Chechem Hah (poison wood river), the cave was discovered by local *chiclero* workers while exploring the dense forest. Inside we felt our way through a damp chamber carved long ago by rivers flowing through the limestone. Wide enough for two or three people to make their way, and as high as eighty feet, the cave became pitch black after a few paces. This was a real departure from life on the surface. I began to grasp the Mayan vision of the underworld, *Xibalba,* home of the nine princes of darkness, the place from which the Maya believed we came and to which we all would go. It was both womb and grave.

The air was breathable, but thick and musty. I had never inhaled anything like it before, and I remembered warnings we'd heard of a mysterious lung disease caused by an airborne fungus. Normally short of breath because of allergies, I wondered nervously how long this journey would be. We came upon several pottery sites, some of the thousand-year-old bowls still intact,

others having crumbled, and a few left upside down with punc-
ture holes to allow ancient spirits to depart. Most were blackened
from time, but some still held traces of painted circles or waves,
and one had a small figure with a severed head.

There were blind scorpion spiders stationed like guards on
the walls, and fruit bats fluttering upside down at one narrow
passage. The darkness was becoming inconceivable. After feeling our way past stalactites and stalagmites, we were motioned
to squeeze through a narrow passage. Climbing through, I
dropped into a round vaulted space, and found myself standing
in an ancient ceremonial chamber, dating back some 1,500 years.
It was perhaps large enough to hold fifty people. In the center
was an upright altar stone, three feet high, protected by a circle
of smaller ones.

I was accustomed to seeing the elaborate and sophisticated
monuments and temples left behind by the Maya. But here was
a stone of sacred simplicity. To its makers, the stone was not a
work of art but a holy presence in itself, without the need of any
artisan's hand. Nor was the natural chamber where we stood an
engineered place of worship. It was simply ceremonial, the aura
of the stone magnetic.

We extinguished our lights, as they seemed to violate this
space. An absolute darkness came over me like never before. I
felt connected to the earth in a nonphysical, nonlinear way. I
tried to imagine a community praying in this temple in the earth.
How could they not believe it was provided by the spirits of
nature for their worship? Even without sight, I was aware of
their life and death. The air was thick with their history. As the

darkness made the physical world drop away, I experienced the cave as an eternal space in the universe. It was the feeling of being a soul.

THROUGH EXPERIENCES SUCH as these, I have crossed the artificial divide between self and natural world. The dissolution of boundaries is important to how we define the environmental crisis. Those intent on managing the environment can only see pollution as an external physical problem, solved by applying the managerial mind as a tool. But the environment is not outside ourselves waiting to be managed. A different approach can only come from closing the gap between culture and nature.

The true solution to the crisis exists in our perception, our hearts, our habits. If we view nature (or another person) in a detached manner, we are in danger of missing their interior. We thus manage individuals as objective units of production, consumption, or in other mechanical ways. Similarly, if nature is outside us, we trim its offending branches, dam its rivers, level its forests. But if we have an intimate relationship with nature, we will seek to heal and harmonize, not simply manage it as a resource we think we are superior to.

This redefining of the self meets powerful resistance in our culture, where the self is institutionalized as a fortress against nature. We need what Joanna Macy aptly calls a *greening of the self.* There has been little support from the institutions on which we depend for intellectual and spiritual guidance for such a redefinition. The guidance professionals—the psychologists, the teachers, the media, and, above all, the clergy—have tended until very recently to deepen the divide instead of offering the wisdom that could heal the wound between humans and the natural world. Until an environmentally driven generation that has awakened spiritually transforms these professions and institutions, the divide will be perpetuated for our children.

Reuniting Nature with the Psychological Self

The need to overhaul our sense of self in nature is evidenced by a look at *Psychology*, a textbook that devotes only 10 of 700 pages to "environmental psychology." Moreover, these ten pages trivialize the subject of the self and environment. For example, they teach that dancing couples will enjoy noise levels up to 140 decibels at a disco, but that lower noise levels "can decrease the feeling of attraction"! A real environmental psychology would explore the effects of songbirds on our moods, not how to manipulate crowds at discos. Theodore Roszak, in *The Voice of the Earth*, calls for a new discipline of *ecopsychology* to confront the bankruptcy of the existing profession that splits the inner life from the outer world, "as if what was inside of us was not also inside the universe." He notes that the listing of mental illnesses in the *Diagnostic and Statistical Manual of Mental Disorders* (the profession's bible) lacks even "a single recognized disease of the psyche that connects madness to the non-human world in which our environmental responsibility is grounded."

The belief that the psyche is pitted *against* nature was central to the approach of Sigmund Freud, who defined the human condition as one of suffering under the "superior power of nature." Freud wrote, "nature rises up against us, majestic, cruel and inexorable; she brings to our mind once more our weakness and helplessness." Indeed, for Freud, "the principal task of civilization, its actual raison d'être, is to defend us against nature."

In *Civilization and Its Discontents*, however, Freud for once glimpsed a more creative and benign evidence of nature within the Self. He discussed the "oceanic feeling," a "sensation of 'eternity,'" described by many patients, an "intimate connection with the world around them from an immediate feeling." Admitting he had never experienced this feeling in himself, Freud had trouble accepting its existence "since it is not very easy to deal with feelings." He only briefly speculated that "originally the ego includes everything [and] later it separates off an external world from itself." The ego, thus separated from nature, might be a "shrunken residue of a much more inclusive . . . feeling which corresponded to a more intimate bond between the ego and the world about it . . . a *bond with the universe*" (italics added).

Unfortunately Freud rejected this path of inquiry. Instead he concluded that any weakening of the boundaries between ego and external world might cause pathology. The "oceanic feeling," he speculated, was an infantile resurgence of childish attachments. From this perspective, any nature-based belief system was primitive regression. Our Western understanding of human behavior has yet to recover from this Freudian necessity of the Self "going over to the attack against nature and subjecting her to the human will."

Another giant of modern psychology, Carl Jung, comparing modern with "archaic" communities, wrote that civilized man "must strip nature of psychic attributes in order to dominate it." Jung approved the role of baptism in distancing humans from any attachments to nature. Baptism was of "the greatest importance for the psychic development of mankind" because it "lifts a man out of his archaic identification with the world and changes him into a *spiritual man who stands above nature.*"*

Even Abraham Maslow, parent of the modern-day humanistic psychology so influential on the environmental movement, tended to disregard the environmental context in his promotion of "self-actualization." He explicitly wanted to focus therapy on "that portion of the psyche which is not a reflection of the outer world." Only in the 1968 preface to his last work, *Toward a Psychology of Being,* did Maslow suggest the need for what is now called ecopsychology to complement his humanistic priority. He wrote of the need for a transition to a psychology "centered in the cosmos," following a tradition going back to Thoreau and Walt Whitman:

* There is a roundabout Jungian way to understand how an ecological Self might develop. Jung's theory of a collective unconscious was based on archetypes that were unconscious images of actual human instincts. A Jungian might argue today that humans are in the process of developing new instincts, and therefore are developing new archetypes for guidance in response to environmental warnings. This is similar to Leopold's observation in *The Land Ethic* that an ethic is a "community instinct in the making."

> Without the transcendent and transpersonal, we get sick, violent
> and nihilistic, or else hopeless and apathetic . . . (we need)
> something "bigger than we are" to be awed by and to commit
> ourselves to in a new, naturalistic, empirical, non-churchly sense.

The "oceanic feeling" of compassionate association with the
universe is precisely the quality that needs cultivation. Maslow's
call for a "transcendent" but "non-churchly" approach "centered
in the cosmos" is the seed that has now begun to flourish in the
new ecopsychology movement. After nearly a century of obsession with severing the ego from its roots in nature, we may be
on the threshold of a more nature-based image of the self.

Ecopsychology could help harmonize the individual with nature and labor in a new way. The "oceanic feeling" would not be
repressed but encouraged as an intuitive identity with nature.
The self would be defined as a unique focus of nature's energies.
In addition, the meaning of work would be harmonized with
sustaining, rather than conquering and exploiting, the natural
world. Mental health and maturity would be defined as adjusting
the individual to the "web of life." The oil industry executive
who dismissed the Arctic wilderness as a "flat, crummy place"
could be given counseling for incipient schizophrenia, not employed as an Alaskan resource official (as he was). The timber
industry consultant who compared old-growth forests to cemeteries, claiming that they are "extremely self-centered in that
they care only for themselves and no one else," might be seen as
suffering from a tendency to self-projection.

To retain a child's appreciation of nature is integral to healthy
personal development, not regression. The child does not dis-

tinguish a moral hierarchy among trees, flowers, animals, and human beings. In the child's heart, the parent is special, of course, but all the rest are also alive and full of possibilities.

When we associate maturity with diminishing a child's enthrallment with nature and the universe, we foster apathy and dualism. Most spiritual and ecological teachers have suggested that wisdom comes to those who retain a childlike, innocent dimension. The *Tao Te Ching* says that "one who possesses *te* (vital energy) in abundance is comparable to a new-born baby." Ralph Waldo Emerson wrote that "the lover of Nature is [one] who has retained the spirit of infancy into adulthood." Rachel Carson observed that

> a child's world is fresh and new and beautiful, full of wonder and excitement. It is our misfortune that for most of us that true instinct for what is beautiful and awe-inspiring is dimmed and even lost before we reach adulthood.

Carson wished for each child a "sense of wonder" that would be

> so indestructible that it would last throughout life, as an unfailing antidote against the boredom and disenchantments of later years, the sterile preoccupation with things that are trivial, the alienation from the sources of our strength.

Instead of fostering this childlike awe into, say, a poetic sensibility, the function of the educational system is all too often to suppress it.

Reforming the Environmental Illiteracy
of Public Education

For many decades our educational system has perpetuated the division between self and natural world. Endless debates over educational reform all but ignore the environment. Throughout the U.S. educational system, ecology is relegated to the elective or voluntary corners in the curriculum, supported by a small number of caring faculty. Moreover, if religion is discussed at all in public schools, there is little, if any, mention of earth-based spiritualities.

There continues to be a reductionist definition of students as little machines receiving educational input in order to become more productive for when they join the workforce. The nuclear power and oil industries have targeted the elementary grades with such "educational materials" as *Mickey Mouse and Goofy Explore Energy* (by Exxon) and *The Atom, Electricity and You* (Commonwealth Edison). A 1993 survey revealed chemistry books that lacked any mention of toxic contamination, economics texts that classified the environment as a resource "used to produce what we want," and the following passage on conserving our natural resources:

> If we cut down too many trees the forests will disappear. Then there will be no trees to use to build houses or to make paper.

Ecology needs to become an integrative framework in the curriculum and the very process of learning, not a feeble branch separated from the entrenched disciplines. What needs to be restored is John Dewey's insight in *Knowing and Known* that:

> intelligent activity . . . is not something brought to bear upon Nature from without; *it is nature realizing its own potentialities* . . .
>
> "Environment" is not something around and about human activities in an external sense; it is their medium . . . [and] narrowing of the medium is the direct source of all unnecessary impoverishment in human living. (italics added)

And what of the raging debate over values in American education? Nothing better illustrates the devaluation of the environmental crisis than its absence from the agenda of such "reformers" as William Bennett, Allan Bloom, Lynne Cheney, and E. D. Hirsch. These professed saviors of Western culture perpetuate a dualistic mentality in which nature is purely an unimportant background to culture and civilization. For example, Bennett's best-selling *Book of Virtues* contains exhortations to every conceivable virtue except kinship or stewardship toward nature. The former U.S. Secretary of Education's overriding concern is for the "control of appetites," an obsession that leads him to include an essay on the virtues of cleanliness, but not a word about controlling our appetite for nature's resources.

In Bennett's punchy companion volume, *The Index of Leading Cultural Indicators: Facts and Figures on the State of American Society,* there is a parallel myopia to the state of the American environment. The closest that Bennett comes to the subject is a worried note that American students were at the bottom of a world survey in their knowledge of geography. Hirsch's best-selling *Cultural Literacy* is similarly empty on the subject of nature. Its five thousand "essential" names, phrases, dates, and concepts does not include the environment. The neoconservative theme of a "return to basics" constitutes a retreat from addressing the environmental crisis at all.

The Media: Where Is the Daily Planet?

The media is arguably the most important institution for visualizing our relationship with the planet and sounding the alarm for its health. For the first time ever, a global population has seen powerful images of endangered species, rainforests burning, and extraordinary photographs of the planet itself.

But the media fails to address the environmental crisis as headline news. The closest to environmental news, ironically, is the weather report, in which a modern telegenic shaman tells us whether nature will be friendly or hostile.

The height of media attention to the environment was Earth Day 1990. Yet during the one-year period beginning in spring 1990, network television devoted only 1.5 percent of its news stories to the environment. Daily newspapers committed 2 percent of their coverage during the same period. ABC's "Nightline," considered an in-depth source of important commentary, featured the environment in just six of 130 programs analyzed during a six-month period of 1989, leading up to Earth Day. Of the fifteen guests on those "Nightline" environmental programs, most were government and corporate representatives, and only two were from environmental organizations.

Only in recent years have major newspapers assigned top reporters to cover the environment at all. Even then, compared to political events, corporate mergers, sports, or entertainment, nature is considered a minor category. In 1995 the *Los Angeles Times* dropped the environment as a hard news beat in Sacramento, just when the Governor was attempting to gut the Endangered Species Act. The environment was "just not in the equation," a *Times* representative said. The public was deprived of important daily news, and the *Times'* talented environmental reporters were assigned to write occasional feature stories. The *New York Times* in the 1990s replaced Philip Shabecoff, an environmental reporter with fourteen years' experience. According to Shabecoff, he was told that his writing "was considered pro-environment, whatever that means." The *Times,* Shabecoff said, criticized him for describing the killing of dolphins as "slaughter." The *Times'* new environmental reporter, Keith Schneider, reported favorably on the first stirrings of what became an anti-environmental backlash, climaxing with a front page, five-part series in 1993 that implied that many environmental threats were exaggerated. Schneider quoted unnamed scientists that "as many as two-thirds of the compounds deemed carcinogenic would represent no danger to humans," as if there should be no worry about the cumulative effects of thousands of unanalyzed chemicals in our midst.

By contrast the Persian Gulf war of 1992 was reported and televised around the clock by hundreds of on-the-scene reporters and so-called experts who conveyed the unified message that we were fighting a clean and necessary war. The environmental dimensions—the raging fires, the massive oil spills, the effects of chemical weapons on humans and other life, our excessive dependence on Persian Gulf oil, President Bush's personal family investments in Kuwait—were little explored. It took Greenpeace to begin uncovering the toxic toll.

I wonder what might happen to human consciousness if, day after day, our news was dominated by dramatic and visual stories about the precipitous decline of Chinook salmon or blue whales, the steady increase of cancers, the growing campaign contributions of polluting industries to individuals running for office. In 1980 President Jimmy Carter was discredited because the television news kept announcing how many days Americans had been held hostage in Iran. What if nightly television news reported how many acres of rainforest were destroyed during the past day, or how few salmon remain in the Atlantic and Pacific runs, or how many children died of contaminated water? Or if the television stations that covered the O. J. Simpson trial closed their evening programs with an image of one of the fourteen nonsmokers who died that day in California from second-hand smoke? In other words, what would happen if there was a real *Daily Planet*?

But the news is not driven to raise public consciousness about the price and profits of pollution. Instead it strives to win ratings wars by emphasizing celebrities, sex, and violence. The networks try to keep their commercial sponsors happy by being the supine vehicles for 3,000 television advertisements daily prompting consumption—commercials that can have a greater effect on culture than the news itself.

The mind of the media is like Descartes at a fast-food counter. The pressure is to divide the self from the world, dissect, devour, and dispose of material as a kind of McNews. The Nature Channel, National Geographic documentaries, Captain Planet cartoons are all welcome relief but do not counteract the dynamic of corporate and editorial choices to turn the environment into background—mere B-roll filler.

I HAVE ARGUED that we are conditioned to grow up in a moral divide between the self and nature, and that our learning institutions (psychology, education, and the media) perpetuate this way of thinking throughout our culture. But where does the moral dimension of the divide originate? How have we become invested with this sense of moral superiority to nature, and how is it justified? Here it is necessary to turn toward our religious traditions, the most powerful authorities for determining our hierarchy of values, our sense of what is moral, what is sacred, and what is not.

So as we shall see in the next chapter, the default of organized religion is that it perpetuates the great divide between self and nature.

3

The Default of
Organized Religion

*God blessed them, saying to them, "Be fruitful, multiply, fill
the earth and conquer it. Be masters of the fish of the sea, the
birds of the heaven, and all living animals on the earth."*

GENESIS 1:28, *The Jerusalem Bible* (1966)

*My responsibility is to follow the scriptures, which call upon
us to occupy the land until Jesus returns. I don't know how
many generations we can count on before the Lord returns.*

JAMES WATT, U.S. Secretary of the Interior (1981)

*It should not be believed that all the beings exist for the sake
of the existence of humanity.*

MAIMONIDES, *Guide of the Perplexed* (1190)

IN 1991 I decided to visit religious bookstores to inquire
whether they included environmental writings in popular
publications describing their faiths. After browsing through
books on Christianity, Judaism, Buddhism, Hinduism, and Islam, all for the common reader, I concluded that the popular
texts either gloss over the environmental crisis or ignore it altogether.

For example, the *Contemporary Catechism* of the Catholic Church in the 1980s featured a chapter called "God, Man and the Universe," which declared that "the sun and the moon, worshipped as divinities by the Babylonians, are simply [God's] creations, and so far from having dominion over the human race, were made by God for the service of man." So, too, the beasts and birds worshiped by the Egyptians were "the work of God's hands and put by him under the control of man."

It was not until 1982, in *Redemptor Hominus,* that a pope took note of the environmental crisis in an encyclical. He warned against our being "heedless exploiters," while still reaffirming the traditional Church view of human beings as "intelligent and noble masters and guardians of nature." The 1994 Catholic *Catechism* marks a modest greening from the past. "Each creature possesses its own particular goodness and perfection," and is "a ray of God's infinite wisdom and goodness," proclaims the updated text. The mandate to "subdue the earth" is clarified to exclude "arbitrary and destructive domination." The U.S. Catholic bishops have also begun to take stands on certain environmental issues for the first time (though not on endangered species as of this writing; "they do not want to oppose anthropocentrism," says one informed religious insider).

The new *Catechism* reaffirms the traditional teaching of a hierarchy of earthly beings with man at the "summit." God has "destined all material creatures for the good of the human race," the text continues, citing the ancient claim of St. John Chrysostom that "for [humans] the heavens and the earth, the sea and all the rest of creation exist." Given the nature of original sin, it is inevitable that humans who believe that the environment exists for them will succumb to selfishness rather than stewardship.

Like this pale green catechism, the environment remains a strictly secondary issue in popular Catholic thought and action. For example, a 1990 volume on modern Catholics by Father Andrew M. Greeley contains not a single reference to the world of nature. In an excellent chapter comparing ideologies such as capitalism and socialism with a Catholic moral viewpoint, the environment is overlooked completely. Greeley even writes a lengthy analysis of anarchism, but not a word about environmentalism. This is a disappointment, since Greeley is one of the more outspoken reformers within the Church.

The 700-page *Oxford Illustrated History of Christianity* (1990) includes less than one page on environmental issues. In a chapter called "The Future of Christianity," it notes that problems of population growth and resource decline lie ahead, but we are reassured that "it seems likely that new discoveries may provide the means for averting the cumulative threats of population explosions and diminishing food or resources." There is no sense of a moral dimension or urgency in this Christian hope for a technological fix.

The 1991 edition of *Judaism*, by Arthur Hertzberg, is advertised as an "anthology of the key spiritual writings of the Jewish tradition." This edition was revised "to take account of the new questions which have been debated in Judaism in recent decades." But in 320 pages, there is not a single reference to the environmental crisis. The only land mentioned is the Promised Land.

I focused in my exploration on mainstream Western religion in order to address the separation of self and culture from nature in our American society. Because of the appeal of Asian religions among many U.S. environmentalists, I chose to explore Buddhism, a faith that has drawn my interest for many years (See chapter 6). To my surprise, Buddhism too is beginning only now to engage the environmental crisis. The authors of *Dharma Gaia* ("teaching of the living earth"), an excellent book of Buddhist essays published for Earth Day 1990, believed it "to be the *first* compilation of environmental themes in the history of Buddhism." Like Western religions, Buddhism has been barren of environmental emphasis until quite recently.

I have neglected Islam and Hinduism in this book to my regret, but it is apparent that both of these great faiths treat the environment as an afterthought as well. The 1991 book *Islam and Ecology* is described by its editor, Fazlun M. Khalid, as "the *first* attempt at a comprehensive presentation of the Islamic position on ecology." Like the other monotheisms to arise in the Middle East, Islam is a hierarchical doctrine positing an external creator and assigning human beings dominion over the natural world. Like Judaism and Christianity, there are scriptural passages that evoke a powerful imagery of nature ("the world is green and beautiful and God has appointed you as his stewards over it"), and there are nature mystics like the animal-rights scholar of the thirteenth century, Izzad-Din Ibn 'Abd As-Salam. But in the end, the tradition of nature in the teachings of Islam has been left undeveloped.

Hinduism, like Buddhism, has a strong tradition of integrating nature in its philosophy from its origins to the present day. The *Bhagavad Gita* celebrates all of creation as a holy banyan tree; Krishna dances with peacocks in the forest; modern Hinduism has given us Gandhi; and, in the 1980s, the Chipko (tree hugger) movement of the Himalayan forests. But these indications of nature reverence have to be retrieved from a long Hindu tradition of viewing the earth as illusion to be transcended, and seen in the context of India's deepening environmental crisis in which even the sacred Vrindavan forests of Krishna have been cut down.

Finally, however, I did examine the celebrated ecumenical work by Huston Smith, *World's Religions* (1989), which is described in its subtitle as "A Guide to Our Wisdom Traditions." Smith, who has been featured on Bill Moyer's television series, "The Wisdom of Faith," issued this book as an update to his popular 1958 work, *The Religions of Man*. He acknowledges changing his newer work to reflect gender issues. But in a text covering Hinduism, Buddhism, Confucianism, Taoism, Islam, Judaism, and Christianity, Smith never once explores whether these wisdom religions include any wisdom concerning the modern environmental dilemma.

From a planetary viewpoint, the discovery and revival of a lost gospel of the earth in all these significant religious traditions is vital. But the main focus here will be on Western religious traditions that continue to shape the consciousness of a Western society that impacts so much of the global environment.

Tenets to Be Overcome

The difficulties faced by the Western religious tradition in confronting the environmental crisis may not be insurmountable, but they are daunting. In the form of a simple outline, the tenets of mainstream religion that we must re-examine are these:

- *The doctrine of an external, original creator,* who set the universe in motion at a certain time in the past, creates a consistent *dualism* between creation/mind and nature/matter throughout Western culture. Even evolution is commonly understood as only a *physical* process and elements such as soul or spirit given Divine origins, as if God skipped evolution to plant these qualities in human beings alone.

  Ecology would suggest, in contrast, that spirit, soul, consciousness, and creativity are part of the mystery of evolution, not outside the process, and that creation is ongoing, not simply an epic event in our past.

- *A moral hierarchy of being, with the human community placed at the top* of the ladder in the image of God, who occupies an eternal dimension. Below humans, typically, are the animals and plants most enjoyed by humans, followed by less desirable species such as insects, with the oldest micro-organisms disregarded altogether at the very bottom. St. Thomas Aquinas

(1225–1274) wrote in *Summa Theologica* that "dumb plants and animals are naturally enslaved and accommodated to the uses of others . . . by a most just ordinance of the Creator."

Ecology casts doubt on any species' moral dictatorship, and implies an interdependence between humans and other life forms, including our "lowly" bacterial ancestors.

- *The transcendence of nature through an ascent to eternal life.* Life is seen as a temporary passage, and earth a temporary place, giving way to transcendence to a separate sacred sphere. For founders of Christianity like the apostle Paul (and for certain fundamentalists today), the end of the world was imminent and so any attachments to the natural world were delusional. Those who held such attachments, while "claiming to be wise," were "fools" to Paul because they gave up the "glory of the immortal God for images resembling mortal man or birds or animals or reptiles." (Rom. 1-22:23)
- *The separation of grace from nature.* Augustine (396–430) succeeded Paul as the great architect of the Church's otherworldliness. In the time of Rome's corruption, he held the view that the temptations of the material world were only evidence of the fallen state. Augustine's vision of an ascending hierarchy of Being required a separation of the state of grace from the state of nature.

These religious doctrines support and complement the concept of a mechanical universe. The universe and the earth are desanctified, abandoned, and left to the uses of science and technology at the hand of humans. In this resulting world view, the core axioms are:

- that while human beings are made in God's image, nature is different, a supporting theater cast for the human drama;
- nature is no more than the sum of its parts, and can be reduced to those parts for use;
- human beings are the measure of all things; nature's role or destiny is to be "developed" into a storehouse of value.

These notions constitute an edifice arising from thousands of years of religious and scientific tradition in the West. Despite recurring descriptions of the "two cultures," the concept of a mechanical universe complements both disciplines.

When Western science separated from religion in the seventeenth century, the partition left science essentially amoral, without an explicit religious context. Instead of challenging the Church's traditional cosmology as unproved dogma, science remained silent, conformed, or secularized the Church's vision of man's "domination" over nature.

Sir Francis Bacon (1561–1626), for example, was both the "father of the scientific method" and a leading member of the Church's Inquisition. His writings were filled with imagery of the mental conquest of nature, drawn from the witch trials of the time. Nature was to be "placed on the rack," "enslaved," "bound into service," and "forced out of her natural state and molded."

Not long after, in his *Discourse on Method* (1637) René Descartes sealed the intellectual separation of self from nature, and mind from natural processes, with the assertion that "I think, therefore I am." The human destiny was to be "masters and possessions of nature." He could then reassuringly explain that animals did not feel pain when being whipped, skinned, or amputated, since they lacked souls. Their screams were only apparent expressions of pain, but in reality just the noises of their body machinery.

Sir Isaac Newton (1642–1727) summed up the universe as a giant machine composed of "impenetrable, movable particles" whose laws could be charted by an external, observant, scientific mind. Immanuel Kant (1724–1804) combined Bacon's method of inquisition with Newton's detached mode of observance in a powerful image of the scientist as the "judge" of nature. He wrote that while Reason must learn from nature, Reason must do so not as a pupil but as "an appointed judge who compels the witnesses to answers questions which he himself has formulated."

Far from outdated, the doctrine of a universe left by God to operate according to mechanical laws recurs in the contemporary thinking of Stephen Hawking, one of the most influential scientists of our time. Hawking seeks to merge relativity with quantum mechanics in a "grand unified theory" that will reveal the whole universe. It appears to Hawking that God has "left the universe to evolve according to [these laws] and does not now intervene in it." God has chosen to leave clues for scientists to discover, and thus the grand unified theory will be "the ultimate triumph of human reason: for then we could know the mind of God."

The universe according to Hawking is without final mystery,

and its God turns out to be a cosmic nerd. "The laws of physics can still determine how the universe began," he asserts. There is no Sacred Mystery, no Creative Spirit beyond the reach of our logic. For Hawking, the universe originated in math. He needs to postulate an original departure point at which the distance between galaxies, which are rushing apart, was zero, and the density of the universe and curvature of space-time were infinite. "As far as we are concerned," says Hawking on behalf of the physicist mind-set, "*events before the Big Bang can have no consequences*, so they should not form part of the scientific model of the universe. We should therefore cut them out of the theory, and say that time had a beginning at the Big Bang . . . if one adopts a positivist viewpoint, as I do, *it is meaningless to talk about an underlying reality.* There would be no experiment that one could perform to determine what this reality was" (italics added). In an essay called "The Origin of the Universe" Hawking clarifies the limits of his discipline thus: "science may solve the problem of how the universe began [but] it cannot answer the question: Why does the universe bother to exist? I don't know the answer to that."

In the mechanical view, mathematical logic replaces mystery, equations are the stuff of stars, and where there are no research grants there is no underlying reality. The universe is to be conquered mentally on the logical path to the mind of God.

Such attitudes entail deep alienation from the earth and universe. Where nature becomes an object of intellectual conquest, physical conquest is not far behind.

The Utilitarian Creed: Nature for Use

The Genesis mandate of dominion combined with the belief in a mechanical universe results in a deep sense of moral, indeed divinely based, entitlement to use nature for our self-interest, to turn mountains to high-rises, rivers into electrical sources, redwoods into condominium decks, oceans and canyons into toxic dumping grounds. The environment is thought to be wasted, vacant, or even uninhabited unless it contributes to the Gross National Product.

As the astute Frenchman Alexis de Tocqueville commented in his 1835 *Journal,*

> The wonders of inanimate nature leave Americans cold. . . . The American people see themselves marching through wildernesses, drying up marshes, diverting rivers, peopling the wilds, and subduing nature.

The very essence, the "cultural core," of being American, says a historian of religious awakenings, is to be "covenanted with God on a special errand into the wilderness." These assumptions are so deep, so unconscious, as to be hardly debatable. They are at the core of our beliefs, not only in the modern world, but the "postmodern" sensibility (defined by Frederic Jameson as "what you have when the modernization process is complete and nature is gone for good"). In the postmodern context, there is no point in trying to save wild nature, for there is none. Nature is appropriated into culture. Wilderness becomes theme park.

In politics, these attitudes are translated into defining nature not as a *source* of life but as *resource*. (Take, for example, the very name of the Natural Resources Committee, which I chair in the California Senate. If I tried to rename it the Nature Committee, my colleagues would worry about me more than they do already). The notion of exploiting nature as a resource for development has become a modern global ideology. In my generation, student activists were raised on the assumption that "development" was an unquestioned good. In the 1962 Port Huron Statement, the founding manifesto of Students for a Democratic Society, we called for "the industrialization of the world" through the use of "decentralized" nuclear power. Our techno-globalism reflected the times; a 1963 United Nations report declared that "natural resources cannot develop themselves; it is only through the application of human knowledge and skill that anything can be made of them." So celebrated is this utilitarian doctrine in our culture that as recently as 1987 Robert Solow won the Nobel Prize in economics for his conclusion that "the ancient concern about the depletion of natural resources no longer rests on any firm foundation . . . If it is very easy to substitute other factors for natural resources, then there is, in principle, no problem. The world can, in effect, get along without natural resources, so exhaustion is just an event, not a catastrophe."

The utilitarian creed is illustrated in the Orwellian definition of the California Department of Conservation's mission, described as promoting "development and management of the state's earth resources by fostering the wise use of California's land, energy and minerals." Conservation here becomes synonymous with development. The term "wise use," the banner of a powerful and deceptive pro-business coalition, is incorporated into state policy.

Section 1600 of the California Fish and Game Code is another example. It declares that "Fish and wildlife are the *property* of the people and provide a major contribution to the *economy* of the state as well as providing a significant part of the *people's food supply* and therefore, their conservation is a proper responsibility of the state."

As another example, the State Forestry Practices Act, passed in 1973, declares that "maximum sustained production of high-quality timber products" must be achieved, while other values including recreation, watersheds, wildlife, and aesthetic enjoyment need only be "considered."

This "maximum yield" goal arises from a national attitude expressed long ago by President Theodore Roosevelt:

> Forest protection is not an end in itself; it is a means to increase and sustain the resources of our country and the industries that depend on them. The preservation of our forests is an imperative business necessity.

Roosevelt was a *conservationist,* it should be remembered, a president who still deserves credit for his appreciation of national parks and wildlife. In his overarching perspective, however, there was little room for wilderness except within the boundaries of parks. Although progressive for the time, this notion is akin to allowing wild animals only in zoos. Having set aside such reserves for recreational enjoyment, the main work was to manage the remaining forests as resources for products such as housing or newsprint.

The first priority in this master vision was "yield," a term rich with images of conquest and extraction of value from a defeated adversary. The forest was to "yield" itself to our industrial priorities. It was to be protected, not for its biodiversity, not for its cooling effect, not for its defense of streams from erosion, certainly not for any intrinsic worth, but simply to "sustain the resources of our country." That goal remains paramount today, despite rising and occasionally successful environmental opposition.

Another example is water. The modern notion of water entitlements in California arose in the Gold Rush years from the mere claim of exercising physical control. In formal language, this was the doctrine of "prior appropriation," or, as the miners put it, "first in time, first in right." The riparian laws that emerged in the 1850s gave entitlement to all water that flowed through a property, aside from upstream uses or diversions for one's farm irrigation. Any water freely flowing from the mountains to the sea was considered "water to waste." A century later Governor Earl Warren declared that "we should not relax until California has adopted and put into operation a statewide program that will *put every drop of water to work.*"

As late as 1978, an official state review of water rights law concluded that "California's groundwater is usually available to any pumper, public or private, who wants to extract it, regardless of the impact of extraction on neighboring groundwater pumpers or on the general community." And in 1979 the California

Supreme Court held in two decisions that the "reasonable use" of water did *not* include retaining water for native plants, animals, and fish.

This narrow doctrine was not challenged successfully until 1983, in a case involving the City of Los Angeles' insatiable thirst for the disappearing waters of Mono Lake. Faced with the likely death of the ancient lake's whole ecosystem, not to mention a passionate environmental outcry, the state Supreme Court held that government could protect Mono Lake as an exercise of a "public trust." The lawyers for Los Angeles denounced this decision as "radical." Though they lost the specific case, the debate over public-trust doctrine continues today.

The doctrine of utilitarianism shows no sign of becoming obsolete. As available and affordable natural resources steadily shrink, the pressure to permit pollution grows. "Scarcities of renewable resources are already contributing to violent conflict in many parts of the developing world," *Scientific American* reported in February 1993. Like any other addiction, the pursuit of those resources will become more obsessive and self-destructive over time.

Forbes magazine describes the philosophy of nihilism that might emerge: "In the end, of course, catastrophe awaits us anyway, whether from the eccentricities of a passing asteroid, or the dying of the sun, but that doesn't change the desirability of postponing the day of reckoning as long as possible." This was an extraordinarily candid admission, written in 1992, of an addiction that cannot be changed, one that seeks only to delay a disastrous "day of reckoning." In fact, this has always been the moral emptiness underlying the promotion of physical growth. At the very peak of the petrochemical age, in 1952, President Truman's Commission on Growth concluded: "Granting that we cannot find any absolute reason for this belief [in growth], we admit that to our Western minds it seems preferable to any opposite, which to us implies stagnation and decay."

The Holy War against Environmentalism

In 1994 the religious and political enemies of environmentalism triumphed in the congressional elections, pledging a "Contract with America" that Speaker Newt Gingrich said would save Western civilization. Revealingly, the "Contract" made no mention of environmental issues. Under euphemisms like "excessive regulation," however, a Republican Christian coalition and its business allies targeted the alternative faith that environmentalists seemed to represent. "They turned Easter into Earth Day and worship dirt," declared conservative presidential candidate Patrick Buchanan. In doing so, Buchanan reasserted the ancient argument for a transcendent monotheism that desanctified the earth and painted environmentalists with the brush of paganism.

The crusade against environmentalists began to assemble its power in the Reagan years. Two Interior Department secretaries invoked biblical rationales for their anti-environmental agendas. One of them, James Watt, testified to Congress that "my responsibility is to follow the scriptures, which call upon us to occupy the land until Jesus returns. I don't know how many generations we can count on before the Lord returns." The other,

Manuel Lujan, termed the story of Adam and Eve "essentially correct" in explaining his official view that "God gave us dominion over these creatures."

Watt and Lujan were echoing the doctrine of "dominion theology" promoted by the Christian right, especially through Regent University and the Christian Broadcasting Network of former presidential candidate Pat Robertson. In this theology, Christians are entitled to dominion over the environment and the world's institutions as temporary "regents" until the second coming of Christ. They interpret the Book of Genesis as mandating "the faithful and righteous application of God's Word to every area of life." The Genesis call to "subdue the earth" is seen to include civil dominion. As Robertson writes in *The New World Order*, "there is absolutely no way that government can operate successfully unless led by godly men and women operating under the laws of the God of Jacob," laws that specifically exclude those he condemns as "animist tree worshipers" and "New Age worshipers of Satan." Some are even more extreme than Robertson, like the theologian Rousas John Rushdoony, author of *Roots of Reconstruction*. Rushdoony, whose influence extends to the right wing of Republican politics in California, calls for the death penalty for "blasphemers," "witches," "astrologers," and "teachers of false doctrine" generally.

A form of "dominion" doctrine has long been shared by the traditional Roman Catholic hierarchy, as well. On Earth Day 1990, New York's Cardinal John O'Connor admonished his flock to remember that "the earth exists for the human person and not vice-versa." In 1993 Pope John Paul denounced Catholic feminists in terms eerily reminiscent of the Inquisition. In a story headlined JOHN PAUL CRITICIZES 'MOTHER EARTH' RITUALS, the *New York Times* reported that "senior cardinals have expressed concern about worship of such concepts as the earth goddess by some feminist American Catholics, saying the practice creates an unacceptable blend of Catholicism with animist faith [and] such worship veers toward witchcraft." Two years later Pope John Paul opposed the democratic election of an ex-Communist in Poland on grounds that he represented a "neo-pagan" philosophy. To be fair, the Pope now decries the "culture of domination" toward the environment. What is missing is a realization of how the Christian tradition has fostered this culture of domination and condemned nature mysticism as sinful or subversive.

Similarly, the prominent Jewish neo-conservative Dennis Praeger claims that Nazism itself arose not from racism, not from national chauvinism, not from the psychic need for a scapegoat, but from nature worship. Judaism, he declares, "came into this world to obliterate [nature worship] with ethical monotheism." Linking the genocidal "blood and soil" nationalism of Hitler with environmentalism is ludicrous. The nature ideology of many Nazi leaders was linked to racial nationalism. And while certain environmentalists today may call callously for population reduction, they are not comparable to the German Nazi Party in the least. Environmentalism wants to preserve soil as a source of life, not the basis of militarism. But for Praeger the green movement is the "new hiding place of evil."

These religious voices have been complemented by editorial

writers for the conservative press, most notably the *Wall Street Journal* and *Forbes*. The *Journal* weighed in with a theological defense of "real religion" against the spooky environmentalists who promote a "pagan fanaticism that now worships such gods as Nature and Gender with a reverence formerly accorded real religions." *Forbes* pontificated with a piece titled "Tom Hayden, Meet Adam Smith and Thomas Aquinas," a lengthy religious argument for the capitalist marketplace. What was intriguing was that *Forbes* reached for a spiritual defense of corporate pollution. The source of their worry was that firms like Exxon were being condemned "not simply for fouling the beaches of Prince William Sound, but for committing a grievous sin against the innocence of nature." Furthermore, "it's not just a few radicals who sound this way" (that's where I came in), but even respectable officials who were throwing around terms like "sacred place" in describing the Alaskan wilderness. The *Wall Street Journal* and *Forbes* were calling on corporate America to support a Christian backlash against the environmental movement. That is exactly what happened.

THE ATTACK OF THE CHRISTIAN RIGHT

The most militant political anti-environmental force has been the Christian Right coalition. In 1990, addressing a cattlemen's convention, James Watt threatened: "If the troubles from environmentalists cannot be solved in the jury box or at the ballot box, perhaps the cartridge box should be used." In 1992 Oliver North denounced U.S. Senator Barbara Boxer for allegedly believing that "spotted owls are higher on the food chain than we are, and that's not how I read Genesis." In the same year Rush Limbaugh decried those who have "replaced religion with secular environmentalism," and wrote: "my views on the environment are rooted in my belief in Creation." Limbaugh's theology included this teaching: "If a spotted owl can't adapt, does the earth really need that species so much that hardship to human beings is worth enduring in the process of saving it? . . . Why, we could even survive without any owls. So what if they are no longer around to kill the mice. We'll just build more traps."

The founders of the Wise Use Movement, a coalition linked to timber and mining interests, the National Rifle Association, and Japanese off-road vehicle companies, among others, call environmentalism "the new paganism," in which "trees are worshipped and humans sacrificed at its altar. It is evil. And we intend to destroy it." In 1993 the Wise Use Leadership Conference declared "spiritual war" against environmentalists.

As the anti-environmental forces gained ascendancy after the 1994 elections, they became more blatant in their theological claims. A Republican congresswoman from Idaho, Helen Chenoweth, said environmentalists "believe nature is God; where we know that God Himself created nature. And there comes the conflict." Another right-wing group called Putting People First denounced public schools for "brainwashing [children] with animal-rights and green ideology. . . . Whether you are a Christian, Jewish, or objectivist, this modern New Age ideology, the enemy of Western culture, is your enemy too."

Limbaugh predicted and, by implication, rationalized violence against environmentalists in a February 21, 1995, radio broadcast:

> I mean there is a—out West, you go out to Nevada, parts of California, there is the second violent American revolution is just about—I got my fingers around one-fourth of an inch apart—is just about that far away. Because these people are sick and tired of a bunch of bureaucrats in Washington driving into town and telling them what they can and can't do with their land, using all of these federal regulations.

A few weeks later, Limbaugh got what he was predicting, when a lethal bomb blast in Oklahoma City revealed the growing presence of armed, government-hating militias, whose "Christian Identity" agenda included a rollback of environmental regulations. Even before Oklahoma City focused the nation's attention, however briefly, on violent right-wing extremists, the environmental movement suffered several years of threats, arson, shootings, and other forms of violence, carefully recounted in David Helvarg's *The War Against the Greens*. A group called the U.S. Militia Association claimed that they turned out a thousand volunteers for U.S. Congresswoman Helen Chenoweth's election in Idaho. In 1994 an armed posse had chased U.S. Forest Service rangers off illegally bulldozed areas in a Nevada national forest. If one of the U.S. rangers had pulled a weapon, a posse member proclaimed, "fifty people with sidearms would have drilled him."

Aside from a 1992 "60 Minutes" report on this localized intimidation of environmental groups, there was little interest expressed by either the national media or the Federal Bureau of Investigation on the subject. For those familiar with religious history, the biblical echoes of warfare against "pagan" nature worshipers were painfully apparent.

While the right wing's declared holy war on environmentalism has escalated, most of organized religion has remained on the sidelines of the debate until quite recently. It would be inaccurate and unfair to imply that mainstream Christianity shares the views of this right-wing Christian fringe. But as a whole, organized religion in America has ignored the plight of the earth for many centuries. Its hierarchical theology, with its indifference to the earth, provides a broad vacuum and narrow doctrinal rationale for the hatred and frustration of the Radical Right in its quest for dominion over its enemies.

The Lost Gospel: The Seeds of Retrieval

We are caught in a cycle of consciousness (or unconsciousness) that once led to growth and now threatens destruction. The cycle begins with the religious overview of Genesis, in which a God in the sky has appointed human beings as his divine regents over nature. The community of sacred things includes God and human beings, nothing more. The rest is a vast earth filled with resources for human development. Since human beings are infected with original sin, or the tendency toward greed, it is inevitable that they will exploit the earth for their benefit. If that vision was viable thirty-five hundred years ago when 5 million people filled the planet, it is catastrophic for a world of 6 billion today.

The vision must change, beginning with our religious framework. Carl Jung explained how powerful our religious traditions are in shaping the vision and psychological assumptions that guide the daily behavior of believers and nonbelievers alike. "We entirely forget that the religion of the past two thousand years," he wrote, "is a psychological attitude that lays down a definite cultural pattern and creates an atmosphere that remains wholly uninfluenced by intellectual denials."

The modern vision of an external God, a mechanical universe, and a utilitarian approach to nature-as-resource arose long ago in debate and war against a seamless spiritually that was centered in the earth and the universe. That lost gospel is what we need to retrieve and examine.

THERE ARE SIGNS the retrieval is beginning. A number of excellent books by independent theologians and scientists on the need for religion to embrace the environment have appeared since the 1980s.*

* Here are a few that have been helpful to me: *Ecology and Liberation,* by Leonardo Boff (1995); *Religion and Environmental Crisis,* edited by Eugene Hargrove (1986); *Baptized into Wilderness, Beauty of the Lord,* and *Hope for the Land,* by Richard Cartwright Austin (1986, 1987, 1988); *Tending the Garden,* edited by Wesley Granberg-Michaelson (1987); *The Greening of the Church,* by Sean McDonagh (1990); *Replenish the Earth,* by Lewis Regenstein (1991); *Covenant for a New Creation,* edited by Carol Robb and Carl Casebolt (1991); *The Environment and the Christian,* edited by Calvin DeWitt (1995); *God Makes the Rivers to Flow,* edited by Eknath Easwaran (1991); *Let the Earth Teach You*

In addition, there are notable efforts to organize on behalf of an environmental agenda within the major religious institutions. In 1987, representatives of five major faiths met in Assisi, Italy, to issue a statement of environmental principles. In 1990, 270 scientific leaders from eighty-three nations signed a petition declaring, "We understand that what is regarded as sacred is more likely to be treated with care and respect. Our planetary home should be so regarded. Efforts to safeguard and cherish the environment need to be infused with a vision of the sacred." Green networks exist within all the major denominations. As Reverend Vincent Rossi has urged, "What is needed is for men and women to feel religious about nature. . . . [W]e need 'monks' and 'nuns' in the temple of the earth. . . ." The Cathedral of St. John the Divine in New York City has taken this mission very seriously. On the birthday of St. Francis every year, the church's massive doors are opened to all of creation: elephants, horses, butterflies, and even tiny insects are brought into the sanctuary for celebration and blessing. Friends at St. John the Divine have mobilized the National Religious Partnership for the Environment, bringing together top leadership of the U.S. Catholic Conference, the National Council of Churches of Christ, major Jewish organizations, and a new Evangelical Environmental Network, with an ambitious program of outreach to 53,000 congregations, staff training, and research and scholarship.

But these initiatives are centuries late and still low in priority

---

Torah, by Ellen Bernstein and Dan Fink (1992); and *To Till and To Tend,* by Rabbi Dan Swartz and others (1995).

for our religious establishment. Compared with the Catholic hierarchy's involvement in stopping abortion, or the Jewish organizational commitment to Israel, or the combined efforts to support social-service programs, the plight of the environment remains a remote and secondary cause. An examination of the budget and staff allocations of the major religious institutions would show negligible investments in environmental programming. For example, funding for the National Religious Partnership's excellent educational and outreach programs was slightly over $4 million in the first three years, most of it coming from secular sources such as the Nathan Cummings, Pew, and Rockefeller foundations.

The most powerful writings on spirituality and the environment have been outside the religious and cultural mainstream. The best-selling 1976 *Tao of Physics,* by Fritjof Capra, for example, attempted to connect modern physics with Eastern mysticism. *The Spiritual Dimension of Green Politics,* by Charlene Spretnak (1986), was an original breakthrough. The mysticism of theologian Matthew Fox (*Creation Spirituality,* 1991) has a wide audience, though in 1994 the Vatican excommunicated the author after thirty-three years in the priesthood. The most prophetic of all these works, in my opinion, is *The Dream of the Earth* (1988), by Father Thomas Berry, who has managed to survive humbly on the margins of the Catholic Church for many years. These works, and others like them, aim at nothing less than the long-term reconstitution of present religious thinking.

So far there is nothing like a spiritual manifesto and commitment to the environment of the sort that Dr. Martin Luther

King, Jr. expressed in his *Letter from a Birmingham Jail* in 1963. Few remember that Dr. King's letter was to the *clergy* of Birmingham who were either defending segregation or sitting on the fence. Dr. King condemned not simply the violent segregationists, but the "appalling silence of good people" whose churches were on the sidelines. In words that could be applied today to the environmental crisis, King wrote that while a few "noble souls" of the religious community had joined the movement, "the contemporary Church is so often a weak, ineffectual voice with an uncertain sound," and he added that "the power structure of the average community is consoled by the Church's silent and often vocal sanction of things as they are." The theological question he asked—"Isn't segregation an existential expression of man's tragic separation, an expression of his awful estrangement, his terrible sinfulness?"—can be asked today about those who willfully defile the environment. Isn't pollution an "essential expression of man's tragic separation" too? Where is the Dr. King of the environmental cause? Where is the "Letter from a Rainforest" or the "Letter from Cancer Alley" from a prophetic religious figure?

While a truly prophetic voice like Dr. King's has yet to ring out, the cause of a spiritual environmentalism has touched important American officials, including even Vice President Al Gore and Interior Secretary Bruce Babbitt. Gore's best-selling *Earth in the Balance: Ecology and the Human Spirit* includes a specific call for a religious ethic of stewardship. Gore was involved in the development of the National Religious Partnership. Babbitt, too, unlike his predecessor James Watt, has expressed a belief in the sacredness of land. Babbitt, a Catholic, confesses that "I always had a nagging instinct that the vast landscape was somehow sacred and holy and connected to me in a sense that my catechism ignored." Babbitt now believes that plants and animals are a "direct reflection of divinity." Gore and Babbitt are cautious in expressing these views, and have not always applied them as absolute standards in politics, but both officials are nonetheless targets of the ever-vigilant Christian Right. Cal Thomas, a columnist and colleague of the Reverend Jerry Falwell, pounced on Babbitt as being "close to animism," which for the right wing seems to be the most dangerous threat since communism. In keeping with his sky-based faith, Thomas declared that "I love my cat, but she is not a reflection of divinity." No wonder felines are suspicious of humans.

Some clergy are beginning to act on the lost gospel of the earth. As I have noted, in 1995 ministers and rabbis calling themselves Clergy for All Creation formed in California to defeat Governor Pete Wilson's attempt to weaken the state's Endangered Species Act. On a grander scale in 1996 a coalition of evangelical Christians launched a similar campaign nationwide to save the federal law protecting endangered species.

And so the battle lines for a new religious debate over nature are being drawn. The Christian Right must be considered the most aggressive and best organized foe. The mainstream denominations are more torpid and distracted by other priorities. But a stirring of believers in the lost gospel has clearly begun. If religious communities join with environmentalists in a spiritual-political crusade like that of the civil rights movement, the lost gospel will return and the potential for profound change will be at hand.

4

The Lost Gospel
in the
Judeo-Christian
Tradition

*The old gods are dead or dying and people everywhere are
searching, asking: What is the new mythology to be, the mythology of this unified earth as of one harmonious being.*

JOSEPH CAMPBELL

LOST NATURE MYSTICISM can be discovered in the Hebrew Scriptures, especially Psalms, Ecclesiastes, and Job. This
vision of all creation as holy was embraced by many ancient
people. It declined with the military and political victory of
monotheism over the older polytheistic and goddess-based religions. But it never died out among lay believers, and was
resurrected by the Christian, Jewish, and feminist mystics of the
Middle Ages. The Inquisition, and later the scientific revolution,

all but crushed nature mysticism for several centuries. But once again it has reappeared with the new interest in preserving the environment and indigenous cultures throughout the world.

The term mysticism derives from the Greek *mystikos*, which means to shut off one's senses and enter the realm of the unknowable. Matthew Fox defines a mystic as "someone who has internalized the experience of a living cosmology," a far different, more vibrant awareness than the modern urban-suburban one. Nature mysticism is the de facto religion of native people everywhere, but it is also a powerful but neglected current in the Judeo-Christian tradition.

Prophets and Saints of Nature Mysticism

The essence of nature mysticism is that the earth and indeed the universe is alive and holy, pregnant with a spirit of creation. Where monotheism invokes a single God in the First Commandment, nature mysticism senses a tapestry of holiness, including the human, the animal, and the plant realms, all woven together by an underlying creative power (that can be called God, too). Where God of monotheism has acquired patriarchal characteristics, the god(s) of nature mysticism often contain a blend of male and female in a larger oneness, or marriage. Here is how nature mysticism of the Etruscans (1000–300 B.C.E.) was described by D. H. Lawrence:

> Behind all the Etruscan liveliness was a religion of life. Behind all the dancing was a vision, and even a science of life, a concep-

tion of the universe and man's place in the universe which made men live to the best of their capacity. . . . all was alive; the whole universe lived; and the business of man was himself to live amid it all. He had to draw life into himself, out of the wandering huge vitalities of the world. The whole thing was alive, and had a great soul, or *anima*; and in spite of one great soul, there were myriad roving, lesser souls; every man, every creature and tree and lake and mountain and stream was animate, and had its own peculiar consciousness.

Lawrence's description of the Etruscans, we shall see, was no different from the first accounts of conquistadors, explorers, and priests when they met the indigenous tribes of the Americas. Similar forms of nature mysticism exist today as the legacy of early native people all over the earth.

It was inevitable that in overcoming this nature mysticism, as well as goddess-worship, the triumphal Hebrews, Christians, and Muslims would absorb some of its powerful themes.

Over time there developed strands of nature mysticism within those monotheisms, especially through the Middle Ages and the periods prior to the Inquisition and scientific revolution. Within the Hebrew Bible, the *hokmah* ("wisdom literature") contained powerful traces of nature imagery that went back thousands of years in folk memory and lore. The wisdom of Solomon as described in the Bible includes nature wisdom:

He spoke of trees, from the cedar in Lebanon to the hyssop that grows out of the wall; he spoke also of beasts and birds, reptiles and fish. [I KINGS, 5:9–14]

The Hebrew prophets were keenly aware of environmental pollution caused by human transgressions, and implied that the earth had qualities of life:

> The world languishes and withers,
> The heavens languish together with the earth,
> The earth lies polluted under its inhabitants,
> For they have transgressed the laws,
> Violated the statutes, broken the everlasting covenant.
>
> [ISAIAH, 24:4–5]

> Fear not, O soil, rejoice and be glad;
> for the Lord has wrought great deeds.
> Fear not, O beasts of the field, for the
> pastures in the wilderness are clothed with grass.
>
> [JOEL, 2:21–22]

Here we can glimpse the transition between the earlier earth-based tradition and the sky-based one that followed. In Isaiah the earth is not merely lifeless matter, but rather alive with feelings of pain and suffering. It is polluted, however, not because its inhabitants have violated environmental precepts but because they have broken the commandments of God. A people who once prayed to gods of nature are hereafter to obey the Ten Commandments. In this emerging vision, environmental catastrophes stem from failures to adhere to a transcendent moral code. Even today national calamities are referred to in law as "acts of God."

"The earth is the Eternal One's and the fullness thereof," the Bible asserts (Psalms 24:1). Here the earth is part of a holy creation and not the possession of human mortals. This ancient view that creation is "good" (the phrasing of Genesis) has become the basis for today's "green fundamentalists," who counterpose themselves to the Rush Limbaugh–James Watt school of self-serving theology.

The earth, by prophetic implication, does not belong to developers, the timber industry, or the polluters, not even to humanity as a whole, for we humans are all "strangers resident" and "sojourners" upon God's good earth (Psalms 24, Lev. 25:24). The prophets were explicit, for example, in saying that "man's late appearance on earth is to convey an admonition of humility; let him beware of being proud, lest he invite the retort that the gnat is older than he." As a Talmudic commentary on Ecclesiastes states, "God showed the first people the beauty of the world and then instructed them: do not destroy or corrupt my world, for if you do, there is no one to set it right after you."

St. Francis of Assisi (1186–1226) wrote in his great *Canticle of Brother Sun, Sister Moon* that all of creation was a family, and spoke of nature's elements as brothers and sisters:

> All praise be yours, my Lord, through all that you have made,
> And first my Lord *Brother Sun*,
> Who brings the day: and light you give to us through him.
> How beautiful he is, how radiant in all his splendor.
> Of you, most high, he bears the likeness.
>
> And praise be yours, my Lord, through *Sister Moon*
> and stars. In the heavens you have made them
> bright, precious and fair.

All praise be yours, my Lord, through *Sister Earth*,
Our Mother, who feeds us in her sovereignty and
produces fruits and colored flowers and herbs.

In today's terms, St. Francis was a kind of Indian of Christianity, speaking to wolves and calling the earth his mother. Less famous over the centuries than Francis was Hildegard of Bingen (1098–1179), whose writings, music, and paintings are finding a new audience today after nearly 800 years of neglect. A feminist for her time, a respected church theologian, painter, musician, and healer who dwelled in the German Rhineland, Hildegard invented the term *viriditus*, ("greening spirit") for the force she saw in nature. The very word of God, for Hildegard, was "all verdant greening, all creativity." She celebrated Mary as *viridissima virga*, the greenest persona of all. Of Jesus, Hildegard wrote that "in the beginning all creatures were green and vital, [and] later the *green figure* itself came down" (italics added). In one of her visions, she quoted the voice of the Holy Spirit thus:

I am the breeze that nurtures all things green,
I encourage blossoms to flourish with ripening
fruits. I am the rain coming from the dew that
causes the grasses to laugh with the joy of life.

In the Jewish tradition, Nachmanides wrote of the book of Deuteronomy that "scripture will not permit a destructive act that will cause the extinction of a species even when it has permitted the use of that species for food." Maimonides, in *Guide of the Perplexed* (1190), explicitly rebuked the utilitarian notion that nature should serve humanity:

> It should not be believed that all the beings exist for the sake of the existence of humanity. On the contrary, all the other beings too have been intended for their own sakes, and not for the sake of something else.

The Hasidic nature mystic Rabbi Nachman of Bratslav urged daily prayer in the fields and emphasized that God was present and revealed in all of creation. Moses Cordovero (also known as Remak) wrote that "the principle of wisdom is to extend acts of love toward everything, including plants and animals." Indeed, the Jewish mystics felt that God placed "sparks of holiness" throughout *all* creation.

The original significance of the Sabbath, it can be argued, was deeply ecological. Every seventh day was one of rest and renewal, as was every seventh year for the land. One of the leaders of today's National Religious Partnership, Rabbi Daniel Swartz, writes that the Sabbath is the time when the harmony of life is reasserted, "the balance between work and rest, between striving and acceptance, between the momentary and the eternal . . . *the Sabbath becomes for time what wilderness preservation is for space.*"

THE ECO-CONSCIOUSNESS OF JOB

The ancient story of Job is, for me, one of the deepest sources of a creation-based spirituality in the West. Job's tale usually is presented as a treatise on the need to submit obediently to God, even when terrible things happen to good people. But there is quite another interpretation, one that humbles us before the inexplicable mystery of creation. An ego-centered universe is rejected for an eco-centered one.

Job is the Lord's favorite servant. But the Accusing Angel believes that Job is obedient to God only because he is blessed. For the Accusing Angel, Job is just another utilitarian human. The test is whether Job will curse the Lord if his blessings are taken away, or whether Job will remain faithful.

God tests Job's faith in every possible way; he takes Job's children, his wealth, his health, for no reason. Job ultimately breaks down in rage, damning the day he was born. In the usual rendering, he loses "the patience of Job."

But reading the story in a creation-centered framework, it is striking that when God finally decides to answer Job's cries, it is through the medium of an awesome nature spirit described as an "unnamable voice within the whirlwind." Such spirits were commonly thought to be present in cyclones and dust storms. The same nature spirit appears elsewhere in the Bible; for example, the God of Psalms 29 and 65, who "thunders over many waters."

Job's sin, it turns out, was *anthropocentrism,* the arrogant and deluded belief that the earth and universe were designed for human benefit and control. If the authors of *Job* are correct, Stephen Hawking might find that the "mind of God" is more like a whirlwind than a physicist.

"Where were you when I planned the earth? Tell me, if you are so wise," the voice in the whirlwind begins scornfully.

Were you there when I stopped the waters,
As they issued gushing from the womb?
When I wrapped the ocean in clouds
And swaddled the sea in its shadows?
Have you ever commanded morning or guided dawn
to its place?

For verse after verse, the voice in the whirlwind rages on, out-
lining all the interdependent elements of creation—the winds,
clouds, thunderstorms, the lightning, lions, antelopes, oxen,
ostriches, horses, hawks, vultures, bulls, serpents. The voice
lashes out at Job's narrow self-centeredness, admonishing that
he never can understand the complexity and functioning of the
planet and cosmos.

Have you seen to the edge of the universe?
Speak up, if you have such knowledge.

This is the very opposite of a universe built for us to manipulate
as we will. Instead of being given dominion over plants and
animals, or a license to subdue nature, Job is told to bow down
and be humble before its dominion over him. He is required to
understand absolute humility. He says at the end:

Now I will speak no more.
I have spoken of the unspeakable
And tried hard to grasp the infinite.
I had heard of you with my ears
But now my eyes have seen you.
Therefore I will be quiet,
Comforted that I am dust.

Job is reconciled to a "dust" that is more than the earth that is cursed in Genesis. This "comforting" dust, from which Job has come, is real soil, the creation of the voice. His ultimate surrender, as Stephen Mitchell has pointed out, is not the sort of mindless obedience wished by some clerical authorities. It is the kind of surrender that is "the whole-hearted giving up of oneself," a giving surrender to the universe, arising from humility that leads to wisdom instead of anthropocentric pride. Job is born again, converted from an ego-centered to an eco-centered consciousness based on awe.

Genesis: The Loss of the Cosmic Garden

The foundation of a nature-based spirituality in both Christian and Jewish traditions is a strong one, as we have seen, but it remains a lost gospel. It is not the dominant scriptural interpretation, not the dominant tradition, and certainly not the dominant practice of these Western religions over the millennia. The "Old Testament clearly and purposely removes any trace of divinity from nature" admits one biblical scholar in developing a Christian basis for environmental ethics. The superb *Jewish Guide to Environmental Studies* includes one essay that states: "It is not acceptable in Jewish law to make an assertion of the independent rights of nature." These acknowledgments, I want to stress, appear in works *defending* a Judeo-Christian environment ethic.

To understand more fully how nature mysticism became so separated from the mainstream that attempted to transcend nature, one has to return to Genesis, where the split originated. In Genesis, the elevation of Man to "dominion," (a license to plunder the natural world) came about through a religious conflict of monotheistic true believers against the pagan nature worshippers—not unlike that promoted by the Religious Right today.

THE VISIONS UNDERLYING Genesis arose from desert tribes struggling toward unification on both national and religious levels. The Ten Commandments begin with a severe insistence on monotheism, a stern order warning people away from following the old religions that sanctified the earth. The people "shall have no other Gods before me" because God is a jealous divinity, and "you shall not make for yourself an idol, whether in the form of anything that is in heaven above, or that is on the earth beneath, or that is in the water under the earth. You shall not bow down to them or worship them." (Exodus 20:2–5)

With the advent of monotheism, God was relocated to a higher station, a throne, outside the earth. Since the Creator was greater than anything created, a transcendent vision of a ruler outside of creation was required. While the commandments of this god specified ethical human behavior, there was no commandment to honor the earth, for that might stir the ancient pagan attachments.

There were savage wars between these tribes in Canaan, especially in the twelfth and thirteenth centuries B.C.E. A vacuum was caused by the exhaustion of the imperial power of the Pharaohs. Beginning about 1200 B.C.E., sea peoples with iron weapons invaded the eastern Mediterranean coast, while Philistines from the coast and Israelites from the desert raced to fill the power vacuum left by Egypt's withdrawal. The conquest of the land of milk and honey was a bloody one.

The triumph over the old religions was not easy to sustain. The Hebrew Scriptures are filled with suggestions that the people of Israel continued to backslide into their former practices.

> And the children of Israel did secretly those things that were not right against the Lord their God . . .
>
> They set them up images and groves in every high hill, and under every green tree:
>
> And there they burnt incense in all the high places, as did the heathen . . .
>
> Therefore the Lord was very angry with Israel and moved them out of his sight . . .   [2 KINGS 17:9–18]
>
> . . . ye shall destroy their altars, break their images and cut down their groves,
>
> For thou shalt worship no other God: for the Lord, whose name is Jealous, is a jealous God.   [EXODUS 34:13–14]

Prior to the sky-based monotheism, the prevailing tribal religions shared forms of nature worship that eventually became known and condemned as paganism, from the Latin *pagani* ("country people") and later as "heathen," from the German *heiden,* for the "hidden" practices of pagan people.

In pagan worship the earth typically was defined as a mother—Gaia ("mother of all, oldest of Gods") to Plato, or Isis in Egypt, Asherah in Tyre and Sidon, and as Earth Mother among native people in other parts of the globe, a tradition followed by Francis of Assisi. The sun in the heavens was also a powerful divinity on which all life depended. People prayed for the earth's fertility and health in seasonal ceremonies, and for the successful journey of the sun across the sky. Often the sky-god was a male figure that awakened the fertility of the female earth with rain and heat.

Deities were present everywhere, as spirits in mountains, caves, forests, rivers, in special places set aside for ritual, and in living creatures. The serpent that appears in the garden story, for example, was a common symbol in the old religions, representing the force of cyclical regeneration. According to the Book of Kings, the Israelites themselves burned incense to the serpent. Serpent religions were polytheistic; serpent gods were both good and evil, cyclical and seasonal, not beneficent and omnipotent, and definitely not gods of transcendence into eternity beyond nature and universe.

The presence of so many gods reflects the tribal pluralism of the religion. With diverse and multiple gods, there could be no single and permanent center of loyalty to authority. The emergence of monotheism, in historian Mary Condren's theory, closely paralleled the emergence of monarchy from tribalism.

In a desert world of polytheistic clans, the people of Israel lacked any central structure. Unity depended on allegiance to an invisible God, Yahweh, and his commandments. Faced with external aggression, the clan system could not respond. A crisis of authority became pressing. The Israelites, having been oppressed by the Pharaoh, had to decide whether they should support a monarchy of their own. Many prophetic leaders were opposed to the notion of a centralized kingship, while priestly castes tended to favor such an order. Their deliverance from Egypt proved the superiority of the monotheistic god Yahweh over the Pharaoh's many gods; by analogy, a monarchy would be the most powerful defense against tribal aggressors.

Monotheism, and the accompanying monarchy, implied a national structure of loyalty that false gods could not be allowed to obstruct. Political loyalties shifted. The nomadic hunter-gatherer culture that wandered the desert in search of the garden/oasis was being replaced by a settled agricultural civilization. Polytheistic clans rooted in ancient rhythms of the Tigris-Euphrates Valley were pressured to become one nation united under one king and one God. The continuance of goddess worship was replaced by patriarchy. Creation no longer was to be based on the serpent's seasonal fertility but on God's word. In the end the powerful, transcendent, unifying vision of the Judeo-Christian God was reflected in models of a patriarchal, monarchical state that endured for centuries.

THE SIGNIFICANCE OF GENESIS

Genesis remains important to nations, cultures, and individuals because they need creation stories as a basis of their identity. Genesis is the most riveting and important creation story of Western culture. It explains the origin of the whole universe, the earth, and the human family. It defines human responsibility as having dominion over nature, issues a covenant that humans are to obey, introduces sin in the world, and informs us that the loss of paradise is the human condition.

The story of the Garden of Eden has infused Western identity. Explorer-conquerors like Christopher Columbus left behind the battered environment of Europe for a new Eden. At the swelling mouth of the Orinoco River, Columbus speculated that he was near the very confluence of the four great rivers described in Genesis. "The terrestrial paradise must be nearby," he confided in his diary.

Genesis became the scriptural rationale for the conquest and settlement of the new nation. As the 1991 account of the *Oxford History of Christianity* states, "a whole continent had . . . *to be subdued and made fruitful,* and . . . it was reckoned a grievous sin to be idle and unproductive" (italics added).

William Bradford, governor of the Plymouth Colony from 1620 to 1635, portrayed his surroundings as "a hideous and desolate wilderness, full of wild beasts and wild men." Nothing could save them "but the spirit of God and his grace." John Winthrop, governor of the Massachusetts Bay Colony, echoed the Genesis mandate in 1629. Americans could not "allow a whole continent to lie empty and unimproved," he declared, for "the whole earth is the Lord's Garden, and he has given it to the sons of man upon a condition: increase and multiply, replenish the earth and subdue it." Cotton Mather went farther in his 1689 "counsel to soldiers" to think of the Indians as the Amalekites in the Book of Joshua, whom the Israelites were mandated by God to destroy.

For the next two centuries, according to a careful historical study, the nation's textbooks "universally upheld the belief that the true story of the earth comes from Genesis." Even after Charles Darwin reported his theory of evolution, the popular *McGuffey Reader* still instructed American schoolchildren that "the Earth was formed by the Creator to be the abode of man during a short life, and the school in which he is to prepare for a life that will never end, . . . all the works of God are founded in wisdom and are intended for some benevolent purpose," and that to think differently was "a very wrong and wicked wish."

Restoring a Mystical Eden

To recover a lost nature mysticism it is crucial to recall that from the time of Columbus there were dissenters against the imperial Conquest of the Americas who clung to utopian images of an unspoiled Eden. They include obscure figures like Francisco Roldan, who led a commoners' rebellion against Columbus to create an Indian-Hispanic state in Hispaniola. There was the famous Father Bartolomé de Las Casas, whose 1552 eyewitness account, *The Devastation of the Indies,* chronicled forty years of genocide in the islands known as paradise. Among the first Roanoke colonists were those who "went to Croatan," joining an Indian tribe close to the Virginia settlement.

Among the dreamers arriving in America was a sect called the Adamites (named after the first earthling), who practiced "going naked for a sign" that they were back in Eden. The mystics of Merry Mount, like Thomas Morton in the 1620s, paraded around maypoles and held interracial assemblies with

Indians. Roger Williams, the founder of Rhode Island, wrote poetry as if he were an Indian mocking the new Puritan settlements:

> We wear no clothes, have many Gods,
> And yet our sins are less:
> You are barbarians, pagans wild,
> Your land's the wilderness.

As late as the mid-eighteenth century, a Frenchman known only as Priber formed a utopian community in Georgia called Paradise, composed of Cherokees, runaway slaves, and debtors. He died in prison, his books and even his first name lost to history. To this day, certain Cherokee descendants are known as tri-racials, possible descendants from this attempted paradise.

Nathaniel Hawthorne later wrote that the future of America as a new Eden was at stake in these early quarrels. If the "grisly saints" of Puritanism prevailed, Hawthorne remarked, America would be an Eden lost, a place "of hard toil, of sermon and psalm, forever." But if the Merry Mount nature spirit took hold, he forecast that a "sunshine would break upon the hills and flowers would beautify the forest."

These experiments in restoring a mystical Eden served as the seeds of an alternative to the dominant Puritan version of Genesis that moved the nation toward its "manifest destiny." The romantic identification with nature and native people continued to survive in the vision of modern environmentalism and human rights movements.

Through the 1960s, symbols of Genesis continued to play a

central role across all dimensions of our culture. There was rebel icon James Dean embodying the curse and fall in the film *East of Eden*. There were the American astronauts in space reciting Genesis and, when Americans landed on the moon, President Nixon claimed it was the "greatest week since Genesis." The romantic theme of kinship resurfaced as well; in her song "Woodstock," Joni Mitchell sang for the sixties generation that "we've got to get back to the Garden."

The Green Genesis

Environmentalists generally are wary of Genesis. The tale is seen as elevating humans to dominance over nature, rather than a source of environmental wisdom. The environmental critique of Genesis began with John Muir, who questioned the conventional assumption that God gave everything in the world to humans. Were sheep created, he asked, to provide wool after Adam and Eve were expelled from Eden? Were whales "storehouses of oil for us" until oil wells could be discovered? He asked: "Why should man value himself as more than a small part of one great unit of creation?" Other creatures, to Muir, were our "earth-born companions and fellow mortals."

This fundamental division between the Genesis tradition and environmentalism was restated in 1967 in a widely discussed article by professor Lynn White in *Science* magazine. Titled "The Historical Roots of Our Ecological Crisis," the essay asserted that the West's pollution crisis was rooted in "the victory of

Christianity over paganism," especially the assertion of a linear creation story leading to a heaven beyond time and space.

White interpreted Genesis to mean that man is "not simply part of nature: he is made in God's image" and that God has "planned all this explicitly for man's benefit and rule. . . . By destroying pagan animism, Christianity made it possible to exploit nature in a mood of indifference to the feelings of natural objects."

Muir and White, living nearly a century apart, both were wounded Christians more than they were pagans or committed atheists. Muir rebelled against the starched Puritanism of his stern father, who was a Scotch Presbyterian minister. Muir longed for recognition of the Creator's presence not in churches filled with straight-backed pews, but in the "cathedrals of nature," his Sierra Nevada. White, despite his hostility to mainstream doctrines of Genesis, proposed that St. Francis be named "the patron saint of ecology."

Is a green interpretation of Genesis possible? If not, environmentalism faces the difficult task of refuting and replacing the key creation myth of Western civilization. But if a greener Genesis is possible, it would be an important new vision for those who would rather not have to choose between their religious faith and their environmental beliefs.*

---

*A 1991 Gallup Poll found that 47 percent of Americans adhere to a "strict Creationist" view, described as "God created man pretty much in his present form at one time in the last 10,000 years." Forty percent believed the "centrist view" that "man developed over millions of years from less advanced forms of life, but God guided this process." Only 9 percent accepted the "naturalist view" that humans "evolved from less advanced forms of life" without God's

Genesis 1: The Story of the Cosmos

The biblical scholar Everett Fox notes that "Genesis 1 is unmistakably reacting against prevailing Near Eastern cosmogonies of the time." These were animistic faiths that located divinities in nature, often in sexual form. The God of Genesis (*elohim*), however, has no gender, origin, or limitation in space or time. There is no dialectic with other forces leading to creation, no sexual act of "begetting" as between male and female deities. This God simply *is*. By God's actions, we are to understand God's character. God is omnipotent, creating order and symmetry. Above all God is a *designing* God; a creator outside the universe and the earth, outside nature.

The philosopher J. Baird Callicott noted that this Genesis "resembles contemporaneous Greek cosmologies virtually point for point." There is in Plato's thought a sharp dualism between mind and nature. The God of Genesis 1 parallels the platonic mind. In the naturalist view, chaos in the universe and wilderness on earth are powerful forces with which humanity must harmonize or coexist. The implication of Genesis 1 is the opposite; only the external God can tame wilderness and chaos, and only when humans are obedient.

---

intervention. Believers in the strict Creationist interpretation have declined, however, from about 67 percent in the early 1960s. From a practical point of view, it appears that Americans will choose to believe the Genesis dominion mandate where it contradicts environmental imperatives, unless Genesis can be reinterpreted in a greener way.

The declaration that each step of creation was "good" is the key starting point for revering the earth as holy, and for retrieving a creation-based cosmology. For Matthew Fox the notion that creation is "good" is the *original blessing* that preceded any original sin and fall. In a creation-centered spirituality, humans would experience creation as *ongoing*, not as a divine act decided long ago. Creation of earthly life would hint at heaven itself, instead of being reduced to a transitional stage of existence.

The major interpretive problem, however, comes with the mandate of dominion given to the humans on the sixth day of creation. This is the turning point in which God seems to retire to absentee ownership of the earth, and appoints us as his overseers. (In the Islamic texts describing creation, incidentally, man is described similarly, as a kind of viceroy serving a kinglike figure of God.)

Both the lordly and stewardship interpretations of "dominion" can be derived from this text. In both models there is a hierarchy in which humans, made in God's image, rule over the animal, plant, and marine kingdoms. The difference lies in how dominion is exercised. *Rada*, the Hebrew for "dominion over," is associated with force and coercion, and elsewhere in the Bible refers to government supervision. In the Hebrew Scriptures the common meaning of *kabas*, the root of "subdue," is used in the context of violence, the subjugation of foreigners, sins being stamped out, and enslavement. The verb *shamar*, also used in Genesis, means to guard or protect against enemies. These meanings support the exploitative model. However, the clear analogy in Genesis with shepherds and their flocks lends itself to a kinder, gentler model of control.

Genesis 2: The Garden Story

In Genesis 2, written centuries earlier than the cosmos story, God places Adam in the Garden "to till and tend it." The modern *Oxford Bible* (1991) says that "human dominion, corresponding to God's rule, is to be peaceful and benevolent." In any event, God has given the natural world to us as an entitlement program. What humans do with this resource is a matter of free will.

This Genesis begins in the desert, the harsh wilderness of nature, where "no bush of the field was yet on earth . . . for God had not made it rain." But then came the rains, the enrichment of the soil, and Adam, the "earthling." Adam is formed of "dust from the soil," but becomes a living being by the breath of the designing God. He is placed in the Garden of Eden, a legendary home of tribes in the Tigris-Euphrates Valley. This was "nature primeval," in the phrase of Callicott, who interprets the Garden story as a lament at the historical shift from nomadic life to settled agriculture. In this original Eden there was no "self," or ego-awareness, differentiated from the seamless whole of nature's process. Eden means "delight," and is the "garden of god." The place was an oasis of both fertility and beauty. This is the symbolic Eden of Merry Mount's revellers, of Joni Mitchell's lyrics, of romantic environmentalism.

At the center of Eden is the Tree of Life, though it is not given great significance in conventional discussions of Genesis. The Tree of Life was a powerful symbol in the old religions. The Tree is nature's means of grounding the human in the universe, with roots in the earth, branches reaching to the heavens, and a center providing strength. The original Tree of Life has been traced to the Chaldeans who lived in the Tigris-Euphrates Valley. In the epic of *Gilgamesh,* which preceded the Bible, the Trees of Life were the giant cedars of Lebanon. For early Egyptians the Tree of Life stood in the center of paradise, providing immortality. For pagan Ireland and Europe, the Great Tree was also a sacred symbol. Ancient native traditions in the Americas placed a sacred tree at the center of the universe. The Mayan people always had a *ceiba* tree at the sacred center of their communities. The Iroquois symbol was the great white pine, whose sachems were known as "pine tree chiefs" because they sprang from the people. To the legendary Black Elk, the "flowering tree was the living center of the sacred hoop."

In the garden story, we can speculate that the Tree of Life represents the nature-based tradition of spirituality. God is thankful that Adam and Eve seem unaware of the holy tree, "lest [Adam] send forth his hand and take also from the Tree of Life and eat and live throughout the ages!" What does this passage mean? What does this God fear? One can make too much of these fleeting lines of Genesis, but it is tempting to think of the Tree of Life as a symbol of nature's eternal organic cycle, abandoned when our human ancestors, burdened with sin, began their linear journey from Eden toward eternal redemption. The possibility of "living throughout the ages" through the eternal cycles of human and natural life was replaced by new transcendent possibilities of monotheism.

The stewardship mandate to "till and keep" the Garden is given on one condition, that the humans not eat from the more famous tree in the Garden, the Tree of Knowledge of Good and

Evil: "you are not to eat from it, for on the day you eat from it, you must die, yes, die." I always have resisted this part of the story, for it seems to require a blind obedience to God or his representatives, under the threat of the first death penalty. Callicott makes the enticing observation that seeking to obtain this "knowledge of good and evil" is the arrogant sin of anthropocentrism—usurping the right to decide universal truths from an ego-centered vantage point. When we "size up the creation in relation to ourselves," Callicott writes, we create an "inevitable alienation from nature."

The serpent becomes the first creature cursed to exist in this new Cold War with humans. Next, Eve is cursed to suffer pain in the natural act of giving birth. Then, because of Adam, the soil is cursed. Thorns and stinging thistles will spring up when Adam tries to take plants from the field. Instead of living in Eden's lush environment, he will endure by the sweat of his brow in "painstaking labor." In the garden story of the fall, the human and the natural world are plunged into antagonism for the first time. This division is also the inner nature of the human. As Paul would say later, the natural world was placed in "bondage to decay" and "groaning in travail"; likewise, human beings would "groan inwardly, as we wait for the redemption of our bodies" (Romans 8:19–23).

Eve and the Serpent

God's effort to create plants and animals as "helpers" for Adam was a failure. The needs of the first human being could not be met by nature. The magic and beauty of the universe were not a cure for male loneliness. Only Eve would do.

The appearance of Eve as the first woman must be seen in the context of the nature-based goddess religions of the era. If woman once was elevated as goddess, now she was nothing more than Adam's rib, a creature derivative of man. Just as Eve was the goddess inverted and overthrown, so too was the serpent a pagan deity brought low, a creature of treachery and deceit. The battle of transcendent monotheism against nature worship and goddess cults was distilled in the curse of God against this subversive conspiracy between the serpent and Eve.

Nearly fifty years ago, Simone de Beauvoir observed that Woman "is the privileged object through which [man] subdues nature. . . . In women are incarnated the disturbing mysteries of Nature, and man escapes her hold when he frees himself from Nature." It has taken centuries of abuse for women to begin to react successfully against the blame and inferiority assigned them by Genesis.* The parallels between women and nature are many.

---

* The Judeo-Christian religion is not the only one to place the female in a subordinate role. Hinduism, Buddhism, and Islam are patriarchal, as well. Nor is the Bible the only source of this negative association of women and nature. Aristotle claimed that the active male, through the "power which resides in the semen," implanted himself in the women's passive "matter," much like a gardener fertilizing soil. But it was Christianity that promoted the inferiority of women as an incontestable theological assertion, not an empirical issue. This misogyny culminated in the Inquisition, in which millions of "witches" were condemned not only for being possessed by Satan, but for nature-based practices of healing.

Similar themes carried over to the conquest of America, whose first colony was named for a virgin (Virginia), and where wilderness was described alternatively as seductive, wild, and needing domestication.

They represent the natural cycles of regeneration, birth, seasons, galaxies. The difference is that the banished descendants of Eve today are able to protest their oppression and demand a reinterpretation of sexist scripture in order to portray a "feminine face of God." Now the analogous question at hand is whether a nature-based wisdom can be retrieved from a Genesis story in which nature is cursed and hostile—and which generations of believers have internalized just as deeply as patriarchy.

Toward a Kinship Interpretation of Genesis

In the end, Genesis leaves us three possible interpretations: lordly dominion, paternal stewardship, and interdependent kinship.

The first—defining dominion as sheer dominance or exploitation—has been the most common in practice over the millennia, down to its use by the Religious Right today. But the scriptural justification for pillaging the natural world is lacking. There are the angry passages in Isaiah 10–11 in which God threatens to "hack down the thickets of the forest with an ax / and Lebanon with its majestic trees will fall." These ravings find

---

The doctrines of possessing the female continue to reverberate today. For instance, a 1970s university law textbook opined that "land, like a woman, was meant to be possessed." The woman who successfully protested this offensive text went on to become the president of the National Organization of Women, Patricia Ireland.

their echoes in the European treatment of native people and their lands over the centuries. But few today would cite Genesis as justification for deforesting the Amazon Basin.

It is true that Genesis assigns humans a higher status than animals and plants, but there is no explicit emphasis on a license to exploit, torture, or harm. Nonetheless that "right" seems to have been claimed by destroyers seeking to justify their conquests and save their souls. Tragically our religious institutions have said little in the past two thousand years to censure or reverse such exploitation of the natural world in the name of God.

Stewardship is a second, more defensible interpretation of how Genesis instructs humans. If people of faith and institutions of religion will accept stewardship sincerely as a moral obligation, the condition of the environment will improve. Stewardship would be a step forward from the blind destruction now carried on in God's name.

But the concept of stewardship raises unsettling ecological and ethical questions. Genesis never explains why the plant and animal kingdoms need our stewardship after several billion years of being on their own. Stewardship implies dualism, hierarchy, and elitism. What is the evidence that human beings know what is best for nature, or that humans are separate from and superior to the natural world? The evidence is that we are interdependent with all of nature, not its paternalistic stewards.

Perhaps an analogy of social behavior will make the point. Society is evolving beyond stewardship models. White people are not the stewards of black and brown people. Men are not the stewards of women. Marriages are based on legal equality, not the husband having dominion over his wife. The old stewardship models are being rejected for a new understanding of the interdependence of all the unique cultures and qualities that make up society. Similarly, the stewardship model ultimately may be replaced by an ecological model based on interdependence and kinship.

I BELIEVE THERE is a kinship model retrievable from Genesis that is deeper than stewardship; a trace of nature mysticism that forms the biblical basis of the lost gospel of the earth. Kinship is the original state of things in the universe and the Garden. Kinship is implicit in the declaration that all creation is good. Kinship is present in the Garden before the fall. And kinship is suggested in part by a rainbow covenant that climaxes the human journey that begins with Adam and Eve and ends with Noah, the last truly good man in this early stage of the human drama, who is assigned to protect the biodiversity of species and start anew.

After the flood, God decided that his curse was too harsh for an innocent earth placed in the dangerous hands of fallen human beings. And so while God repeats the stewardship mandate to "be fruitful and multiply," and take charge of "every living and crawling thing," God also declares a Rainbow Covenant with the earth itself, one independent of the agendas of human beings (italics added):

> This is the sign of the covenant which I set between me and you and all living beings that are with you for ageless generations.

My bow I set in the clouds, so that it may serve as a sign of the covenant between me and the earth.

This Rainbow Covenant was repeated and elaborated by the interfaith gathering of religious environmentalists in Assisi, Italy, in 1986, and adopted at the Festival of Creation at Washington National Cathedral in May 1990 in Washington, D.C. It is the covenant, for Christians at least, that will last until the return of the Messiah, whose reign will be "paradise regained" in the phrase of the *Oxford Bible*. This will be a utopian moment of reconciliation between humans and the natural world, in the vision of Isaiah, when wolves lie down with lambs, when cows and bears shall graze together, when the child shall play by the asp, when none will "destroy my holy mountain, for the earth will be full of the knowledge of the Lord" (Isaiah, 11:6–9).

Does any of this mean we can return to the garden? The expulsion from Eden would seem to be final, not reversible by the Rainbow Covenant. God has cast the humans out, and installed winged sphinxes with flashing swords east of Eden "to watch over the way to the Tree of Life." Return seems hopeless. Banishment becomes the human condition, to be followed by painful labor to extract a living from the hostile soil. With Adam and Eve, the story of uprooted immigrants has begun.

The Return to Eden

The image of the garden contains our oldest memories and legends, of a communal state of nature where humans were free of guilt and the fear of death. This garden, the place of natural kinship, remains the ideal state. In the Christian tradition of original sin and redemption, a future Heaven becomes the substitute for a past Eden. In a creation-based spirituality, by contrast, we do not ascend from Eden, but can return to the garden as part of our original blessing.

We can return, not literally, but through "a higher level of consciousness" based on kinship and humility, as Callicott contends. The key, which Genesis acknowledges, is to follow the way toward the Tree of Life, and thus make our consciousness and our world more like the image of the garden. The tree, the ancient symbol of nature's eternal cycle, contains the seed of living throughout the ages. Instead of ascending to heaven, it calls us back to earth. Instead of alienating us from nature, it reminds us of kinship with nature. The great tree grows from a seed, nourishes life, dies and is reborn through casting its seed into nature's flow.

"I do not believe that a plant will spring up where no seed has been," Thoreau once wrote, "but I have great faith in a seed. Convince me that you have a seed there, and I am prepared to expect wonders." There is a parallel in Job (14: 7–9):

> There is hope for a tree, if it is cut down it will renew itself; its shoots will not cease. If its roots are old in the earth, and its stump dying in the ground, at the scent of water, it will bud and produce branches like a young sapling.

We cannot leave the universe, but we can leave ourselves within its life-giving structure. Life and death are a continuum, not separate states. We can return to the sea as our remains become runoff. We can return to the sky as the sea evaporates. We can return to the earth as rain. We can return to our children as spirits. And our remains can become the stuff of Eden again.

If this lost meaning of Genesis is not the heaven our parents promised, it is still consolation enough for me. Like Job, I am comforted to be the dust of stars and Eden.

5

The Lost Gospel
in Our
Native History

*Every shining pine needle, every sandy shore, every mist in
the dark woods, every clearing and every humming insect is
holy. . . . Whatever befalls the earth befalls the soul of the earth.*

CHIEF SEATTLE, 1854

THE LOST GOSPEL of the earth is inseparable from the
culture and land of native people in the Americas and around
the world. Nature mysticism arises from an imagination rooted
in a place. The Cherokee language has a word, *eloheh*, that means
land, religion, history, and culture, all at the same time, without
dualisms. The journey to discover the lost gospel of the earth
inevitably leads to the ancient, indigenous cultures that were
subjugated by, yet still coexist with, our Western one.

In our quest we will cross the divide that usually separates
modern industrial civilization from traditional society and cul-

ture. We will find that everyone has indigenous roots that have been suppressed, denied, forgotten, or sentimentalized into trivia. The search for the lost gospel thus becomes a deeper exploration of our common identity in a native past. No one is purely settler, or purely native. We are all indigenous somewhere.

In my formal education, I never learned the indigenous histories—cultural or ecological—of the places I came from. But they were all new Edens, and their heritage was lost. My ancestors were emigrants from Ireland, fleeing the Great Famine of the 1840s. Their descendants made homes in rural and small-town Michigan and Wisconsin, displacing the native people who had lived there for thousands of years. With roots in Ireland with its Celtic nature spirituality, they gradually became urban Catholics who passed on to me a religion based on strict obedience to a paternal God in the eternal heavens.

In searching for the lost gospel, it has been necessary to uncover this hidden history of my own family roots. And all of us must seek our spirituality and our story in the same way. Most of us have indigenous roots in nature mysticisms of long ago. The lost gospel lies within us, deeply submerged on the oldest levels of the psychic architecture of our consciousness. This is so, whether we are descendants of African slaves, Mexican farmworkers, Asian refugees, or white Europeans. Many of our ancestors lived organically in tribal groupings, where they learned to practice conservation and embraced earth-based spiritualism. The myths of Eden and expulsion echo beneath the surface of their histories.

Take an example from African-American culture: the traditional art of weaving sweetgrass, which is threatened today by excessive development on the Carolina coastline. Sweetgrass is a long and luxurious grass that was originally used by the basketweavers of west Africa (and by Native Americans). Sweetgrass basket-making continued as a subversive art during slavery, a ritual of spiritual continuity with one's ancestors. The sweetgrass baskets remained central to the coastal culture of African-Americans for three centuries, until subdivisions tripled the population of South Carolina in the past thirty years.

In 1994 the *New York Times* described the urgent effort of hundreds of volunteers to save the sweetgrass by planting two thousand clumps at an inland location away from the natural coastal habitat. Why would citizens of the modern urban world undertake such a seemingly hopeless effort? To maintain a cultural and spiritual identity based on the earth.

Even our most modernist commentators, like the editors of *Time* magazine, express occasional worry at the loss of what they acknowledge is "tribal wisdom." It has been estimated that of five thousand languages spoken on earth today, only a hundred will survive the coming century. In a far-sighted 1991 cover story, *Time* warned of the imminent loss of "an enormous trove of wisdom" as thousands of tribes are threatened with extinction. These vanishing cultures, *Time* lamented, are "humanity's lifeline to a time when people accepted nature's authority." If *Time* is willing to endorse ceremonies honoring tribal shamans, perhaps retrieval of the larger lost gospel is not a hopeless quest.

Celtic Spirituality as the Lost Gospel

My Irish ancestors could be called the Indians of Europe, a people who lived in clans and tribes, were warriors with a heroic view of life, and who communicated with spirits in the land and sea.

The Irish creation stories, going back thousands of years, tell of succeeding tribal waves, each of which comprised an element of a larger Being. The earliest of these mythic races, known sometimes as the companions of Cesair, were pagan idolaters who escaped the flood of Noah's time by secluding themselves in Ireland. Later tribes covered the island, creating the four directions and the sacred center. Those known as the Fir Bholg came in search of liberty. They retreated into the mountains when the legendary Tuatha De Danaan, the people of the goddess Diana, came through the air, introducing the dimension of spirituality. Masters of arts, magic and law, their shamans were known as druids. Five thousand years ago or more, these ancient people created the elaborate centers of community, science, and spirituality at Newgrange, a chambered structure older than the Egyptian pyramids.

These early Irish developed a language sometimes known as *Ogham,* popularized today as a kind of Irish *I Ching* known as runes. The evolution of language and thought was closely based on ancient traditions of knowing places intimately, including natural environments, spirit realms, and human cultures. The Irish-language poet Nualla Ni Dhomhaill speaks of this nature-

and place-based lore, or *Dinnsheanchas,* as a powerful resource for spirituality and the environment. "Through Dinnsheanchas," she writes, "we can possess the land emotionally and imaginatively without any particular sense of, or actual need for, titular ownership. . . . [W]ithout the mediation of this dimension of the human imagination, rocks and grass and water would be for me only rocks and grass and water."

Even today the roots of this Irish world view can be glimpsed in Irish idioms. The common statement "Of course, I don't believe in fairies, but they're there" is an example of this ambiguous mind-set. The poet Seamus Heaney tells of an Irish student writing a school lesson describing a sparrow thus: "[I]t is a migratory bird, and he have a roundy head." The sentence begins with the analytical, detached English-language perception, and then slides into the intuitive Irish animism in which the sparrow has a subjective personality.

THE EARLY IRISH created a culture that was energized and organized according to nature's sacred cycles. On the festival of *Imbolc* (February 1), they lit the sacred flame to awaken the winter sun. On *Beltane* (May 1) their drums heralded fertility through rituals and dancing. On *Lughasadh* (August 1) they revered the sun god, Lugh. On *Samain* (November 1) they celebrated a new year by communing with the spirits of the "otherworld." In all these practices they were little different than other native peoples around the world.

Until the nineteenth century the majority of rural Irish lived in kinship-based clans similar to tribes in America. An Irish *clachan* was a village with communal land-holdings. One's *cui-bhreadh*, or share, was based on kinship and on understanding of environmental limits. The *rundale* system of agricultural production involved collective use of alternating furrows on the same field. The poor depended upon the potato, a crop that originated with native people in the Americas. Far from despoiling the land, one historian says, "these clustered settlements represented a sophisticated environmental response to the farming of marginal lands, and were very successful in reclaiming bog and mountain areas." A description of this life by historian Kevin Whelan is remarkably similar to descriptions of Indian villages in America:

> In this intimate face-to-face world . . . a rich oral culture was encouraged . . . [S]inging, dancing and storytelling emerged as the prized art forms. All this life was intricately interwoven with the cohesive quality of rundale life, with its communal, customary and contextual modes of organization. The vivacity and gaiety of the society, as well as its hospitality, was constantly commented on by pre-Famine visitors.

A GREEN CHRISTIANITY

Even after the Irish were converted to Christianity, their ties to nature spirituality remained so deep that theirs became the "greenest" church in Europe. "Early Irish Christian spirituality is marked by both the intimacy of a tribal society and by a use of nature imagery bordering on pantheism," writes Fintan O'Toole. The great Christian mystic Columba (or Colum) founded his sixth-century monastery in a sacred grove in Derry (he called it "my dear little cell and dwelling"), and declared that cutting down oak trees was profane. He was excommunicated by the Church and exiled for thirty years on Iona, an island made of perhaps the oldest exposed rock on earth. Columba returned once to Ireland in C.E. 574 to defend more than one thousand bards who were being expelled by a Church synod. He was refused when he asked that they be given a place to practice their rituals. It was the end of the druids as recognized priests of the ancient religion.

The subversive power of Celtic mysticism was not defeated, however. It resurfaced in the work of John Scotus Erigena ("John the Irishman, born in Eire"), one of the greatest theologians of the Middle Ages. He was accused of pantheism and saw his work *De Divisione Naturae* burned in C.E. 1210. This ancient pagan Christianity remains alive in Ireland today, much to the discomfort of the established hierarchy. O'Toole predicts that the Irish Church "in the year 2000 will look remarkably like what it was in 1800—a focus for a relaxed but deep spirituality."

English hostility toward Irish culture and customs directly foreshadowed their colonial antagonism toward the Indians of the New World. During Oliver Cromwell's military campaign between 1641 and 1652, thirty percent of the Irish population died of sword, plague, and famine, while much the same fate was occurring among native people across the Atlantic. Just as California Indians would be scorned as lazy "diggers," the Irish peasants were a "lazy" people who depended on a "lazy root," the potato. In this colonial view, cited by Kevin Whelan, the potato was "the crop which fosters, from the earliest childhood,

habits of indolence, improvidence and waste." The British destroyed the *rundale* and *clachan* systems "in the belief that only
individual farms would encourage initiative and self-reliance."
The whole country had to be enclosed in long straight fences,
even running up mountainsides. In a further uprooting, Irish
language was banned and delegitimized. The native Irish
tongue, lamented a nineteenth-century Irish farmer, was the
language of "all that's gone before me—the speech of these
mountains, and lakes, and these glens where I was bred and
born." The language historian Tim Robinson confirms that the
Irish language was "an emanation of the land of Ireland, of this
segment of the earth's surface and its moody skies. . . . The
farmer without Irish is a stranger in his own land." It may be
debated whether the British intended racial genocide or were
merely indifferent to Irish starvation; but there is no doubt that
the Irish language, with its implications for nature and culture,
was the target of complete eradication.

In the Great Hunger of the 1840s, while British ministers
were describing Ireland as a savage wilderness, 1 million Irish
died of starvation or famine fever while at least a fourth of the
entire population (or 2 million) was forced to emigrate. A new
system and world view—an enclosure system that consolidated
property in fewer hands and maximized immediate yield at the
land's expense—were imposed on the ruins of the indigenous
culture. The official *Report of the 1851 Census* even declared that
Ireland had *benefited* from the famine. A British finance minister
agreed that the catastrophe was all for the good: "Except for a
purgatory of misery and starvation, I cannot see how Ireland is

to emerge into a state of anything approaching to quiet or prosperity."

Subjugating the Irish was an experimental exercise on the English path to the conquest and creation of America. "Ireland was a sort of apprenticeship," writes historian Frederick Turner, "the Irish natives serving the English as the Moors and West Africans had once served the Portuguese and Spanish. Irish campaigns were schooling in savagery and in them the 'wild Irish' forfeited their lives and lands by reason of cultural differences." The *London Times,* speaking of the Irish-speaking Connemara region of western Ireland, drew the connections between the conquests of Ireland and America directly: "In a few years, a Celtic Irishman will be as rare in Connemara as a Red Indian on the shores of Manhattan."

The Irish mourned and raged against their expulsion from Eden. "A sea-guarded Garden pines and faints in the throes of hunger, in the shame and torture of tyranny," wrote the nationalist paper *The Nation* in May 1851.

The old nature spirits seemed to have failed the Irish people in their moment of crisis. After the famine, the countryside was devastated for generations. Traumatized silence replaced song and dance. Nature mysticism declined. The language nearly disappeared altogether. Unmarked graves covered the landscape. Only now, 150 years later, is the Great Hunger beginning to be recalled and commemorated officially. One of its deepest legacies, besides the decline of the nature gods, was an alienation from the environment.

Irish Times writer John Waters wrote in 1995 that "we have constructed an ideology of progress which has turned concepts of 'land' and 'soil' into four-letter words, and thereby cut us off from the very means of our own survival. . . . We have turned Ireland into a polluter's paradise, selling off our birthright earth to the multinational sector. . . . But even here, the evidence of our pathology seeks to emerge from the language and hit us between the eyes. The phrase 'make the landscape pay,' so much in favor among the current crop of modernizers, has about it an irony. . . . It is as though we were seeking to take revenge on the earth for the horror it inflicted upon our people 150 years ago."

FROM THE LOST GOSPEL
TO THE NEW RELIGION

In *The Uprooted*, his great classic of immigration, Oscar Handlin wrote that "the migration to America had destroyed the context of the peasants' natural religion."* The new life was separated from the soil, requiring that the emigrant "reconcile himself to a life away from the earth, that he cut himself off from the process of birth and death, from the cycle of growth, aging and regeneration that once had given meaning to his being."

But the passivity of their peasant cultures stayed with the immigrants, making "the texture of their Christianity an oth-

---

* Stannard notes, however, that Handlin failed to stress the link between the immigrants and native people in America, instead perpetuating myths common among historians of the time. Handlin, writes Stannard, "referred to thoroughly populated and agriculturally cultivated Indian territories as 'empty space' . . . [and] makes more references to the Indians' 'quickly developed taste for firewater' than to any other single attribute." (See Stannard, *American Holocaust*, 12–13.)

erworldly fatalism." The newcomers to America were reduced to those religious institutions they could bring along: "'Well, the trolls and fairies will stay behind, but the church and priest at very least will come.' The more thorough the separation from the other aspects of the old life, the greater was the hold of the religion that alone survived the transfer."

The Irish emigrants were a major chapter of Handlin's universal story. They were often defined as a subhuman, animal-like race like the Indians or the African slaves. In 1860 a Cambridge historian and minister classified them as "human chimpanzees"; in 1863 the founder of the Children's Aid Society in America called the Irish mentally deficient because their skull size was closer to the African than the English. The average period of survival on reaching America was only six years. A disproportionate number of Irish filled the lunatic asylums of New York and Boston. Dumped into squalid urban ghettos, living in streets and basements, they were as far from the natural world of pastoral Ireland as one could imagine. The dangerous work that was available to Irish laborers—in mining and the building of canals and roads—laid waste to the New World's environment. To make the bottom rung of whiteness, the Irish had to compete for menial jobs with blacks in the cities or become Indian-fighters on the frontier.

This emigration was spiritual as well as physical, an erasure or denial of the Irish native past that might have linked them with the lower classes, the freed slaves and the Indians of America. Their spiritual emigration required, as Handlin pointed out, the repression of their old nature mysticism in favor of a faith that offered an otherworldly theology of a better life beyond this vale of tears, possible only through the separation of soul from nature. "Poor thing that he was, his soul was yet a matter of consequence," Handlin observed. Thus the eternal aftermath to life increasingly became a consolation to a people who previously had rooted their spirituality in the seasons of the earth. Given their helpless condition, the only practical hope for these emigrants was to follow the Church, leave the past behind, and assimilate into a new identity altogether.

But the price of this Irish-American assimilation was high: deprivation and amnesia about their spiritual and tribal origins rooted in the land, a displacement from the village on earth to a heaven in the sky.

MY FAMILY IDENTIFIED success in America by the distance our peasant roots and spirituality were left behind. They taught me nothing of a past that they considered shamefully primitive and from which they themselves were severed. I never knew that my namesake, Thomas Emmett, was banished to America under a death sentence in the early 1800s, and became a leader of the Irish nationalist cause in New York. I knew nothing of the rolling hills of Monaghan County, from where my Irish ancestors fled while half the population was being decimated in the 1840s. I was born and raised in the bubble of modernity, floating away from this Irish past. Though I was a descendant, an orphan, from a social and environmental trauma of epic proportions, the story of the Great Famine was absent in my family (and in many

Irish-American families) until I began seeking a deeper understanding of my own roots after the upheavals of the 1960s.

Shortly after the confrontations in the streets of Chicago in 1968, at a time I was feeling particularly uprooted, I watched on television as Irish people were gassed and beaten on the streets of Derry while singing "We Shall Overcome." For the first time in my life I felt a connection to my Irish heritage. In search of those roots, I flew to the southern Republic, expecting to drive to Belfast and Derry in the North. Acting on U.S. and British intelligence, the Irish authorities questioned me for twenty-four hours in Shannon Airport, then expelled me from the country as a potentially subversive revolutionary. My romantic desire for roots had met a stern rejection. The name of the Irish official who signed the expulsion order was Garity, my mother's maiden name.

The expulsion only deepened my resolve. I decided to resurrect my mother's Irish name. My wife, Jane, and I bestowed it on our son, Troy, in 1973. We felt we were keeping something alive in that name, something more than my mother's memory. Perhaps there was a trace memory of the expulsion of my ancestors from the garden that Ireland once had been, and in naming our son Garity, there was a desire for return. I wonder today if the experience of expulsion from our own ethnic gardens doesn't reverberate as an unhealed pain in our own memories. Naming our son Garity was a step in the recovery of memory and healing of loss.

It also was then that I began to understand how an Indian in America must feel.

THE JOURNEY CONTINUED:
NATIVE SPIRITUALITY IN THE MIDWEST

My Irish ancestors arrived in Wisconsin and Michigan in the 1840s, fleeing the famine. Like millions of others, they crossed the ocean in vessels so dangerous that they were called "coffin ships." Tens of thousands of emigrants died of sickness and fever during the crossings, and were buried at sea.

The survivors arrived at a quarantine island called Grosse Ile in the St. Lawrence River, a treatment center for the exhausted and feverish. Today a monument on the isolated island reads that "in this secluded spot lie the mortal remains of 5,294 persons, who, fleeing from pestilence and famine in Ireland in the year 1847, found in America but a grave."

Those of my kin who survived came to pastoral Sullivan, Town 6 North, in Jefferson County, Wisconsin. There, on April 30, 1853, my great-grandfather Owen Garity paid $50 for forty acres of wooded lands, which the U.S. government was making available to pioneer homesteaders in Indian country.

I have tried to trace these ancestors through the available sources, primarily the genealogical society of the Mormons, which keeps close track of the souls of the deceased. The Mormons provide an undated typewritten history called *Sullivan, Town 6 North*. It contains several chapters of Jefferson County history, the first of which is titled "In the Beginning," and opens with a full recitation of the garden story from Genesis.

It then describes Sullivan as a new Eden, "and it was very

good," noting that "evidence of God's wonderful creation was everywhere." The Mormon volume rapturously visualizes the meandering river, the oaks and maples, the tamarack and the deer, all listening to the whisper of Genesis. "Soon man would come and claim the land and plant seed." The official account concedes that, before the pioneers, this "primeval forest" belonged to the Winnebago, whose word for "meeting place of the waters" became translated into the state name, Wisconsin.

There is no way of knowing Owen Garity's attitude toward the Indians. He was a principled man; during the Civil War his farm served as a station on the Underground Railroad of escaping slaves. But the Indians of Sullivan had vanished before his arrival from Ireland. They "ceded" their hunting grounds in 1832 but, according to the sanitized history, "they continued to linger, reluctant to leave the land of their forefathers." In 1841, the story continues, a company of U.S. Dragoons "passed through the area, gathering up all the Indians they could find and removing a large number of them."

This account of expulsion from Eden, so like the history of Ireland, is matched by the local history of what happened to the ecology: "Today the land is changed. The tall, thick stands of timber have yielded to the pioneer's ax, and cease to exist. Only a few clumps of woods, resembling cattle crowded together during a rain storm, dot the countryside. The soil, after more than a hundred years of cultivation, has lost its natural quality, and needs to be bolstered by fertilizers in order to produce a sufficient crop."

I spent all my childhood summers in Wisconsin towns with Indian names without ever hearing this history. Finding their still-numerous arrowheads and tools in the local woods conjured images of Indians as ghosts on the land. Local gossips said that Oconomowoc, the town where I spent my summers, was named after an old Indian who said, "Oh, I can no more walk." We thought it was funny at the time.

I grew up in Michigan, never knowing it was a deforested land. It seemed only natural to me that there were factories in Detroit, circled by suburbs, with an outer ring of pleasant farm-lands. No one told me that the autoworkers were descendants of lumberjacks, that the Au Sable River I fished as a youth had been a major logging stream, that millions of acres of white pine forest had been cut down in the first seventy-five years of the state's existence. Only forty-nine acres of that old-growth forest exist today, in a state of some 37 million square acres.

I cheered the University of Michigan Wolverines, while never knowing the state animal had been killed off in the state (though two were in the zoo). Nor was I taught that Michigan was the killing ground of the last passenger pigeons, once so numerous that they blackened the sky. Those who destroyed the passenger pigeons in their vast nesting grounds did so for urban consumption, for hogfeed, for sport. Since each bird lay only a single egg each year, their numbers crashed. Their final great nesting was in Petoskey, Michigan, in 1878; soon after, they were extinct from the earth and sky.

The Three Fires Confederacy

Nor was I told that a "copper culture" existed as long as ten thousand years ago in Michigan's Upper Peninsula, or that long before the Europeans there were tribes that called themselves the Anishnabeg. The whites came to name and know them as the Ottawa, Potawatami, and Ojibwa.

These tribes, eventually known as the Three Fires Confederacy, settled several thousand years ago (when Rome was in its infancy) from the southern Mississippi Valley up into Ohio and southern Michigan, building vast religious centers, which prompted anthropologists to name some of them "mound builder" cultures.

With the region's warming after the Ice Age, from 6000 to 3000 B.C.E., there emerged vast forests abundant with deer and bear. The acorn, which I thought of only as the name of my high school newspaper, covered the soft forest floors of the whole state.

These aboriginal people coevolved with their environment. They fished, harvested acorns and wild rice, made syrup, grew plants for sustenance, domesticated their corn, and hunted, using what they killed for food, clothing, housing, and tools.

They had a rich cosmology. According to their descendants, the Genesis story of the Anishnabeg was as follows:

> In the beginning, there was only darkness. Kitche Manitou [the Creator] began to fulfill a vision of crimson sunsets and starladen skies, a vision of various forms of beings living together and sharing the bounty of the creation.

Kitche Manitou made rock, water, fire, and wind. From these four basic elements, the sun, the moon, the earth and the stars were formed.

To complete the vision, Kitche Manitou created the plant beings, and then the animal beings.

The last act of Kitche Manitou's vision was the creation of man. And so, the world of the Anishnabeg began.

Every being in the Anishnabeg world had *manitou,* an "unseen power or spirit" that accompanied every physical or human form. Life depended on a balance with the manitou in all things. The whole natural world with its unseen spirit was treated not as an object to be mastered, but as a related realm to be treated with respect.

In an Ottawa story, the earth was covered in a great flood; in another version, "the first world was a world of dreams and mist." The creator being, called Nanabozho, was a force of nature who could create mischief or grave harm, as well as things of nobility and beauty. In the story, Nanabozho created the earth from a grain of sand given him by Otter. When animals perished, human beings were created from their remains. Thus human beings were linked by kinship to the animal world, and particularly to the *Ododem* ("totem") animal from which they arose.

The Anishnabeg governing structure was based on an elaborate network of clans and councils. The Midewiwin, or "medicine society," played a crucial role, similar to druids in Ireland or shamanic figures throughout the native world. The Midewiwin were plant specialists, healers, psychologists, spiritual sto-rytellers, and a fearsome threat to Christian missionaries.

The Anishnabeg were a powerful confederacy, rooted in prin-ciples of mutual consent in decision making, sharing of food and wealth, and interconnectedness with the natural world. They dominated the trade routes of the Great Lakes. Their legendary leaders included Pontiac, who led a massive rebellion against the British in 1763, and Tecumseh, a cultural and spiritual nation-alist, who occupied my hometown of Detroit during the War of 1812. And then it all unraveled. By the 1830s glowing assessments of timber and mineral deposits were exciting the forces of greed and attracting settlers to the Midwest, including my great-grandparents. In 1837 Michigan became a state of the Union, and as a condition of statehood, Indian lands were transferred to the state, leaving the Anishnabeg on marginal reservation lands.

This native history was erased from my culture and schooling as systematically as the Anishnabeg were removed from their lands. I grew up in a suburb named Royal Oak, having no understanding of the spiritual significance of the great Michigan oaks to the Anishnabeg (not to mention the Irish tradition, which venerated the oak groves; the word druid derives from *dru-wid,* meaning "knower of oak trees and steadfastness"). In becoming a proud "native son" of Michigan, I was raised in separation from its actual native past.

The Lost Gospel in California

I now live in the celebrated Eden of California and, some say, its fallen garden, the city of Los Angeles. For twenty-five years I have lived near the coastline of the Pacific, close to the site of an old native village. The idyllic past of this place is obliterated now, but an environmental movement still fights to defend an image of Eden against the serpents of urban sprawl and pollution. The protest, however, is mostly a holding action against the rate of growth. Failing to reverse the trend, people retreat from the city to the suburban valleys, then to the distant foothills, only to find that the serpent follows them.

The twentieth-century developers of Los Angeles actually promoted the city as a new Eden, importing palm trees to create the look and lifestyle of the Garden. Since then, Los Angeles has shaped the global trend toward megacities, new urban empires of several million people, which draw their water and power from distant rivers, and dump their excrescence in deserts and abandoned mines. For everyone in the world to consume energy at the per capita level of Los Angeles would require five planet Earths, it has been estimated. Even this level of growth and energy consumption has not solved the crisis of poverty and misery (inner-city Los Angeles is 105 square miles of census tracts deemed officially poor by the federal government).

The visionaries of the new urban colossus assume that the natural world, as well as human populations, should be subdued and managed, and that endless development is sustainable. The Los Angeles River is cemented and channeled, mountainsides are subdivided, open space is redefined as the mall, and even the beaches are artificial constructs of dredged sand. The original beauty of the place is reduced to background, a skyline here or sunset there, a view of the natural landscape that once inspired natives and settlers alike. An engineered synthesis overtakes the natural order. In the inner city there is nothing natural left at all. The environment is seen as an external place, which one visits on weekends. The Natural Resources Defense Council published a book called *The Amazing LA Environment!* to remind the public that the city indeed rests on an eco-system.

When a centralized bureaucracy manages people and resources, the public loses any sense of neighborhood or community with ties to the land. With the loss of nature and community there is inevitably a loss of imagination, as well. This culture of frenzied growth causes a spiritual emptiness and stress. Los Angeles generates many sensations, including ambition, pleasure, excitement, greed, fear, and loathing, but is rarely mentioned as a great cultural and intellectual center (or a "city of angels"). The psychological dynamic of its growth involves a stimulation of nervous energy that replaces the inspiration of the soul. In terms of Genesis it is a focal point for the fallen. While millions, even billions, of people are attracted to its possibilities, they also dread the price in beauty lost and values deformed by envy-driven consumption. Perhaps above all, they sense the cost in historical memory that comes with living in a culture that only emphasizes the moment, a rootless place that prizes the ability to invent oneself anew through media. The newest escape from nature by postmodern Los Angeles is City-Walk, a massive outdoor mall that captures and transforms the ethnic and environmental assets of the city into artifacts. Owned by MCA, Inc., it attempts to replicate Los Angeles without crime, congestion, or chaos. Santa Monica Bay, for example, is miniaturized into an exhibit with electric-powered tides and waves. The architect of City-Walk says of his work that "the theme of Los Angeles is that there is no theme." Can one imagine a native American designing a village to have no theme? Or declaring that the meaning of life is that there is none? That is the point of City-Walk, called a "controlled environment" and the "essence of Los Angeles" by its developers at MCA.

The entertainment-based megacity is total, promoting a message that there is no alternative, that its nature is the nature of the modern world. The past is dimmed, retained in museum collections and archives. The loss of the past is the loss of the dreams and ideals of the original place. We live in a stressed and polluted urban universe, not a city of angels, not in the universe itself, as native people always did. We are in danger of losing the sense that nature is connected with the meaning of life. This is a loss of the spiritual resource that could be the basis for a challenge to the modern consecration of development without end. That resource is the lost gospel of the native people who lived here for thousands of years before the conquest that became California.

Before Los Angeles

As anthropologists long ago demonstrated, native California peoples such as the Wintu found it difficult even to express personal domination and coercion in their language, so foreign were those concepts to their ways of life. And for most of California's Indian peoples those ways of life were directly tied to the great bounty that nature had given them."

DAVID E. STANNARD, *American Holocaust* (1992)

In 1542, just down the street from where I now live, Juan Rodríguez Cabrillo sailed past, the first European to observe the California coast and its native inhabitants. Cabrillo didn't anchor in Santa Monica Bay, but he described in his diary the Indians in "fine canoes," and commented that "they live well."

> They have round houses, well-covered down to the ground. They wear skins of many different animals, eat acorns and a white seed the size of maize which is used to make tamales.

Cabrillo sailed on, leaving Sebastián Vizcaíno to lead the first expeditions ashore in 1602. These later explorers often became violently ill and, as frequently occurred in the first period of contact, were aided by the native people. The diary of Fr. Antonio de la Ascensión recorded that the Indians "showed all the kindness possible."

They called themselves *tongva*, meaning "people." What is now Los Angeles they called *Kuruvungna*, and there is evidence of human settlement dating back at least ten thousand years.

Two tribes inhabited the area in which I live today, the Chumash and Gabrieleño. An estimated 13,000 Chumash populated the bountiful areas of the Santa Barbara coast down to Topanga and east to Frazier Mountain. The Gabrieleños, who lived around Santa Monica, were related to the Hopi and Nahuatl cultures of the south and east.

Anthropologists describe these tribes as "highly accomplished practical botanists and zoologists" who were connected with nature "in a different way, a way directed at understanding nature in such a manner as to use it without destroying it." They cultivated some 175 plants for food and medicine: the laurel as an insecticide, alders for stomachaches, the mugwort for headaches, creosote bushes as tea, and so forth. Acorn meal provided up to half their food.

They lived at the very center of powerful forces: where a river flowed to the ocean and the tides met the mountains. Quickly dropping to great depths, the sea became a rich marine environment, filled near the shore with surf fish, clams, mussels, and shellfish. Salmon migrated in and out of the vast tributaries that fed into a bay, which today is an internationally known example of pollution.

To fish, trade, and travel to the Channel Islands, the Chumash invented elegant and durable ocean-going canoes, called *tomols*, of pine or redwood logs that drifted down from the north. They made a variety of baskets, described by an eighteenth-century visitor as having "long inscriptions . . . by the illiterate people with a degree of exactness that was really astonishing." From their dreams they painted vivid pictographs on rock walls—often deep in caves—colorful portrayals of supernatural beings, lizards, and wild creatures, circles to represent the seasons, and symbols of fertility. Today their most famous painted cave has been locked shut like a prison cell in the mountains above Santa Barbara to avoid vandalism. The canoes and baskets sit in Santa Barbara's Mission Museum, artifacts from another world.

The Chumash story I love most celebrates the earth goddess *Hutash* during the acorn harvest in the fall. Hutash was married to the Milky Way. The Chumash believed that their people originated on Santa Cruz Island, a lush land of Eden off the southern California coast, which Hutash created with seeds of a magic plant. The original Chumash crossed to the mainland of California on a rainbow bridge made by the goddess. If any Chumash lost their balance on this rainbow and fell into the sea, the goddess transformed them into the first dolphins. This creation fable differs from the story of the Fall in that human life originates in a blessing, rather than in a sin. The birth of life comes from an ecstatic union of the earth goddess in the spiral arms of the Milky Way. The first people are made with a magic plant, not from lifeless dust. The rainbow is a bridge of life, not a covenant to be obeyed. And the dolphins are our lost brothers and sisters. What a different vision of the world from that which dominates California today. Yet I suspect most Californians would be touched at its telling; its ancient wisdom is sorely needed in grappling with modern issues like offshore oil drilling and dolphin protection.

The sea was central to Chumash cosmology. In their oral

tradition, a great flood transformed the first ancestors into plants and animals, and later the humans were created. There were three worlds: a sky world inhabited by the sun, the eagle, the coyote spirit, and others; a middle world of islands on the sea, including this land where the Chumash made their home; and a lower world filled with the dangerous creatures. The soul and the sea were linked in eternity. The Chumash believed that the soul, after death, departed for eternity through a sacred place known now as Point Conception, west of Santa Barbara.

These tribes lived in a covenant with nature, and maintained a kind of environmental etiquette. They held rituals of supplication, appreciation, and condolence for the help that humans received from the natural world. They believed that animals made the world ready for humans, and that all living things were capable of feelings. The Europeans, they believed, were reincarnations of souls that had gone across the sea. "The world is a single congregation, the noble principles of the soul are the same," a Chumash elder once told me.

The Gabrieleños lived freely on what is now prime southern California real estate, from Santa Monica to Newport Beach. They, too, lived in watersheds by the sea, where whole villages bathed together at dawn. To obtain visions of the universe, which was inhabited by the crow, eagle, raven, jaguar, and spider as well as the sun, moon, and stars, the Gabrieleño drank from *toloache*, the jimsonweed. They honored a mythic founder named Chingichnish, who emerged after an archaic time of chaos and cruelty to create the shamans and, out of mud, a new race of people.

By 1900 the official histories declared the extinction of the Gabrieleño, who had disappeared more suddenly and completely than the Chumash. In the past two decades, however, the tribe has reappeared, and now numbers approximately three hundred. As part of their reemergence, they tend and guard a sacred spring in West Los Angeles, once the center of a Gabrieleño village and now the grounds of University High School. They claim the original human settlement of Los Angeles was Kuruvungna, now the property of the state university at Long Beach. Both sites are the targets of development.

The Dream before
the "California Dream"

The story of the first white men to enter the Yosemite Valley is filled with the symbolism necessary to understand the replay of Genesis in California.

On March 27, 1851, Yosemite Valley was "discovered" by fifty-eight armed members of the Mariposa Battalion, a California volunteer force engaged in punitive attacks on local Indians. That year the Governor of California had endorsed a "war of extermination" against the native tribes. The Mariposa party commanded by the aptly named Major James *Savage,* was hunting down the Yosemite Miwok tribe, in a valley the Indians called *Paradise.* Among the raiders was a twenty-seven-year-old named Lafayette Bunnell, who later wrote an account titled *Discovery of the Yosemite and the Indian War of 1851 Which Led to that Event.*

Savage confronted the Miwok leader Teneiya and demanded

a Miwok retreat, noting that Satan himself had once entered a place known as Paradise. After shooting Teneiya's son in the back, the Mariposa unit captured the chief. Anticipating the more famous speech of Chief Seattle in 1854, the captured Teneiya made a prophecy over his son's body, which was written down by Bunnell:

> Kill me, sir captain! Yes, kill me, as you killed my son, as you would kill all my people if they would come to you . . . But wait a little; when I am dead I will call to my people to come to you . . . to avenge the death of their chief and his son.
>
> You may kill me, sir captain, but you shall not live in peace. I will follow in your footsteps, I will not leave my home, but be with the spirits among the rocks, the water-falls, in the rivers and in the winds; wheresoever you go I will be with you. You will not see me, but you will fear the spirit of the old chief, and grow cold. The spirits have spoken. I am done.

It is stunning to contemplate that this was the first entry of white men to Yosemite, not only a geological wonder of the world but an inspiring, sacred place for many generations before and after. In Bunnell's account, there is no evidence that the Mariposa party was awed by the sheer natural beauty of Yosemite. They were obsessed instead with removing the Indian devils from the path of the Gold Rush.

California was an echo of the American creation story, which itself harked back to Genesis.

The earliest European myth of California was directly reminiscent of Eden. A 1510 Spanish novel cast a spell that would last: "Know ye that on the right hand of the Indies there is an island called California, very near the Terrestrial Paradise," a land of black female Amazons and a single metal resource, gold.

The conventional California myth or creation story represses the memory of the natural world as it once was and the near extermination of its native inhabitants. Instead the Indians are depicted as a small handful of primitives who unfortunately inhabited lands valuable to the completion of Manifest Destiny. This version of history speaks of lovely and orderly Spanish missions that bloomed on the dormant California coast to organize the new state into a bustling agricultural civilization. The truth is that, like the biblical story, California was conquered by a band of religious proselytizers, the Jesuits, accompanied by muskets and swords where the cross was not enough.

"Better than the utopias of the ancients," crowed the *Los Angeles Times*, "is this modern utopia of the Pacific, better than the Garden of Hesperides, with their golden fruits, the gardens of this sunset land." The official cry of California's conquerors became "Give us men to match our mountains," and the Eden Dream, the American Dream, was reborn as the California Dream. At the time there were some 100 tribal communities, consisting of 300,000 people, living in this newly discovered paradise. No area of comparable size anywhere on the continent, or perhaps even the world, contained such a diversity of languages and cultures as did aboriginal California, according to the history of James Rawls.

Where the capital city of Sacramento ("city of the Sacrament") now sits, there once was an inland sea much like the ancient confluence of the Tigris and Euphrates. During the rainy season, the Great Central Valley became a body of water one hundred miles long. When the water receded, the valley floor was blanketed with ocean sediment and sharks' teeth. Bunchgrass savannas and valley oaks filled the foothills and waterways. A forest of tules covered the basin. Trout and salmon choked the streams, millions of geese and ducks came and went, and massive herds of elk prowled the land along with grizzly bear. There were as many as 100,000 Indians, speaking thirty languages, living in what they called "the plains of the world," but what the pioneers called swamp.

Into this original paradise came the leviathan of the bureaucratic state that created the greatest physical alteration of a natural water system in the world. The winter snow and rainfall of the north are trapped today in 1,200 reservoirs. Los Angeles receives 300 million gallons of water daily through aqueducts stretching north. Half the fresh water that once flowed from the eastern Sierra across the Delta to San Francisco Bay is diverted to irrigate farms and cities built on deserts. This flow represents 25 percent of nation's water supply.

In the glow of this awesome technological achievement, the memory of our loss is dim. Long gone is the grizzly bear. The salmon, as we know, are facing extinction. In March 1996 the *Los Angeles Times* reported charges that cattle owned by a brewery in the Owens Valley were "running roughshod over a magnificent wilderness, and in the process, driving the exquisite golden trout, California's state fish, toward extinction." When the trapper Jedediah Smith entered the Central Valley in 1826, he camped on Tulare Lake, some 700 square miles in size; today it is entirely gone. A 1996 study by 100 scientists found the whole Sierra Nevada range on the precipice of collapse: one-fifth of the animals in decline, two-thirds of streambeds degraded, robins disappearing at 3 percent a year, ponderosa pine dying of pollution, and 90 percent of the oldest trees forever gone.

The Yokuts, the largest tribe, were typically generous to the first trappers and missionaries, but proved intransigent to conversion to the new religion. When asked who they were, people in the Sierra foothills answered with the name *Maidu*, which, according to one scholar, meant not simply "people" but "beings." Animals, birds, and fish also were *maidu*. Thus, when asked their identity, the Maidu would answer "we are beings," expressing their immediate kinship with all of creation.

The Yokuts' religion has been described as a "vitalist cosmos," as captured in this Yokuts shaman's song:

> my words are tied in one   Do you all help me
> with the great mountains,   with supernatural power
> with the great rocks,   and you, day,
> with the great trees,   and you, night!
> in one with my body   all of you see me
> and my heart.   One with this world.

All over California hundreds of native tribes had lived "one with this world." As the southern Chumash glimpsed eternity in the sea, the Maidu saw a cosmic rhythm in the meeting of ocean and fresh waters, and the Yuroks considered the center of their world (*Uu-nek*) to be the convergence of the Klamath and Trinity rivers. The A-juma and Atsugewi people believed that the spirit called *Mis Misa* in Akoo-yet (Mount Shasta) kept the elemental forces of Wonder and Power in balance, like the ends of a single canoe paddle. Because of *Mis Misa,* an elder said, "all of nature seems to be in balance, with some completeness, some wholeness that most humans are denied access to."

Subduing the Savages

Despite the rooted cultures and developed religious visions of the native tribes, the early explorers almost uniformly repeated the blind Puritan perception of the place as nothing more than a wilderness filled with wild savages. Far from a terrestrial paradise ruled by benign padres, the real California creation story was one of brutal assaults on Indian and environment, a story that has been glossed or denied to present times.

An early Spanish explorer, claiming to be a scientific son of the enlightenment, described the California Indian in 1791 as dominated by "animal instincts . . . [which] degrade him, make him stupid." An otter hunter named William Shaler in 1804 saw "little to distinguish them from the four-footed inhabitants of their forests." The author Richard Stevenson wrote of the Gabrieleños that he "never saw any [Indians] so miserable, so abject, so spiritless, so nearly allied to the brute." During the same period, Father Geronimo Boscana denounced Gabrieleño religious customs as "horrible, ludicrous and ridiculous," and wrote that the "Indians of California may be compared to a species of monkey." The Indians, like the Irish earlier, were scorned as "diggers," rooting around in the dirt. In fact, they were gardeners turning over soil with digging sticks and planting potatoes.

As California approached statehood in the 1840s, an early annexationist from New England, John Marsh, observed that "the mind of the wild Indian . . . appears to be a tabula rasa, on which no impressions, except those of mere animal nature, have been made." The value of this backwardness was that the Indians would "submit to flagellation with more humility than the Negroes," and "nothing more is necessary for their complete subjugation but kindness in the beginning, and a little well timed severity when manifestly deserved." It was widely held that the Indians were not human, but a race of simians intermediate between humans and "lower" animals.

The labor necessary for the economy of this new golden state was based on a system of involuntary servitude. Indians, including children, were bought and sold for slavery or pleasure and, when no longer essential, became subject to "a war of extermination," as endorsed by governors in both 1851 and 1852.*

This system of servitude began with the Spanish missions,

---

* The first governor, Peter Burnett, sent a message to the Legislature in 1851, declaring that "the white man, to whom time is money, and who labors hard all day to create the comforts of life, cannot sit up all night to watch his property. . . . After being robbed a few times, he becomes desperate, and resolves upon a war of extermination." Such a war must "continue to be waged between the races until the Indian becomes extinct." Following up, his successor, Governor John McDougal, repeated that if the Indians would not relinquish their lands the state would "make war upon [them], which must of necessity be one of extermination to many of the tribes."

where Indians and the environment were subject to the domination of cross and sword. While some were converted voluntarily, the majority of Indians were coerced to join or remain within the mission system. Their personal living spaces were two-by-seven feet, and their caloric intake has been estimated as less than African field hands in the Confederacy. They were accompanied to church services by soldiers who whipped anyone who was late.

Two-thirds of these original people died in the six decades between 1769 and 1834, when the missions fell to secular Mexican rule. Overall the numbers declined from approximately 310,000 to fewer than 100,000 by the eve of the Gold Rush. According to a recent study, two-thirds of the Chumash children in missions died before reaching five years of age.

By the late 1970s, the California Indian was reduced to 1 percent of the state population, possessing .54 percent of the land. Since the Indian was the prime keeper of the lost gospel of the earth, the survival of that living wisdom was nearly erased as well.

America and the Loss of Eden

Recounted above are the lost visions of the people who lived with attachment to a living land in the places I have dwelled. But the stories of the Irish ancestors and their native kin in Michigan, Wisconsin, and California can be found in every corner of the vast North American continent. The particular stories are chapters of a larger book of wisdom that must be retrieved from a history that has long been repressed and distorted. In my parents' time, the distinguished historian Francis Parkman, writing of Pontiac's rebellion, described the Indian as "man, wolf and devil all in one." The 1974 ethnocentric history of Harvard historian Samuel Eliot Morison is little changed:

> Never again may mortal men hope to recapture the amazement, the wonder, the delight of those October days in 1492 when the New World gracefully yielded her virginity to the conquering Castilians.
>
> [The Indians were] pagans expecting short and brutish lives, void of hope for any future [comparable] to the many instances today of backward peoples getting enlarged notions of nationalism and turning ferociously on Europeans who have attempted to civilize them.

COLUMBUS AND THE ORIGINAL SIN

The traditional saga of 1492 focuses on the desperate crews of the Niña, Pinta, and Santa María, bobbing their way bravely toward the discovery of America, led by their great navigator, Christopher Columbus. The truth, of course, is that Columbus was lost.

The further truth is that rainforest destruction did not begin when environmentalists and the media discovered it in the 1980s. It began with the journey of Columbus and the conquerors who followed him. As Columbus himself described the old-growth tropical forest in his diaries ". . . it is the greatest wonder of the world how much diversity there is. . . ." In one generation, the island forest he discovered was gone.

Columbus himself was discovered and saved by the people he mistakenly called Indians. In Peter Matthiessen's lovely alternative telling, the term "Indios" may have referred not to the East but to Columbus's sense of the people he met as "una gente en Dios," a people in God. Our collective memory must recover an image of these Arawak, or *Taino*. Generations before, the Arawak had made a long journey by canoe from the Amazon River to the islands that became known as the Greater Antilles. In the Arawak creation myth, the people came from a cave into the world of light, guided by a moon goddess named Atabeyra who governed the inner tides of both women and the sea. A volcano god accompanied them, providing the nurturing gift of the manioc plant, teaching them how to remove poisons from the plant so that it could serve the people as food (as it does for millions today).

"They are the best people in the world and, above all, the gentlest," Columbus wrote of the Arawak. "They are so . . . free with all they possess that no one would believe it without having seen it. Of anything they have, if you ask them for it, they never say no; rather they invite the person to share it, and show as much love as if they were giving their hearts."

Peter Martyr echoed this tale of Eden Found in his account of the 1504 journey to what is now the island of Cuba: "among them, the land is as common as the sun and the water . . . Thine and Mine (the seeds of all mischief) have no place with them . . . they seem to live in a golden world, without toil, living in open gardens, not entrenched with dikes, divided with hedges or defended with walls."

These tales of Eden would be marred by subsequent events,

such as the killing of an explorers' party Columbus left behind, who apparently provoked the island natives into a fatal conflict. But the initial generosity of these tribes who lived harmoniously in a state of nature was noted consistently by the European settlers. In a later century, many American revolutionaries were tempted by the life they observed among the Indians as well. "To understand what the state of society ought to be, it is necessary to have some idea of the natural state of man, such as it is at this day among the Indians of North America," wrote Thomas Paine, who learned the Iroquois language and attended Indian councils. Paine added that "government, like dress, is the badge of lost innocence," a necessity arising from original sin.

In a tragic version of the Eden story, the innocent Adam and Eve were demonized as heathen savages. But the original sin of America, as we look back, was our ultimate rejection and pollution of the garden that was this continent.

This original sin began with Columbus. "They are naked and defenseless," Columbus noted, and "hence ready to be given orders and put to work." Blind to the Arawak nature-based religion, Columbus believed "they would easily be made Christians because it seemed to me that they had no religion."

The destructive history that followed is told in histories by Kirkpatrick Sale, David Stannard, and others. The important lesson is that the promise of Eden was destroyed again. In less than thirty years, the Arawak people were extinct, victims of Spanish violence, slavery, and infectious disease. The New World had no immune system to protect against the cross, the sword, and the gallows.

Before long, writes Stannard, "reports were circulating that

Satan himself resided on one of those islands in the Caribbean Sea. . . . the New World's Indians were creatures of a subhuman, Caliban-like nature." As discovery turned to aggression and conquest, the image of the native changed from innocent to fiend, from Adam to Serpent. It was widely held that wilderness was a consequence of sin, inhabited by Satanic forces. The likes of Cotton Mather wrote of the woods and forests of the New World as "the Devil's Territories." Where nature was beautiful and pliant to human touch it illustrated God's care and benevolence. Wilderness, by contrast, was evidence of his power and capacity for wrath.

Hernán Cortés, who arrived in 1504 and by 1524 had subjugated the natives of what is now Mexico, summarized the callous new philosophy toward the land in his diaries. His men did not want to stay in the areas they occupied, and treated the land as "they did with the islands first populated, namely to *exhaust* them, to *destroy* them, then to *leave* them" (italics added). The Garden was to be ravished as a virgin frontier.

ECOLOGICAL IMPERIALISM

Exhaust them, destroy them, leave them they did. The alteration of the native environment began in the 1500s and spread to California with the arrival of the Spanish and Russians at the end of the eighteenth century. This "ecological imperialism," as Alfred Crosby labels it, had the effect of destroying resources that Indians required for subsistence. Most of the animals, flora, and fauna of the first colonies were "Europeanized" by the seventeenth century. The euro-crops and euro-animals included wheat, barley, oats, pigs, horses, sheep, goats, and, of course, weeds. When de Crèvecoeur wrote his *Letter from an American Farmer* in 1782, nearly every living thing he extolled was European, except for the passenger pigeon, which soon became extinct.

By the 1800s Henry David Thoreau was already writing of mass extinction, though the nation was only two generations old. "When I consider that the nobler animals have been exterminated here," Thoreau wrote of New England, "the cougar, panther, lynx, wolverine, wolf, bear, moose, deer, the beaver, the turkey, etc. etc.—I cannot but feel as if I lived in a tamed and, as it were, emasculated country."

This destruction was reimagined as cultivation and domestication in the service of God's will. Similarly, the massive death toll of the Indian population was seen as predestined, in accordance with divine providence. While countless Indians died in front of his eyes, Governor William Bradford noted in 1634 that "by the marvelous goodness and providence of God not one of the English was so much as sick, or in the least measure tainted with this disease."

Stannard concludes that "of all the horrific genocides that have occurred in the twentieth century . . . none has come close to destroying this many—or this great a proportion—of wholly innocent people." No one can say how many died, but estimates range in the tens of millions through all of the Americas.

The cultural identity and spiritual ecology of people who had inhabited the continent for at least 10,000 years nearly died, as well. Later histories almost completely erased the lost gospel of the Native Americans.

The Indians knew well that genocide and ecocide were one

process. They believed that the land had soul, and therefore to be removed from the land, to be "developed," meant a spiritual death. For the Cherokee the term *ishtohoozzo* meant the "holy cause" behind all things. For the Lakota *wankan tanka* meant the "great mystery," from which everything arose. For the Iroquois the term *manitou* meant the "maker of all breath." Each of these basic concepts implied an earth in which a supreme being was manifest in all things. "Each step should be as a prayer," Black Elk taught. In contrast, the Christians prayed to the new god with fingers pointed to the sky.

THE LOST GOSPEL OF CHIEF SEATTLE

The most famous expression of the lost native gospel is the speech of Chief Seattle, or S'ealth, of the Duwamish tribe, given in a U.S. courtroom in 1854. The technical accuracy of Seattle's speech has been rightly challenged. The first oration was altered in translation, and the content edited in more recent times by a screenwriter. The significant fact, however, is that the substance and style of Seattle's vision is so authentic that contemporary Indians people embrace the words as prophecy. (In the same sense, the biblical gospels are considered authentic, though written and rewritten by more than one hand.)

Chief Seattle spoke as the U.S. government was purchasing the land of his people in yet another step toward Manifest Destiny. Seattle acknowledged white people as "shining brightly, fired by the strength of the God who brought you to this land and for some special purpose gave you dominion." But from this dominion would come desolation.

When the buffalo are all slaughtered, the wild horses are tamed, and the view of the ripe hills blotted by the talking wires. Where is the thicket? Gone. Where is the eagle? Gone. And what is it to say goodbye to the swift pony and the hunt? The end of the living and the beginning of survival.

Seattle's alternative to the conquerors' vision was based on spiritual ecology. He described a "web of life."

Every part of this earth is sacred to my people. Every shining pine needle, every sandy shore, every mist in the dark woods, every clearing and every humming insect is holy in the memory and experience of my people. The sap which courses through the trees carries the memories of the red man. . . .

Whatever befalls the earth befalls the sons of the earth. Man did not weave the web of life; he is merely a strand in it. Whatever he does to the web, he does to himself.

How can you buy or sell the sky? The warmth of the land? The idea is strange to us. If we do not own the freshness of the air and the sparkle of the water, how can you buy them?

Defeated, Seattle accepted banishment from Eden to the reservation, so that his "people might live out our brief days as we wish." Then he offered this prophecy:

When the last red man has vanished from this earth, and his memory is only the shadow of a cloud moving across this prairie, these shores and forests will still hold the spirits of my people.

And when the last red man shall have perished, and the memory of my tribe shall have become a myth among the white men, these shores will swarm with the invisible dead of my tribe . . . and when your children's children think themselves alone in the field, the store, the shop, upon the highway, or in the silence of the pathless woods, they will not be alone.

At night when the streets of your cities and villages are silent and you think them deserted, they will throng with the returning hosts that once filled, and still love, this beautiful land. The white man will never be alone. Even the white men cannot be exempted from the common destiny. We may be brothers after all. We shall see.

THE FIRST ECOLOGISTS

One could say that ecology was an Indian idea. In the analysis of Kirkpatrick Sale, Thomas Berry, Paul Shepard, and others,

- The Indians were the first to develop medicine from plants, totaling in the hundreds. Though the petrochemical and pharmaceutical industries today try to manufacture synthetic drugs, there is increasing recognition that our medical supplies are rooted, literally, in ancient forests and cultures.

- Instead of a deadly agricultural monoculture, using plows to tear up and expose the soil, the Indians employed farming techniques which conserved the soil, and were able to generate crops that still make up half the world's food: corn, potatoes, beans, pumpkins. Building on this experience, the use of organic farming and preservation of wild genetic stocks has become a major environmental priority for the future.

- Although there were exceptions, the Indians usually hunted down and killed only what they needed. As with agriculture, they did not overuse technology. To reinforce the concept of limits, they employed ritual to offer respect and thanks to the animals they killed for food. These approaches are reflected today in wildlife conservation programs and animal rights movements everywhere in the world.

In addition, the Indians knew that personal stages of life had to be patterned after ecological cycles. For birth, puberty, adulthood, marriage and death, there were specific ceremonies and rituals to teach the meaning of the passage. Lacking such rituals today, Paul Shepard has argued, we push ourselves steadily into alienation. We disconnect from the earth, or take life to be an existential absurdity. The Indian lived in nature, in the universe. The Indian life took a physical toll. We live in an artificial world of *psychic* toll.

As Thomas Berry expresses it, we have lost "interior communion with the archetypal world of the collective unconscious." Indian rituals including the sun dance, vision quest, and the sweat lodge, helped to sustain this primal connection with origins and history.

Having said all this, it is also important that we not indulge an understandable tendency to romanticize the Indian, create a new "noble savage" myth, reject all modern technology, or fantasize about retreating to an earlier time. The Indian did not live always in a blissful state of equilibrium before Western conquest. The very reason for the Iroquois Confederacy was to reduce the bloodshed from periodic tribal wars over power, religion, and resources. Such struggles occurred in many parts of the continent, sometimes with serious ecological consequences. Great leaders like Tecumseh, who attempted to unify the Indian nation against the European threat, were unable to heal the many rivalries.*

Native people often were driven by superstitions, dangerously false interpretations of their world view. Many attributed the European technology, for example, to supernatural power. The Haida believed the sailing ships were creatures from another planet. The Aztecs mistakenly took Cortés for a deity. One should not confuse superstition with spirituality.

Nor is it necessary to blindly or literally accept Indian cosmology. For example, the concept of an Earth Mother is human-centered and may carry the danger of projecting our cultural stereotypes of women (female as the nurturer who patiently suffers neglect and abuse) onto the planet itself. The important point is not whether the earth has a gender, but whether we have an intimate, familial relationship with the earth or an alienated destructive one.

Unfortunately our present problem is not that we sentimentalize the Indians but that we ignore the native experience and instead sentimentalize technology. We must recover access to the painful and traumatic chapters of our collective past, where

* The distinguished conservation biologist Michael Soulé summarizes archaeological and radiocarbon evidence thusly: ". . . the ancestors of the American Indians probably exterminated most of the native megafauna (75 percent of the genera of large mammals, including mastadons, ground sloths, camelids, equids, and indirectly their large predators) of the New World about ten thousand years ago." In this subtle observation, the ecological practices of native Americans may have been a learned response to earlier ecological crises. See Soulé's essay, "The Social Seige of Nature," in Soulé and Gary Lease, eds. *Reinventing Nature: Responses to Postmodern Deconstruction* (Washington, D.C.: Island Press, 1995, 137–70).

the destruction of the indigenous people and environment began the present-day rupture from the natural world. No doubt the effort to restore this shielded memory will be painful. But often the most painful episodes of our past life can be our greatest resources for finding a path to health. The restoration of the lost gospel of native America should be a liberating experience, not an occasion for guilt and blaming.

THE ONGOING EXTINCTION

One reason it is important to know this history is that the long assault on native people and their environments is not over, but is coming to a climax today.

If the past is past, if we really can "move on," why are native Americans still the most impoverished people in America, with their lands ransacked by strip mining, nuclear power, and toxic waste dumping?* More importantly, we need to ask why indigenous people and their natural environments are being threat-

---

* The native historian Donald Grinde has documented the ecocide of recent decades. Parts of Navaho country have been defined as a "national sacrifice area" in a National Academy of Sciences report. Coal-gas plants in the Four Corners rip up sacred land at Black Mesa, and draw billions of gallons of water from sacred Hopi springs for a coal slurry pipeline. Uranium mines desecrate the Black Hills. The most costly Superfund site in the United States is in upper New York state, condemned by the Seneca as a "decimation of the philosophic center of society." In Canada's James Bay, an area the size of Oregon was flooded during the 1970s, leading Cree elders to declare that "the holocaust of Discovery is still going on." As recently as 1988, the U.S. Supreme Court upheld the government's right to destroy Indian sacred ceremonial sites if necessary to develop, mine, log, or manage land (*Lyng v. Northwest Indian Cemetery Protective Association*).

ened with extinction across the planet. Often this extinction is carried out through an exact replay of the Wild West, as in Brazil where armed settlers are killing the last of the Yanomami and assaulting rainforests. In a larger sense, this destruction of indigenous people occurs because of the continuing echo of Manifest Destiny, the ideology of indiscriminate growth, which says that the creation of an artificial technological civilization is both inevitable and desirable. The believers in this orthodoxy may fret over rainforest destruction, feel guilt pangs for the Indians, even send a check to Greenpeace, but still remain enthralled by the inevitability of this destiny, trapped in the belief that it is progress.

Guilt alone will never be sufficient to save native people or native land against the forces of modern destruction. What is needed, beyond guilt and grieving, is a profound understanding that the loss of the indigenous world impoverishes and threatens the loss of the quality of life of all people in the modern world.

As ecocide and genocide take their toll, the world loses access to ancient wisdom, art, religion, language, medicine, and the cultural and biological diversity that is needed for basic existence. The death of diversity threatens the survivors. We cannot return to the past, but we can change our lives to preserve the "resident genius" of the land, as novelist Mary Austin described Indian poetry in the 1920s. The resident genius is where the dream of the continent is most alive.

The Dreaming of North America

Out of our relationship with the earth and the universe arises our capacity for dreams, visions, and spirituality. When that relationship is open, uninhibited, and wild, our dreams are powerful, dramatic, and energy-giving; when that relationship with nature is damaged and diminished, our capacity to dream shrivels too. We are losing the original dream of spiritual well-being to a narrower dream of material ambition.

Dreaming is a source of the lost gospel. In *Arctic Dreams*, nature writer Barry Lopez notes that native people have always sought to achieve a "state of high harmony or reverberation" with their environment and "a conservation of the stories that bind the people into the land." In *The Dream of the Earth*, Thomas Berry writes that "in the beginning, was the dream." Humans came into being in a "lyric" period of the earth's history when nature was achieving its "full florescence," when trees and rainforests, songbirds and flowering plants were awakening our consciousness to a sense of the divine. The human imagination was triggered by the spirituality of place, and still is, when we walk alone in redwood forests, sit on ocean cliffs, lie under the big sky, come upon a wildflower on a granite surface, watch a hawk in the desert, spy a blue butterfly in the forest, or hear a sparrow at dawn. We are that being in Creation with organs for dreaming.

The dream of our continent cannot be expressed completely in words, any more than Van Gogh's paintings can be captured by descriptions. There is no single dream, but myriad dreamings that arise from the seasons and bioregions into a greater harmony.

What we can say, however, is that this continent has evoked powerful and sustaining dreams of creation among those who have sought to live here instead of conquering it. Unlike the deserts of the Middle East or the tropical forests of India that produced singular religious visions, the North American environment contains enough of a diversity of natural wonders to awaken all levels of consciousness at once. Oceans surrounded the land, mountain pinnacles arose from it, forests, deserts, plains, great lakes, and rolling rivers covered its expanse. There may have been more to awaken the human imagination here than any place on earth. The tragedy was that human insecurity in the face of nature's power led to dreams of conquest and sovereignty instead of harmony and beauty.

"America the Beautiful" is often sung as a national anthem in praise of the land. The opening lines about beautiful and spacious skies, amber waves of grain, and purple mountains' majesty, convey a sense of natural blessing. But the anthem reverts to a celebration of conquest:

> O beautiful for pilgrims' feet
> Whose stern impassioned stress
> A thoroughfare for freedom beat
> Across the wilderness

This narrower American Dream of triumph over wilderness was erected like a farmhouse or suburban tract on a prostrated nature—a dream that fired individual ambition instead of awe, that offered the seduction of a virgin continent, that even promised escape and security from nature's laws. That dream mapped, conquered, settled, zoned, urbanized, subdivided, dammed, irrigated, paved, dynamited, razed, and grazed virtually every inch of the land. But it has not created sustainable communities or economies, or yet provided a vision that speaks to our souls.

We assume we can mold and engineer the land and, when we zone ourselves in harm's way, we blame nature for the toll of floods, fires, and earthquakes. We are the only species unable to employ ourselves fully; everything else in nature has a function. Fifty thousand Americans die in car accidents every year, and many thousands more from the tobacco, alcohol, and drugs that we take to steady our nerves. All these disorders of the modern world arise from our striving against nature, which stems from the arrogant false consciousness of being lords of the universe. The time has come to transform the hostile dream of conquest in the larger sacred dream of kinship that nature offers.

Australian Dreamtime

Several years ago, I struggled with the concept of dreaming held by the Australian aborigines, who are possibly the most ancient people on earth. I was in Australia for the odd purpose of playing in a baseball tournament meant to excite Australians about our national pastime. At a clinic for high school students, I found myself staring at an aboriginal youth who showed up with his white classmates. Not only were his dark features strikingly different, but his young face appeared ancient, a kind of throw-back from modernity. The white students, while friendly, treated him as another species from another time on earth.

I became fascinated with aborigines and the vision that had allowed them to survive for so many thousands of years before the coming of Irish and European emigrants to their island continent. Both aboriginal and white Australians told me not to try, that aboriginal dreaming was beyond the grasp of my Cartesian mind. "We come out of the dreamtime of our creative ancestors, and still are in dreamtime," one elder told me matter-of-factly. There is a *guruwari,* an imprint of the seed of the ancestors in all things on earth, he tried to explain. My understanding of his perspective was blocked because I kept imagining an ancestor in the form of an external creator-god, as in the West, dreaming up the earth and its inhabitants before creating them.

I finally had an intuition of dreaming when I walked around Ayers Rock, the vast dome that emerges in the center of Australia's outback. The aborigines consider this huge rock to be the holy center where life originated. I walked through the bush for three miles toward the rock, and was startled by its changing colors, from brown to purple to bright red, from soft blue to brown. When I came close, I experienced a vibration in its presence, like walking through waves. The natives say that the creative ancestors sang the world into existence, and that the vibrations I sensed are present in everything that exists. The pulsing power of the rock was full of creative forces, or what a Westerner might simply call energy fields. When one is aware of this vibration in all things, I was told, one is connecting with the original "song" of creation, written and embedded in the earth itself. I had never before thought of God as an "ancestor."

There is a wonderful analogy to aboriginal dreaming in Susan Griffin's book, *A Chorus of Stones*. She writes how the original cells of life have the same fundamental form after several billion years, and how life traces maps of its history on the earth. "It is said that the close study of stone," for example, "will reveal traces from fires suffered thousands of years ago. . . . Perhaps we are like stones; our own history and the history of the world embedded in us, we hold a sorrow deep within and cannot weep until that history is sung." I would only add that we contain joy and song, not simply sorrow and tears, embedded in the chorus of stones and life.

Recovering the Indigenous Dream

As the universe produces our consciousness, our consciousness evokes the universe.

ALAN WATTS, *Tao: The Watercourse Way* (1975)

This deep experience of the earth and universe as filled with original vibrations of our creative ancestor is shared by all native cultures and is central to renewing the gospel of the earth. Living in direct communion with natural environments enabled native people to develop a very different sense of meaning from ours. They acknowledge, celebrate, and never deny the cycles of nature, including death. They know that every element of the universe is related. They visualize the cycle of human life in the cycle of nature. As Matthew Fox has noted, atheism is unheard of in native cultures, for everyone accepted a spiritual universe.

If such ancient dreams are fading, it is more through the advance of sterile reason than the guns and plows of conquest. We are becoming dreamless. We confuse fantasy with dreaming, while mentally we detach from nature's source of dreaming. We cannot recover on our own the imaginative power that our basic connection with the continent once gave us. We need a dream-maker, a modern shaman, to evoke in us what has been lost to our conscious grasp. Thomas Berry has written of a reverse dependence of Westerners and native people: "Survival in the future will likely depend more on our learning from the Indian than the Indian learning from us. In some ultimate sense we need their mythic capacity for relating to this continent more than they need our capacity for mechanistic exploitation of the continent. . . . The fate of the continent, the fate of the Indian, and our own fate are finally identical."

Our present identity suffers from the loss of our original dreaming capacity and its replacement by misleading and ego-centric creation stories. The reconstruction of the lost gospel requires rethinking how we came to be, on three levels:

1. *We need to establish a meaningful story of the universe,* rooted in the native sense of a sacred creation. The story of our universe has been reduced from a sacred drama to one of two mechanical dogmas: in the first, the religious story in which an external God turned on the sun, created the earth, and

billions of years later reached out and planted Adam in a garden, and then, when Adam was lonely, added Eve; or second, the scientific version, in which life is a meaningless accident or mutation in a random universe. Both of these creation stories remove sacred meaning from the universe and leave us to either follow an unbelievable Genesis myth or experience life as ultimately meaningless. By contrast, native people (and the West's nature mystics) always have embraced *cosmic* stories of human participation in a creative and interdependent universe.

2. *We need to revise the creation story of America.* Like Genesis, the conventional popular myth requires a suspension of all our senses, to believe that America was a virgin wilderness awaiting our discovery and settlement. The orthodox story that Columbus discovered America, that the rest was our Manifest Destiny, is a fantastic denial of our real history and identity. But any serious alternate story is accused of being un-American, subversive, the whining of the politically correct minority. Anyone who questions the dominant myth is made to feel like a stranger in their own country.

In the face of this denial, we need to restore the real creation story of America, which began some 10,000 years ago when our ancestors first learned how to live in this land. Their discovery was more heroic, more arduous, more important to us than any of those we officially honor today. Instead of a tale of conquering the fearful wilderness, a new creation story of America would concur with Henry David Thoreau that "in wildness lies the preservation of the world." It must restore the ancient sensibilities our forebears held toward nature for thousands of years before the desanctification of their world.

3. *Each of us needs to rediscover the creation story of our immediate place,* as I have tried to illustrate in exploring the histories of Ireland, Michigan, Wisconsin, and California. Wherever we live today, we need to see through the town monuments and street signs and below the pavement to re-imagine the original place and its original inhabitants. To take a simple, superficial example, why is there no Tecumseh street in Detroit, Chumash park in Los Angeles, John Muir building in Sacramento? Why are so many properties named after conquerors or developers? Because the deeper roots of our personal native histories are sealed off by the doctrines of Manifest Destiny, progress, modernization, racial superiority, and entitlement to nature that make us blind to the original spirit of the places we inhabit.

Realizing the Dream

The fostering of these new creation stories is not only a matter of internal awakening, but of action in the world as well. There must be a politics of restoration to accompany the retrieval of this lost consciousness. Action can take many forms: restoration of the natural environments in our cities by a massive conservation corps, making organic agriculture a priority, promoting renewable sources of energy like the sun and wind, saving endangered species like salmon by removing destructive dams and restoring watersheds, returning species like buffaloes, wolves, and grizzly bears to lands now ravaged by cattle grazing and mining.

The new creation stories will not gain ground without a struggle against the defenders of Manifest Destiny. It is no accident that Speaker Newt Gingrich, for example, teaches a televised lecture series entitled "Saving Western Civilization," which attempts to protect the old dogmas. Or that William Bennett and other conservatives have selected "traditional values" as the core of their politics. They have chosen to perpetuate the continued denial of what happened to native people and the natural environment (or at best sentimentalizing the story), precisely because multiculturalism and environmentalism threaten the myths on which their power rests.

But the future cannot be built from amnesia. New frontiers must be more than escape routes from a hidden past. We cannot be sustained on a fantasy that law-abiding Americans are the apple of God's eye and always assured more entitlements from nature's bounty. As a culture we suffer from inhibited experience, the tendency to suppress and transmit to future generations the hidden horrors of the past that are too painful to face. This forgetting helps us survive the present, but promotes the same behavior into an even more painful future.

America is a great country with democratic freedoms, a standard of living and scientific accomplishments admired the world over. But that guarantees nothing for the future. Our standard of living and environmental degradation are not sustainable, and our creation stories will provide us with little guidance tomorrow. Our accomplishments are threatened by our unwillingness to come to grips with the devastation we have wrought on native people and their environment. Instead of a neoconservative agenda that promotes even greater denial, we will need to transform our views of nature and spirit to recover ancient nature wisdom as a medicine for modern life.

6

The Lost Gospel
in Buddhism

We can learn the Dharma from an oak tree.

THICH NHAT HANH

*Compassion for suffering lives must be enlarged to the scale of
a whole watershed, a natural system, a habitat.*

GARY SNYDER

As a young man searching for answers I became intrigued
with Buddhism. It seemed cosmic, not restrictive; spiritual, not
religious; anti-materialist in a time of consumption; anti-ego in
an era of selfishness. It seemed to be rebellious and against the
mainstream, as was I. In recent years its most visionary leaders,
like the Dalai Lama of Tibet, have spoken about environmentalism from their hearts. For all these reasons, Buddhism has
attracted many Westerners, particularly environmentalists, as a
possible green alternative to our orthodox faiths.

The Spiritualist Quest

My favorite novel has always been Hermann Hesse's *Siddhartha*, written in 1922. I am surprised at the new meanings I have discovered reading the story at different stages of my life, undoubtedly because *Siddhartha* is about a journey. It follows the stages of a young man's life from the time he drops out of established society. He attempts first a quest for spiritual purity, much like members of the counterculture of my youth. That stage fails and is followed by joining the system of power and status. That is empty as well, and Siddhartha finally becomes a bodhisattva, or enlightened one, living a life of service to others in harmony with the natural world.

The story was Hesse's version of Buddhism. When I first read the book, however, it was a kind of spiritual guide to the early 1960s. Everyone I knew was reading *Siddhartha*. I related to the story of the young man leaving the comfortable world of his parents, searching for authentic purpose, and almost immediately encountering human suffering and misery. Like many others, I had dropped out of middle-class life to join the civil rights struggle in the deep South and in northern ghettos. My father disapproved, and refused to speak to me for many years. I became an outsider as a way of life.

I learned much from those years of living on the edges of society. I saw again and again how a redemptive energy could grow from the human potential that was hidden beneath hierarchies. I experienced what I thought was compassion for the first time. But I never felt that an answer to suffering, pain, and death was being revealed. If anything, the horrifying assassinations of public leaders, the invisible deaths of millions in Vietnam, and the new awareness of environmental crises, became almost too much to bear.

In Hesse's story, Siddhartha also reached a point of no return as an outsider. Having learned what he could and still searching for the answer to suffering, he changed his life and entered the worldly domains of commerce and politics. It was through relationship with a beautiful courtesan, a kind of Barbarella of the time, that Siddhartha entered the world.

Like Hesse's Siddhartha, I eventually felt the limits of being an outsider. I came to participate in the very system I had shunned. Like Siddhartha, who could not "rid [him]self of the self," I could not lead a life of purity and self-denial. So in the mid-1970s I left the streets of the 1960s and explored the corridors of the mainstream. The lure was subtle and powerful. It appeared in those days after Watergate that the established system was thawing, changing, becoming open, even rewarding, to prodigal ones returning from the cold.

Just as Siddhartha entered worldly affairs, I entered electoral politics. I learned how the world of power works and how to influence it. It seemed justified because I could accomplish worthwhile reforms for people. I had access to the resources of the privileged. But like Hesse's character, I still tended to "live the life of the world without belonging to it." I was looking for something else, asking the same questions that were asked in the sixties.

But there were no answers. I was *in* the establishment, but not really *of* it, an outsider on the inside, constantly at odds with my political colleagues. This life was the mirror opposite of the outside alienation of the 1960s. But it could no more cure the suffering of the world than the life of withdrawal. It was possible to spend money on good causes, but not to bring about fundamental change. The main craving of successful people, I began to think, was like any other incumbent class, to achieve more accumulation, the treadmill that Buddhists call *samsara*. Hesse's hero mused that *samsara* was a "game which was perhaps enjoyable played once, twice, ten times—but was it worth playing continually?" After several years of his court life, "Siddhartha knew the game was finished, that he could play it no longer."

He did not spurn or deny this phase of his life, just as he had not treated his outsider years as fruitless or irrational. Incorporating and transcending both experiences, he discovered a kind of spiritual balance in nature. Siddhartha came to identify with the dynamics of the whole universe, in which the drama of human suffering is but a part. He became a simple ferryman on a vast river (symbolic of the larger flow of nature and the universe). It was a river he had used for much of his life, traveling as a young man to its farthest shore and crossing back later on a business trip.

The ferryman, I believe, was Hesse's metaphor for the Buddhist bodhisattvas, those who realize that their enlightenment cannot be complete without the enlightenment of others. The riverboat was the vehicle, just as Buddhism is a vehicle, for the "great crossing" (*dana paramita*) over the waters of daily existence. But instead of reaching the other shore and leaving the flow, the bodhisattva ferryman constantly returns to help others make the crossing. Siddhartha could not become enlightened if he left anyone behind. The river with its endless flow to the sea was the outer setting for this inner awakening to the cycle of nature and life.

Is Buddhism Green?

And so through *Siddhartha* I came to an interest in Buddhism that has lasted over the decades. We need bodhisattvas in this world. The part of suffering that is concrete—discrimination, a lack of income and power—can be addressed by action for social justice. But the effort is draining, the temptations many, a bodhisattva's spiritual grounding necessary. There is a deeper suffering, too, that ordinary politics cannot address. This comes from feeling alone in a seemingly meaningless universe, which requires a bodhisattva's embrace of natural laws.

But is Buddhism really green? Is it the lost gospel?* Despite

---

* Regrettably I am omitting a discussion of Hinduism, the other great religion of Asia. While I have a beginner's grasp of Buddhism, my experience with Hinduism is even more limited. Originally a forest-based religion, Hinduism includes a holistic vision from its earliest *vedas* (scriptures) to twentieth-century prophets such as Gandhi, and to modern environmental movements such as the Chipko struggle in northern India. Chipko, which means "to embrace," was the name taken by women whose civil disobedience in the 1970s consisted of "tree hugging" in the face of chainsaws. *Staying Alive,* by Vandana Shiva, is a brilliant analysis of environmentalism, feminism, and the Chipko movement for any who wish a deeper account. But a scrutiny of the texts, teachings, and practices of Hinduism over the centuries seems to reveal the same neglect of ecology that is found in other global religions. See, for example, *Hinduism and*

my affinity with Hesse's story, I still struggle with the question of whether the lost sutra (the closest Buddhist word to gospel) of the earth lies in Buddhism, or whether Buddhism has failed to fulfill its environmental potential as much as any Western religion. Since hundreds of millions of people live in Buddhist cultures under worsening environmental conditions, the question has far-reaching global implications.

My conclusion is an ambiguous one, which I will relate through observations on the story of the Buddha, the scriptures and stories of Buddhism, and the case of Buddhist culture in Japan. I believe there is a vibrant lost gospel in Buddhism. But it seems as lost as nature mysticism in the West. Despite my affinity for Siddhartha, and despite my expectations, what has surprised me in this exploration is how similar Buddhism is to Western religion in its secondary regard for nature.

THE STORY OF THE BUDDHA

Let me examine whether there is a lost gospel in Buddhism by starting with the story of the Buddha himself. The Buddha (which means "enlightened one") was born as Siddhartha Gautama in the Himalayan foothills in the mid-sixth century B.C.E. Like Hesse's Siddhartha, who is patterned on the Buddha story, this Siddhartha was from an exclusive aristocracy. He grew to be a seeker, compelled finally to leave his cloistered estate.

Ecology, whose authors write that "all over India people have become estranged from their natural surroundings and have forgotten the time-honored ecological values of their culture."

Siddhartha was stunned by what he found on the streets: sick people, elderly and infirm people, corpses being wheeled away. Humanity seemed the prisoner of an inescapable wheel of suffering, a natural cycle of sickness, old age, and death. His life was transformed by this understanding. He slipped away from his compound, devoted to finding the cause and remedy for all this suffering.

He disappeared into the forests, following the ways of ascetic monks and yoga teachers. For six years he practiced every form of self-denial, in extreme reaction to his previous life of privilege. Having failed to find the answers, he turned to the opposite path of worldliness, embracing the life of the courtesan and the disciplines of commerce and statecraft. But in the end, the seeker could not find escape from the wheel of suffering on either path. Exhausted, having given up on all teachers and doctrines, the future Buddha decided to meditate on the problem of suffering under a *bodhi* tree. As he meditated, his right hand touched the earth. After six days and nights, he was enlightened by the inspiration of a morning star.

I find this story both touching and familiar. The *bodhi* tree recalls the Tree of Life in the Garden of Eden and all the sacred trees of wisdom in native cultures. The Buddha pointed down to touch the earth, not up to an imagined heaven, experiencing enlightenment within and through nature. Charlene Spretnak, who was one of the first contemporary writers to reconnect spirituality with nature, has argued that the Buddha was restoring a nature-based meditation practice that had existed in India "long before the cattle-herding Aryan invaders arrived and installed their omnipotent sky god." He was a descendant, she continues, of the *bon* tradition of Central Asia, in which a central rule was to not cut down trees.

The Buddha's central teaching was that suffering could be transcended. Suffering was the key problem for human beings, because all life is transient, ending in pain, loss, and death. The state of restless dissatisfaction that arose from the experience of this condition he called *samsara*, the wandering described earlier as being on life's treadmill.

The cause of this suffering, he went on, is the *craving* that arises from consciousness of ourselves as a lonely and isolated ego in the universe. Ridding ourselves of this craving is possible if human beings could clear their minds of greed, hatred, and delusion. This could be accomplished by focusing on an eight-fold path of understanding, speech, mindfulness, action, livelihood, effort, attentiveness, and meditation or *samahdai* (*zazen* in Zen Buddhism). A life thus led became one of compassion.

Those who believe in a green Buddha must confront the fact that the core of these teachings was about the condition of human beings in society, not about the plight of the natural world.* Like Jesus, the Buddha embodied compassion as a re-

---

* The Korean spiritual concept of *Cheong*, explained in a brilliant paper by Dr. O. Young Lee of Seoul, means an intimate connection between individuals as opposed to the Cartesian division of self from others. The emphasis is seeing from more than one's own perspective or interest. For example, the Korean food kimchi is both natural and cultural. It is fermented, intermingled, harmonized in a natural process in a jar. Like the concept of compassion, *Cheong* can be the basis of healing our relationship with the natural world. But it has been limited primarily to a way of relating between human beings.

sponse to suffering and injustice. In its preoccupation with suffering, Buddhism stresses the *human* condition more than the *planetary* one. And like Christianity, Buddhism became primarily a *social* philosophy, not an ecological one, though its moral axioms could be extended to nature. With both traditions, we may assume that the compassion of these two great teachers would have extended to all of nature today. But that has rarely been the emphasis.

THE BUDDHA-NATURE OF ALL THINGS

There is a key reference to nature in the Buddha's teachings that is the embryo of a lost gospel. It is the admonition to practice "kindness and pity for *all* living beings." In this perspective, living things have a "buddha nature." In much of Buddhism, this concept has applied only to sentient beings, those with feelings and consciousness, not to the broader natural environment. But some have expanded the concept to the whole of nature by the claim that what is not sentient is inextricably bound up with what is sentient and alive.

This is what Zen poet and ecologist Gary Snyder means when he argues that compassion for suffering lives must be expanded to the suffering of natural systems. Thich Nhat Hanh, an exiled monk from Vietnam with a large following in the West, emphasizes the precept "to cultivate compassion and learn ways to protect the lives of people, animals, plants, and minerals." The whole universe can be said to have this Buddha-nature.

There is a clear distinction in Buddhism from the desert monotheisms and sky-gods of Christianity, Islam, and (to a lesser extent) Judaism. Buddhism contains no covenant with an externalized deity, and no dimension of divinity outside the basic stuff of the universe. Where Middle Eastern monotheisms are based on divine revelations that occurred in historical time, Buddhism claims that history travels in cycles, and revelation is a continuing possibility lying in the depths of our own consciousness.

A useful illustration is the *Jewel Net of Indra,* a story from the Hua-Yen school of Buddhism in seventh-century China. The net of the god Indra stretched into infinity. In each eye of this infinite net was a jewel. When a person looked at a single jewel in the net, it reflected all the others. Similarly the cosmos is a context of infinitely repeated relationships, mutual causality, mutual identity, without external causation.

THE EXPERIENCE OF MIND IN NATURE

Silent contemplation is at the center of Buddhism's way of dissolving barriers to the experience of the natural world. Having emptiness of mind means allowing the clutter of thoughts, images, and fragmentary associations to fall away, to feel the way things really are without trying to subdivide or gain a result. To Alan Watts, the eloquent American Zen Buddhist, it was "not so much a mind empty of contents as a mind empty of mind." The key difference between Western and Eastern thought is having a grasping, Cartesian mind, versus having a receptive, absorbing one. The first is premised on nature as an outside force to be dissected, while the latter "goes with the flow" of nature.

Buddhism assumes an interdependent universe based on energy flows, much like the universe imagined in modern systems theory or the new physics. As Fritjof Capra pointed out in *The Tao of Physics*, the intellect in such Asian philosophy is a means to clear the way for the direct mystical experience of oneness, not a tool for endless filing of data. All being arises in the context of nonbeing, just as objects only exist in relationship to space, like particles and waves. Everything exists in a state of what Thich Nhat Hanh calls *tiep hien*, which means "interbeing."

> Without all of the non-flower elements—the sunshine, the clouds, the earth, minerals, heat, rivers and consciousness—a flower cannot be. That is why the Buddha teaches that the self does not exist. What we call "self" is made only of non-self elements.

Unlike Western dualism, Buddhism is rooted in this interplay between seeming opposites, a metaphysics going back to the ancient Chinese concept of the two poles of nature, *yin* and *yang*, which fluctuate in a unity that is also duality. The Buddhist concept of this interbeing was known as *dharma-dhatus pratitya-samupada*, which translates as "the interdependent arising of the universe." In Taoism it is known as *hsiang sheng*, or a kind of mutual arising. Things are said to have "emptiness" and "fullness" (of emptiness) at the same time.

Sixth-century Buddhist philosophers argued with farsightedness that

> when we speak of all things, why should exception be made in the case of a tiny particle of dust . . . there is no water without

waves; there are no waves without wetness . . . there is only the one, undifferentiated nature.

In the universe of Indra's net, everything counts and nothing should be thrown away, just as John Muir and Aldo Leopold said of nature's elements.

For example, in one old story, a young man once threw away his chopstick on a temple grounds, and was confronted by an angry monk who asked him: why have you done this, is the chopstick unusable? When the young man agreed it was still usable, the monk said: "And yet you threw it away, you killed this chopstick. There is a proverb that he who kills another digs two graves. Since you have killed this chopstick, so you will be killed by it." The point is that even to discard a single chopstick is to establish a hierarchy of value that in the end will destroy us.

OVERCOMING CRAVING AND WASTEFUL CONSUMPTION

Buddhists attempt to detach themselves from craving material things, permanence, or immortality—a spiritual path with important environmental rewards. To achieve *wu-yu,* a kind of objectless desire, is the Buddhist alternative to consumption based on craving. As an eleventh-century monk wrote, if people could

> see through material objects and cut through attachments at one stroke, then all things will be empty to them and they will be

free. Not obsessed with food and clothing, not in a turmoil over worldly affairs, letting all vexations and problems run their natural course. . . .

The capitalist consumption ethos is based on the stimulation of psychological envy of others and craving for possessions, which in turn can lead to shopping as an addiction. Statistics show that consumption trends have increased since the 1970s when environmentalism became widely popular. Advertising, the stimulant of consumption, has more than doubled per capita since 1965. Newspapers devote 65 percent of their space to ads, and the typical American child sees 360,000 television commercials before high school graduation. While consumption climbs, living standards do not. There are as many as 35,000 deaths from hunger in the world every day. Such contradictions are rarely cited by the conservative protectors of American culture, because their economic ideology requires the promotion of endless consumer demand.

Buddhism, on the other hand, is not opposed to material comfort but to the deliberate multiplication of artificial wants. Craving cannot be appeased even at the Body Shop. Craving may be psychologically necessary for consumerist capitalism, but it undermines personal serenity and happiness. Shopping is not an answer to personal emptiness. Shopping is an addiction to what Buddhism calls *samsara*. Buddhism offers a powerful spiritual argument against the pathological patterns of behavior that are draining viable natural systems for the sake of psychological addictions.

THE BODHISATTVA ETHIC

The Buddhist ideal of becoming a bodhisattva, an enlightened one, is a powerful model for environmental practice. Engaged Buddhists vow to save all beings everyday, including the birds and the trees. For Alan Watts, "the state of liberation is not away from the state of nature." An example of a monk acting in a bodhisattva way is that of Prajak Kuttajitto in Thailand, who led an arduous struggle in the last decade to save the ancient forests of the northeast. Prajak lived in the forests, where he "ordained" whole groves of teak trees as "children of Buddha." Living like St. Francis among sparrows, butterflies, deer, and other animals, Prajak led daily "monk patrols" to watch for illegal logging. Villagers, and sometimes even logging crews, were unwilling to see such holy trees cut down. Without his efforts, he told reporters, the Dong Yai forests "will be all golf courses and plantations." He added that

> the forest is the source of everything in the world, the dharma, the natural law. It is the university of our life and understanding, the place where Buddha first had a revelation, [where] monks first came into existence.

According to news accounts, Prajak is "branded as a spiritual outlaw by traditional Buddhists who think monks should keep their noses out of politics." Nevertheless, the world needs more green bodhisattvas, monks who preach and live according to the lost gospel. Buddhism can be a growing source of such men and women.

The Emergence of Visionary Buddhism in the West

In recent years both the Dalai Lama and Thich Nhat Hanh have spread a powerful environmental message to the West, deepening the green roots of Buddhism in America. The Dalai Lama proposes a visionary liberation of his people:

> ". . . my dream [is] that the entire Tibetan plateau should become a free refuge where humanity and nature can live in peace and harmonious balance."

Unique among national independence leaders, the Dalai Lama directly connects the subjugation of his people under Chinese rule with the ecological ruin caused by that same occupation. He has acknowledged that Buddhism has neglected the environmental crisis as a spiritual issue as much as any other religion, and is deeply committed to the greening of Buddhism. So is Thich Nhat Hanh, the exiled Vietnamese Buddhist living in France, whose many works emphasize nature, reminiscent of St. Francis. He writes, for example, that "the sun is our second heart." Connecting ancient spiritual insight with evolutionary biology, Thich Nhat Hanh has concluded that:

> In our former lives, we were rocks, clouds and trees. We may have been an oak tree ourselves. This is not just Buddhist; it is scientific. We humans are a very young species. We appeared on earth only recently. We were plants, we were trees, and now we have become humans. We have to remember our past existences and be humble. We can learn the Dharma from an oak tree.

I have wondered whether the lost gospel in the Buddhist tradition is held most closely by Buddhist exiles, spiritual wanderers without ties to official institutions like nation-states. It is true in the cases of the Dalai Lama and Thich Nhat Hanh, and no less so in the Buddhism that has been transported into America. Rick Fields begins his history of Buddhism's journey to America with two prophetic quotes, from the Buddha and Henry David Thoreau. "Twenty-five hundred years after I have passed away into Nirvana," the Buddha once said, "the Highest Doctrine will become spread in the country of the red-faced people," meaning North America.*

Thoreau, the great environmental outsider, was also the first translator of the *Lotus Sutra* into English. During his 1846 retreat to Walden Pond, he "realized what the orientals mean by contemplation and the forsaking of works." Watching the ice of Walden Pond cut into large blocks for export to India inspired in him a revelation that wisdom came from a common well: "the pure Walden water is mingled with the sacred water of the Ganges," Thoreau noted in his diary.

Western interest in Buddhism has risen sharply since the 1960s. The Trappist monk Thomas Merton was deeply involved in dialogue between Christian mysticism and Zen Buddhism at the time of his tragic death in 1968. The pioneering writings of Alan Watts, the life works of Gary Snyder, the poetry of Allen

---

*An eighth-century teacher, Padmasmambhava, echoed the Buddha's prophecy: "When the iron bird flies, / And horses run on wheels / The Tibetan people will be scattered / Like ants across the world / And the Dharma will come / To the land of the red man."

Ginsberg, and the creative efforts of Joan Halifax, Joanna Macy, and Charlene Spretnak to fuse Buddhism, feminism, and environmentalism have influenced a growing audience. Buddhism has taken root in many places in America: the San Francisco Bay Area (where Zen Buddhism was transplanted through the Beat poets of the 1950s), the Tassajara center in Big Sur, and the Naropa Institute in Boulder—the first accredited Buddhist university in America, which also offers special degrees in environmental studies.

The Environmental Default of Mainstream Buddhism

But for centuries traditional Buddhism, like the religious traditions of the West, has buried or marginalized its reverence for nature. The struggle to uncover and restore this lost sutra of the earth bears many similarities to efforts to recover a lost gospel in the West. It is extremely important to global environmental efforts that this lost gospel also be recovered in non-Western religions.

The environmental inadequacy of Buddhism begins with the notion of the earth as impermanent, transitory, an illusion. In the 1950s Alan Watts complained that Asian religion was falling

> into the very trap which it should have avoided: it confused the abstract world of *maya* with the concrete world of nature, of direct experience, and then sought liberation from nature

in terms of a state of consciousness bereft of all sense experience. . . .

In [meditation] it cultivated prolonged exclusive concentration upon a single point—*avidya*—in order to exclude sense experience from consciousness.

The perception of the impermanence of life and all reality is crucial to the Buddhist avoidance of craving. If everything is in constant flux, why seek fulfillment in the accumulation of things that are fleeting by their very nature. But the same notion of impermanence also contributes to distancing the Buddhist from the feelings of organic connectedness with nature as described by Western environmentalists like John Muir, Aldo Leopold, and Rachel Carson. When a Buddhist truly dissolves the self into a dimension of nonself in meditation, the sense of rootedness in the living earth can be lost. The belief that in meditation lies the salvation of the world is different than Thoreau's credo that salvation lay in wildness.

The Dilemma of
Buddhist Social Action

Once I interviewed a Buddhist scholar in Kyoto, Japan, who began a lengthy environmental analysis with the observation that "the earth is dying in any event." While he was certainly right in the time frame of several billion years, a perspective like his can lead to indifference toward taking action to slow the pace of destruction. In *Dharma Gaia*, the text of Buddhist nature writings published on Earth Day 1990, one writer noted that:

given its view of the power of greed to dominate and corrupt the human mind, Buddhism is certainly not optimistic about a sane ordering of the world and has for the most part resisted positing a utopian vision. Traditionally, this view has led to a reluctance by Buddhists to involve themselves too closely with social and political change.

While currently subject to intense debate, the Buddhist emphasis on *wu-wei*, or "nonaction" (or perhaps "nonassertive action"), has fostered a tradition of nonengagement in worldly affairs. "We are stereotyped as navel-gazers," says one Buddhist at Naropa. Since individuals are, in Buddhist author Robert Aitken's definition, "just bundles of sense perceptions, with the substance of a dream or a bubble," it is logical that a life of monastic renunciation of personal action might follow. And since all things already are known to us, and all beings are part of us, it might be concluded that liberation consists simply of the personal act of sitting in meditation.

Teachers like Thich Nhat Hanh are deeply concerned that one's inner state be purified before taking action so as to avoid making a bad situation worse. He once wrote that "instead of saying, 'Don't just sit there, do something,' we should say the opposite, 'Don't just do something, sit there.'" Rick Fields explains a similar attitude among American Buddhists during the Vietnam War:

For the most part, opposition was an individual matter [for American Buddhists]. Buddhists as Buddhists did not follow the path of social action as so many Christians did. In the midst of all the turmoil, it seemed that sitting still might be the most effective and practical thing anyone could do.

Ironically, however, the most powerful protest of the Vietnam War came from Buddhist monks in Saigon who burned themselves to death in lotus positions. Theirs was an act of engaged compassion more profound than many Americans could understand. Their act lingers, even today, as an ultimate act of defiance and truth-telling.

Even if few of us have the same courage as those monks, we can appreciate their sitting as total engagement, not withdrawal. This is an ultimate act of the bodhisattva in the world, not an act of release from the wheel of *samsara*. But does Buddhism promote an ethos of social action to the same extent as Western traditions, an ethos that most environmentalists share? The answer is no. Dharmaloka, an American Buddhist monk, says that while politics alone cannot save the environment, neither is "the overcoming of greed, hatred and delusion a project which can be carried forward solely in a lecture hall." The tradition of religious social action may be the contribution that North Americans make to Buddhist tradition.

BUDDHISM AND THE STATE IN JAPAN

Where Buddhism has become engaged fully in the world of official institutions and power, it seems to have suffered a fate comparable to that of Western religions, becoming accommodated into the status quo of state power rather than standing as a spiritual alternative.

I visited Japan a few years ago seeking to understand what role its Buddhist culture played in promoting environmental values. What I learned was that despite a long nature-based tradition that preceded even Buddhism, there was little or no religious-based opposition to Japan's disturbing environmental policies. Japanese environmentalists, like those of the West, were political activists acting outside traditional institutional spheres, including religious ones. When a Japanese environmental movement exploded over the question of deadly mercury in fish in the late 1970s, many lay Buddhist students were in the forefront of protests, while institutional Buddhism was on the sidelines. During my research two decades later, I found religious scholars and lay Buddhists alike questioning mainstream Buddhism as a weakened religion increasingly relegated to ceremonial functions.

Long before Buddhism, the Japanese practiced a nature religion called Shinto. In the Shinto creation story, deities known as *kami* came from spirits who created the islands. Foremost among the *kami* was the Sun goddess. In the sixth century, an emperor ordered the forests cut down for shipbuilding. The people resisted strongly, because they believed the forested mountains were sacred to a thunder deity. The emperor therefore declared that the empress was a deity herself, and a stronger one than the thunder god. The authority of the emperor prevailed over the old religion and the ships were built.

Today Shinto is woven with Buddhism throughout the cultural fabric of the country. And yet despite these origins in nature-based traditions, the modern Japanese nation-state has acted like any other industrial predator searching the globe for resources. It is bent on the massive development of nuclear power plants. It leads the world in the destruction of whales. It imports much of the world's ivory from the tusks of endangered elephant herds, and is the greatest importer of tropical hardwoods. Ironically the world's forests are being cut partly to provide millions of throwaway chopsticks, despite the ancient Buddhist admonition. The Buddhist hierarchy has no more condemned these policies than the American religious hierarchy has criticized similar policies here. Institutionalized religion, whatever its prophetic origins, seems to coexist in accommodation with the state.

One story from Japan's nuclear program will illustrate this problem better than any statistics. For decades Japan has been developing fast-breeder nuclear reactors in the hope of reducing its energy dependency. The technological promise of the breeder reactor is that it can produce more nuclear fuel than it consumes. In an effort to convince the people to support the program, Japanese nuclear proponents created television advertisements that claimed that plutonium is safe to drink.

Meanwhile critics said that breeder reactors are too great a risk, too expensive, and may contribute to nuclear proliferation. Japan's program fell into crisis in December 1995 when a nuclear leak occurred in the coastal city of Tsuruga. Plant officials covered up the catastrophe, though it permanently shut down the plant. One company official jumped to his death from the eighth story of a Tokyo hotel. Not only had the state protected the fast-breeder industry with a curtain of lies and secrecy, but with the cloak of religion as well. The nuclear breeder facility was named Monju, after the Buddhist divinity of wisdom.

RECOVERING THE LOST GOSPEL
IN BUDDHISM

The process of retrieving a lost sutra of the earth in Buddhism is comparable to the effort to find a lost earth gospel in Western religions. The first element is to revive a scriptural basis (which in Buddhism is the buddha-nature of all things). The second is to restore a lost tradition of natural mysticism, which exists in numerous strands of Taoism and Buddhism. The third and most promising element is the existence of modern currents of revival, most notably in Tibetan and North American Buddhism. An engaged, nature-based Buddhism seems to be growing more rapidly than the new currents of eco-spirituality in the Judeo-Christian spheres.

The Buddhist conception of nature is more compatible with environmentalism than the technological dualism of the West. Buddhism's ethical emphasis on simplicity and the end of craving are powerful antidotes to overconsumption. The emergence of figures like the Dalai Lama as global voices for spiritual ecology is vitally important, and has no parallel so far in the West. The blending of Asian Buddhism with Western spiritual traditions, begun in our time by Thomas Merton, promises to create a greater spiritual focus blending environmental with social justice.

STEPHEN MITCHELL, AUTHOR of *The Enlightened Heart* and *The Enlightened Mind*, once told me that, in Buddhist terms, the environmental crisis is our generation's koan. The koan is a kind of riddle story, a paradox, that is insoluble to the mind, used by students of Buddhism as tools in the quest for enlightenment. Any attempt to grasp the answer to the question fails, for the self is trying to maintain control. Similarly, any attempt to control or manage the environment as a resource fails because it perpetuates the dualism of self against nature. For Thomas Merton, the answer to the koan lay in simply letting go, but that approach, he knew, was "alien to the Cartesian and scientific consciousness of modern man." We attempt to solve the environmental crisis by clinging to whatever technical fixes allow us to continue our dysfunctional behavior a while longer. These false remedies will leave us stuck like a Zen student trying to master a koan until, in letting go, we experience an insight that transforms our perceptions. The agony of this frustration, this Buddhist dark night of the soul, can either keep us stuck or be a prelude to enlightenment and transformation.

It is the same with the lost gospel. It is there like a koan. We cannot prove with our minds that the earth is alive, or that a sacredness inhabits it. Nor can our selfish egos accept a kinship dependency on nature. Instead we fill the shelves of our libraries and our minds with proposals for technological fixes to the environmental crisis. We pull out one after another, like Japan's fast-breeder reactor, only to discover the emptiness in the promises of such quick fixes. Like any addiction, the fixes become more expensive and more dangerous when the real solution is simpler but harder, like letting go of the vain attempt to mentally master the koan. Resolving our environmental koan requires that we let our minds surrender and give our feelings a chance. If we *feel* any kinship or sacredness with the earth, the feelings create a new perspective in which we will choose environmental paths that harmonize with nature instead of imposing technical fixes against nature's grain.

Until we sense what the Buddhists call the buddha-nature of the earth, which is the lost gospel of the earth, the environmental crisis will remain an external projection of our frustrated inner desire for mastery of mysteries we cannot understand.

Our religious, economic, and political tradition in the West has been about dominance and control. The delusion in this dominance was noted by Lao-Tzu thousands of years ago:

> Those who would take over the world and manage it,
> I see that they cannot grasp it,
> For the world is a spiritual [*shen*] vessel
> And cannot be forced.
> Whoever forces it spoils it.
> Whoever grasps it loses it.

7

The Lost Gospel, Environmentalism, and Politics

FOR PRESIDENT CLINTON'S inauguration on January 20, 1993, the poet Maya Angelou wrote the official poem. It is a powerful rendering of what I have called the lost gospel, especially in the lines cited here.

> *On the Pulse of Morning*
>
> A Rock, A River, A Tree
> Hosts to species long since departed,
> Marked the mastodon,
> The dinosaur, who left dried tokens
> Of their sojourn here
> On our planet floor.

Any broad alarm of their hastening doom
Is lost in the gloom of dust and ages.

But today, the Rock cries out to us,
Clearly, forcefully,
Come, you may stand upon my
Back and face your distant destiny . . .

Across the wall of the world,
A River sings a beautiful song. It says,
Come, rest here by my side.

Each of you, a bordered country,
Delicate and strangely made proud,
Yet thrusting perpetually under siege,
Your armed struggles for profit
Have left collars of waste upon
My shore, currents of debris upon my breast.
Yet today I call you to my riverside,
If you will study war no more.
Come, clad in peace
And I will sing the songs
The creator gave to me when I and the
Tree and the Rock were one.

Before cynicism was a bloody sear across your brow
And when you yet knew you were still nothing.
The River sang and sings on.

There is a true yearning to respond to
The singing River and the wise Rock.
So say the Asian, the Hispanic, the Jew,
The African, the Native American, the Sioux,
The Catholic, the Muslim, the French, the Greek,
The Irish, the Rabbi, the Priest, the Sheik,

The Gay, the Straight, the Preacher,
The privileged, the homeless, the Teacher,
They hear, they all hear
The speaking of the Tree . . .

The horizon leans forward,
Offering you space
To place new steps of change.
Here, on the pulse of this fine day
You may have the courage
To look up and out and upon me,
The Rock, the River, the Tree, your country.
No less to Midas than the mendicant.
No less to you now than the mastodon then.

Here on the pulse of this new day
You may have the grace to look up and out
And into your sister's eyes,
And into your brother's face,
Your country
And say simply
Very simply
With hope —
Good morning.

I pray that the poetry of Maya Angelou will hopefully be the politics of the next century.

THE LOST GOSPEL is not only a challenge to existing religion, but also the basis for a new vision of politics that honors the earth. All politics today serves to degrade the earth as a physical resource. The transition must be to a politics that is spiritually grounded in respect for the earth as the source of our life, not a storehouse of raw materials.

We must understand how deeply the utilitarian view of nature is embedded in our historic notions of political economy and how an alternate political vision needs to be resurrected with the lost gospel as its inspiration. All political economies harbor hidden assumptions about the meaning of the universe and the environment we inhabit. In the case of American political economy, the utilitarian view of nature came from religious and scientific philosophies in vogue at the time of the Revolution.

The Politics of the Fall

The first world view, derived from Genesis, was based on the Fall from the Garden of Eden, but also the manifest destiny of Redemption, the possibility of a chosen people making a new Garden. The major Christian works on politics and government, Augustine's *City of God* and Thomas Aquinas's *On Princely Rule*, started from the premise that we are prone to evil as a result of the Fall.

In the sixteenth century when Niccolo Machiavelli laid the foundations of modern political philosophy, he described the human temperament as "insatiable . . . shifty . . . and above every other thing, malicious, iniquitous, impetuous and wild."

In *The Prince*, Machiavelli's classic advice to the incumbent ruler was that government is not about justice, but about appeasing interest groups, a premise that has been followed by politicians for five centuries. Machiavelli asserted that there was a fundamental division between morality and statecraft, that indeed amorality ought to be the practice of politicians. "The fact is that a man who wants to act virtuously in every way," Machiavelli warned, "necessarily comes to grief among so many who are not virtuous." This utter absence of virtue in government derived from the fallen state of human nature, an attitude that continued through the Enlightenment. According to Henry Steele Commager, the Enlightenment mind conceived that "only man in a state of nature was happy . . . Man before the Fall."

The Politics of the Machine

Machiavelli's concept of politics as the achievement of equilibrium among interest groups foreshadowed the second great influence on American constitutional debates, the idea of government as a machine, fostered by the scientific giants of the early seventeenth century. The discovery of America occurred as Johannes Kepler published his *New Astronomy* in 1606. Galileo's telescope had already uncovered the satellites of Jupiter, and his vision of a geometric universe greatly influenced Thomas Hobbes's work on statecraft, *Leviathan* (1651). Taking Galileo's notions of motion and rest, Hobbes asserted that "life is but a motion of limbs . . . what is the heart but a string; and nerves, but so many strings; and the joints, but so many wheels . . ."

Isaac Newton (1642–1727), in *Principia,* argued an axiom that became central to political theory, that "every body continues in its state of rest . . . unless it is compelled to change that state by forces impressed on it . . . and to every action there is always opposed an equal reaction." The image of the state as a vast machine balancing contending interests became pervasive, from the atomistic marketplace of Adam Smith, to the checks and balances of pluralistic democracy, and eventually to the dialectical materialism of Karl Marx. In all of these conceptions, the earth was matter to be molded into things of value, not to be revered in itself. The idea of the political machine, with politicians as technicians of power, became conventional wisdom.

Power in the Lost Gospel

Power in America could have been imagined differently if the founders had listened more carefully to the Indian perspective. The foundation of native society and government rested on traditions such as the Great Law of Peace of the Iroquois, or the Sacred Pipe of the Sioux, in which the *communal* dimension of arrangements was stressed and where power had a *healing* and *creative* meaning; power was rooted in concepts other than fallen human nature or the universe as a great machine.

The Great Law of the Iroquois provided for the election of "pine tree chiefs," who were said to have risen from the people in the same manner as the great white pines under which council meetings were held. Among the Michigan tribes, the cosmos was held together by a great medicine tree, the white cedar. In the Ojibwa language, the word for white cedar was "light." Its tall branches broke through to the light of the sky, but also a light fell on those who gathered to deliberate beneath it. Historians of the Anishnabeg define power as being manifest in the land itself, "the transformative presence in cycles of day and night and the seasons, in the fecund earth and in the vision and deeds of spirits, ancestors and living people."

To native people (and perhaps to all mystics, including Taoists and Zen Buddhists), therefore, power was a medicine that could be summoned and received out of the forces of nature itself. And if power was medicine, government could be organic, devoted to healing. Power was possessed by chiefs, great warriors, shamans, by anyone able to align their being with the energies of the natural world. This power was available potentially not only to leaders but to individuals and to whole tribes. In many cases, to follow the power of a chief was a voluntary act rather than one of submission or obedience. The leader had a power of spirit and example, not of bureaucracy or physical resources.

As Jefferson wrote in *Notes on Virginia*, the Indians never "submitted themselves to any laws, any coercive power [or] shadow of government." According to Benjamin Franklin, "all their government is by Counsel of the Sages . . . There is no force; there are no prisons, no officers to compel obedience, or inflict punishment." Thomas Paine, who was invited to the Great Council fire, the center of Iroquois deliberation and decision making, marveled that "there is not, in that state, any of the spectacles of human misery which want and poverty present to our eyes in all the towns and streets of Europe."

On the European continent as well, Jean-Jacques Rousseau

flirted with the notion of a spiritual superiority in a state of nature. In *The Social Contract* (1762), he asked ironically: "When we see among the happiest people in the world bands of peasants regulating the affairs of state under an oak tree, and always acting wisely, can we help feeling a certain contempt for the refinements of other nations, which employ so much skill and mystery to make themselves at once illustrious and wretched?" But Rousseau also held that humans in a state of nature were "stupid and unimaginative" animals who had to be elevated to the status of civilized beings through the social contract. Nature is replaced by culture and institutions as the proper context for humans, in Rousseau's ultimate conclusion.

Whether in Europe or the colonies, what was missing in this frequent distinction between the "natural state" of the Indian and the "civil state" of the Europeans was an understanding that the Indian perspective, far from being "stupid and unimaginative," included broad negotiated arrangements like confederations as well. The Iroquois and other tribal nations recognized the negative side of human nature, and invented their own mechanical structures like the confederation based on achieving a balance of power. The Six Nations did so to establish peace, and urged a similar framework to the colonists. What was really at stake was not a primitive tribalism versus a sophisticated federalism, but the guiding values that the Indians embraced. They favored communal property-sharing arrangements, mutual respect for spiritual traditions, and even intermarriage, which the emerging colonial society strongly rejected. The colonists preferred the philosophical and legal arguments that the frontier was *vacuum domicilum* (wasteland) and the pseudo-scientific claims of racial superiority, which allowed them to avoid a society of shared power in which the creative potential of native people was respected.

It was perhaps inevitable that the early Americans thought of power as a malign tendency arising from original sin more than as a spiritual medicine arising from the creativity of the universe. They had experienced oppression from the abusive power of both monarchic and ecclesiastic establishments. A government of checks and balances and the personal independence promised by private property were seen as the antidotes to the arbitrary rule of kings.

Even in this choice, they often cited the tribal models around them and consulted the Indian sages. Franklin in 1754 commended "the strength of the League which has bound our friends the Iroquois together in a common tie which no crisis, however grave, since its foundation, has managed to disrupt." In 1778 the Continental Congress invited the Delaware nation to consider becoming a state. And a Delaware chief named Tammany, considered a spirit of nature and protector of fisherman, became the symbol of the Sons of Saint Tammany fighting for liberty. From this early identity with the Indians and nature, this colonial experiment grew into the first political machines and the Democratic Party.

THE AMERICAN POLITICAL VISION

In the end, despite any romantic attractions, the colonists rejected the state of nature the Indians represented, and defined the nature of the state as a machine model of frontier expansion. In doing so, ironically, many of those same colonists with roots in the clans and tribes of Europe decided to adopt a centralized model of government looking very much like the Roman Empire that had once been their oppressor.

In this balance-of-powers perspective, power had no creative dimension and was seen primarily as a danger requiring containment. Government became the machinery for the attainment of equilibrium. James Madison, in *Federalist Paper 14,* extolled the "great mechanical power in government" through which a republic's energies could be "concentrated," like a tool, toward "any object which the public good requires." The task was to engineer a "constitutional equilibrium" to prevent the abuse of that same power. In *Federalist Paper 51,* Madison emphasized the principle that "ambition must be made to counter ambition." According to the historian Clinton Rossiter, the new American leaders believed that God "had set the grand machine of nature in motion" according to laws "as certain and imperative as those which controlled the movement of the universe." God was, in Rossiter's image, "the great Legislator" of all nature.

Thomas Jefferson believed that the universe showed "a conviction of design, consummate skills, and indefinite power in every atom of its composition." He recognized and loved the organic energies of the earth as a gift of nature, but felt they required the labor (or "occupancy") of man "to direct their operation."

Adam Smith, in *The Wealth of Nations* (1776), wrote that his purpose was "to expose the basic laws of motion" that he thought governed the economy. Smith observed approvingly that human societies "in many respects resemble machines." The new capitalist market was a great advancement, Smith observed, from "the lowest and rudest state of society, such as we find it among the native tribes of North America." He praised Americans for turning "the rude forests of nature into agreeable and fertile plains, and [making] the trackless and barren ocean into a new fund of subsistence."

Alexander Hamilton's 1791 *Report on Manufactures* defined the economic direction of the coming century. The first steamboat had rocked in the Delaware River at the time of the Constitutional Convention. The locomotive and electrical power lines were soon to follow. Most first- and second-generation Americans were swept up in hopes of a mechanized deliverance from the hardships of the wilderness. By the early nineteenth century, America was being developed, expanded, and developed again, with trains, paddlewheelers, and talking wires, all forging through the garden. The machinery of government, in this view, rested upon the infinite supply of raw materials found in the frontier of the new nation. The balancing of factions rested on government's ability to expand its boundaries. This vision of expansion, buttressed by the Genesis mandate of dominion, would justify the conquest of the entire continent.

But expansion was one of the most hotly debated of the Federalist doctrines. The French philosopher Baron Charles de Montesquieu, for example, expressed the view that democracy could flourish only in a human-scale state. He feared that a frontier society would lead to the unchecked power of a bureaucratic leviathan. The destiny of the environment may have been different if Montesquieu's advice (and that of many anti-Federalists) had been followed. In Montesquieu's democratic state, the environment would have been cultivated and protected in a steady state, not exploited and left behind. Peaceful coexistence with the native tribes would have been necessary as well.

But the Madisonians feared a future confined by geographic boundaries. It reminded them too much of Europe, without an escape valve from class wars, plagues, and ruined environments.

In making the fateful choice to be an expanding frontier nation relying on machines, America's founders rejected an alternate vision of living within environmental limits in sustainable, community-based governing structures. "Indian society may be best," Jefferson concluded, "but it is not possible for large numbers of people."

The Lost Gospel of Romantic Environmentalism

I wish to speak a word for Nature, for absolute freedom and wildness, as contrasted with a freedom and culture merely civil—to regard man as an inhabitant, or a part and parcel of Nature, rather than a member of society. I wish to make an extreme statement, so I may make an emphatic one, for there are enough champions of civilization: the minister and the school committee and every one of you will take care of that.

HENRY DAVID THOREAU, *Walking*

The lost gospel tradition is rooted in the deep-seated attachment to a village culture connected to the land. This attachment remains with us even in the modern age of megacities, since it has been the context in which we have evolved for thousands of years. It partly is a nostalgic attachment, for we cannot return to a world we have obliterated. But it is not so much a reactionary or obsolete attachment as a *longing*. The decentralized village-based tradition is not only an important resource to salvage from our history, but also a crucial alternative to the relentless and unsustainable growth of the centralized megacity. Countless urban as well as rural neighborhoods today are attempting to regain the *character* of a sustainable village in the shadow of bigness and pollution.

The sustainable village was not only a part of native cultures, but also the vision of the grass-root, romantic, and democratic movements integral to the American revolutionary process. The Levellers, the Merry Mount revellers, the Quakers, and other utopians came from a seventeenth- and eighteenth-century tradition of local self-government and the pursuit of happiness apart from property, which envisioned America as "nature's nation," thus laying the foundations for environmentalism.

European romantics like Thomas Carlyle were also raising their voices in spiritual protest against the modern machine age. Hearing only "the monotonous sound of the perpetually revolving wheel," he warned, modern man "never develops the harmony of his being." Carlyle described humanity as having "grown mechanical in head and heart, as well as in hand. Not only the external and physical plane is now managed by machinery, but the internal and spiritual also."

———

A UNIQUELY AMERICAN romantic vision of nature surfaced in the post-Revolutionary generation of Ralph Waldo Emerson, who recommended the study of nature as a "cure" for the cultural dominance of England. His 1837 speech, "The American Scholar," which joined love of country, love of nature, and love of the spiritual realm, was described as "our intellectual Declaration of Independence" by Oliver Wendell Holmes. What Emerson proposed was that a spiritual and scientific identification with nature was central to the American character itself.

Yet Emerson was still not free of the Genesis view of nature as subservient. He wrote at one point that "Nature is thoroughly mediate. It is made to serve. It receives the dominion of man as meekly as the ass on which the Savior rode." He once extolled the notion that "this great savage country should be furrowed by the plow."

But Emerson's circle, meeting in Cambridge, was the beginning of a new spiritual environmentalism among Americans. They called their vision "the Newness"; in time, it would be described as Transcendentalism. Its powerful personalities included Margaret Fuller, Bronson Alcott, Theodore Parker, and many others; three stand out as the founders of American environmentalism: Emerson, his younger colleague Henry David Thoreau, and their spiritual descendant, John Muir.

Emerson's powerful presence spanned five decades, including the publication of *Nature*, his groundbreaking 1836 volume, his thirty-year relationship with Thoreau, and his 1871 encounter

with Muir in Yosemite. Emerson was the most celebrated philosopher of the three. Thoreau, fifteen years younger, became
Emerson's handyman in Cambridge, and editor of the *Dial,* the
magazine produced by the circle. While Emerson only wrote of
"Self Reliance," Thoreau attempted to put it into practice during
a two-year vision quest at Walden Pond, at the foot of Emerson's
property. Muir, three decades later, knew every word of Thoreau's nature writings, and held Emerson in an awe reserved for
gods. Their Yosemite meeting apparently did not go well; Emerson refused to camp out, and Muir declined Emerson's invi-
tation to come to Harvard. But Muir still shared the vision of
Emerson and the self-reliance of Thoreau, translating both into
organizational practice when he founded the Sierra Club at an
1892 meeting in San Francisco.

They were not without their limits. Emerson, although he
became an abolitionist, once wrote that Africans, Irish, and
Indians were less capable of high achievement than Caucasians.
Despite an emerging feminist movement, few women were included in the Cambridge circle (Louisa May Alcott, Bronson's
teenage daughter, served coffee and cleaned up after their philosophical sessions). Just one of the three, Thoreau, took a militant
stand against slavery and war with Mexico. They shared a phobia
of cities that came to separate environmentalism from urban
populism. They were generally aloof from populist movements,
tending to put their faith in a vanguard of intellectuals.

THE LYRIC WRITINGS of these men have inspired many
succeeding generations, and could be collectively issued as an

American gospel of the earth. Not only did they defend the wilderness during America's first love affair with growth and technology, they articulated a spiritual philosophy that can serve environmentalism today.

Thoreau believed that the American environment was an expanded Eden: "I should be ashamed to think that Adam in paradise was more favorably situated than the backwoodsman in this country." The assault on this garden by self-interested commerce called for a spiritual response, but none was forthcoming. Emerson, Thoreau, and Muir were disaffected Christians, condemning Harvard Divinity School as "the ice box."

Emerson was a Unitarian minister who resigned from the church in 1832. Muir was a minister's son who ran away from home. Christianity, they felt, had become a hand-me-down faith. "But why," Emerson asked, "should we not enjoy an original experience of the universe?" Echoing Emerson, Thoreau argued that "God himself culminates in the present moment, and will never be more divine in the lapse of all the ages." Muir, too, denied that creation was complete with Adam and Eve; "We too live in Creation's dawn." Emerson insisted that revelation was possible through nature: "We too must write bibles, to unite again the heavens and the earthly world."

The common vision was that the creator was present in nature, that enlightenment was more possible in a forest than a cathedral, and that the preservation of wilderness was essential to human creativity. While at first Emerson (like Walt Whitman) considered the possibilities of uniting technology with nature, these environmental founders were ultimately bonded in a spiritual dread of the machine age dawning everywhere around them. While most American leaders were rhapsodizing about telegraphs and locomotives, Thoreau warned that "we do not ride the railroad, it rides upon us."

They also countered deductive science with what Emerson called a "poetical sense in the mind," that enabled them to intuit connecting patterns and wholes instead of seeing only externalities and parts. Muir wrote that "I only went out for a walk and finally concluded to stay out . . . for going out, I found, was really going in." A landscape might be made up of private farms, Emerson noted, but there was also an integrity about the whole horizon to which "warranty deeds give no title."

These were not self-appointed stewards overlooking nature, but believers in a kinship model. Other creatures are our "earth-bound companions," Muir proclaimed. Thoreau compared the hum of mosquito, "singing its own wrath and wanderings," with an "Iliad and Odyssey in the air." Emerson's book *Nature* was published in 1836, not long before Charles Darwin's *Origin of Species*. While Emerson was enthusiastic about the discoveries of science, his essay on "Spirit" resisted any interpretation of nature as purely physical:

> Behind nature, throughout nature, spirit is present. . . . it does not act upon us from without, that is, in space and time, but spiritually, through ourselves: therefore, that spirit, that is, the Supreme Being, does not build up nature around us, but puts it forth through us, as the life of the tree puts forth new branches and leaves through the pores of the old.

Muir built on the same themes, rewriting Genesis to formulate a creation gospel that, even today, rivals any scripture for inspiration and eloquence:

> From the dust of the earth, from the common elementary fund, the Creator has made *homo sapiens*. From the same material he has made every other creature, however noxious and insignificant to us. They are earth-born companions and our fellow mortals.
>
> This star, our own good earth, made many a successful journey around the heavens ere man was made, and whole kingdoms and creatures enjoyed existence and returned to dust ere man appeared to claim them. After human beings have also played their part in Creation's plan, they too may disappear without any general burning or extraordinary commotion whatever.
>
> All the merry dwellers of the trees and streams, and the myriad swarms of the air, called into life by the sunbeam of a summer morning, go home through death, wings folded perhaps in the last rays of sunset of the day they were first tried. Trees towering in the sky, braving storms for centuries, flowers turning faces to the light for a single day or hour, having enjoyed their share of life's feast—all alike pass on and away under the law of death and love.
>
> Yet all are our brothers and they enjoy life as we do, share Heaven's blessings with us, die and are buried in hallowed ground, come with us out of eternity and return into eternity.

These writers were conscious of the connection between ecology and native culture. For his whole life, Thoreau studied the Indians from Maine to the Black Hills, leaving behind thirteen unpublished notebooks. At a time when most Americans believed that "the destiny of the Indian is extermination" (the words written by ethnographer Lewis Henry Morgan in 1851), Thoreau defended Indian life as "practical poetry." According to William Ellery Channing, Thoreau's last words were "moose" and "Indians," as if he was linking his death with the fate of Native American life. Muir, too, identified with the aboriginal world, especially when he canoed to Glacier Bay in Alaska in the late nineteenth century, where he wrote that he "never felt more at home" than in Indian villages. Along with his foreboding at the death of wilderness, Muir feared that Indians would "lose their wild instincts, become very nearly nothing, and gain a hymnbook."

For all of them, experiencing the depth and quality of life took priority over consumption and commercialism.

Muir wrote that "our crude civilization engenders a multitude of wants that lawgivers are ever at their wit's end devising." In this sentiment and others, he echoed Thoreau, who had written that "a man is rich in proportion to the number of things which he can afford to let alone." For example, Thoreau added, "I could easily do without the post office," insisting instead on a life of "Simplicity, Simplicity, Simplicity." In one of his most remembered passages, he declared "I went to the woods because I wished to live deliberately, to front only the essential facts of life, and see if I could not learn what it had to teach, and not, when I came to die, discover that I had not lived."

The Vision of the Transcendentalists

We can realize from the transcendentalists that American environmentalism had its beginnings in a spiritual vision, not a political and managerial one. These are different times, of course, if only because the right to vote has been expanded. Even so, it is hard to imagine that Emerson, Thoreau or Muir would trade their spirituality for political power. More likely, their spirituality would undergird and give fire to their action.

Emerson spoke eloquently of the "party of the future" against the "party of the past," but more in cultural terms than electoral ones. Thoreau condemned politics as "the cigar smoke of man" and called for citizens to "cast your whole vote, not a strip of paper merely, but your whole influence. A minority is powerless while it conforms to the majority; . . . but it is irresistible when it clogs by its whole weight." Muir met with presidents and politicians, lobbied for national parks, wrote lengthy articles in the national press, but always insisted that "politics saps the foundation of righteousness." If these founders had a common strategy, it was to challenge the dominant order on the level of vision, personal commitment, and, in Thoreau's case, civil disobedience.

As for political economy, Emerson, Thoreau, and Muir were forerunners of participatory democracy, a long tradition of direct personal and community involvement in decision making that surfaced again in the 1960s. This tradition has three elements that affect the treatment of nature:

1. Politics is *inspirational,* calling people to a connectedness with natural or universal laws. It is inherently spiritual, arising as it does against any system that deadens the human soul, or the soul of the earth. As a corollary, nature and wilderness have an inherent moral value, which is also of redemptive importance to society.

2. Participatory politics is *anti-bureaucratic,* opposed to systems that purport to manage resources or people. It rests on direct participation in the preservation of communities and natural bioregions.

3. It is *opposed to economic empire,* to systems that require the infinite acquisition of resources by expansion and development. It is supportive of only that development that is sustainable and restorative, and technology that is appropriate to the environment in which it is used.

Against the dominant vision of centralized bureaucracy, expansion-based economics, and the promotion of conspicuous and endless consumption, the themes of the transcendentalists suggested self-reliant communities, self-sufficiency in economics, sustainability of natural systems, and voluntary simplicity as the best approach to attaining a spiritual quality of life.

The Decline of Spiritual Environmentalism

By the end of the nineteenth century, the romantic impulse of Transcendentalism seemed more and more anachronistic. The emergence of America as a great power, the achievements of the physical sciences, and the growth of bureaucratic government all seemed desirable and inevitable. The Romantics were defeated.

The last of them, Muir, fought bitterly with Gifford Pinchot, the Chief of the U.S. Forest Service (appointed by President Theodore Roosevelt), who insisted on developing and managing natural resources in the public interest. Pinchot's pragmatism prevailed. Muir's beloved Hetch Hetchy Valley, a second Yosemite, was dammed and flooded to provide water for San Francisco. The attempt to save Hetch Hetchy was Muir's last crusade. "These temple-destroyers," he cried out, "instead of lifting their eyes to the God of the mountains, lift them to the Almighty Dollar. Dam Hetch Hetchy! As well dam for water-tanks the people's cathedrals and churches, for no holier temple has ever been constructed by the heart of man."

Some say Muir died as a result of losing Hetch Hetchy. The Transcendental spirit surely did. The next few decades saw the damming of the West's great rivers, the irrigation of the Western frontier, the logging of the ancient forests, the spread of private mining and grazing on public lands, all in the name of conquering, domesticating, and developing the power of nature into a new nature of power itself, exercised through a scientific administrative state. This administrative state rested atop the electoral one, a vast and remote empire of delegated authority in the hands of managers who claimed an objective knowledge (that happened to coincide with private development interests).

As the nation became more industrial and urbanized, the

romantic voices were replaced by urban reformers, social work-ers, labor organizers, populists, socialists, and radicals, all of whom concentrated their zeal on social and economic issues. Well documented in Robert Gottlieb's *Forcing the Spring*, these reformers understood pollution in terms of coal dust, urban sewage, poisoned food, and dilapidated slums. The question of preserving wilderness was secondary to achieving social justice. The outer environment became the concern of the more com-fortable gentry, who were distant from the daily crises in the urban environment. The question of human justice became sep-arated from the issue of the environment. Most reformers, con-ditioned by ideas of progress, assumed that the environment could generate wealth indefinitely, and therefore turned their attention to the unfair distribution of that wealth. The views of Emerson, Thoreau, and Muir were too spiritual for the emerging secular age. The outlook of Transcendentalism was too distant from the slums, too radical for privileged environmentalists, and too spiritual for the left, to integrate the social, environmental, and spiritual agendas.

The subsequent Progressive Era traced its roots more to the secular Enlightenment than to the mystical consciousness of the Romantics. The new forces of the Left—the labor movements, the Communist and Socialist parties—drew their strength from immigrant ethnic communities, which had become uprooted from the soil and their peasant origins. Even those religious figures who preached the Social Gospel focused more on the labor and urban struggles of the day than on restoring any wider cosmic spirituality.

THE RETURN OF THE SPIRITUAL

As the age of American growth peaked in the mid-twentieth century, the Romantic ecological message was revived most notably by Aldo Leopold and Rachel Carson. Both were natural scientists who held a spiritual reverence for the land and sea. They exerted a powerful counter-influence during a century of growing belief in urbanization and technology. Leopold's *Sand County Almanac* (1949) and Carson's *Silent Spring* (1962) became required reading for an environmental generation.

Leopold's best-known essay, "The Land Ethic," argued that the sphere of an "ethical community" had expanded continually among humans (for instance, through the abolition of slavery) and would be extended to the realm of nature through a gradual realization that the biotic community had integrity and beauty. He faulted the "Economic American" for thinking that "Growth is the number of ciphers added yearly to the national population and the national bank-roll." Quantitative economics, he lamented, would lead humans to the fate of the "Gigantosaurus," a species which perished for following growth to excess. In a 1924 essay, "The River of the Mother of God," he dismissed the mere growth of ciphers, dollars, and population. "There has been just one really new thing since the Gigantosaurus. That new thing is Man, the first creature in all the immensities of time and space whose evolution is self-directed. The first creature, in any spiritual sense, to create his own environment."

Rachel Carson, a marine biologist with the U.S. Fish and Wildlife Service, is remembered mainly for her early warning of the toxic threat of pesticides. But her own mysticism shines through in *The Sea Around Us* (1951), in which her science yielded to this expression of awe:

> But even with all our modern instruments for probing and sampling the deep ocean, no one now can say that we shall ever resolve the last, the ultimate mysteries of the sea.
>
> . . . that other concept of the ancients remains. For the sea lies all about us. The commerce of all lands must cross it. The very winds that move over the lands have been cradled on its broad expanse and seek ever to return to it. The continents themselves dissolve and pass to the sea, in grain after grain of eroded land. So the rains that rose from it return again in rivers.
>
> In its mysterious past it encompasses all the dim origins of life and receives in the end, after, it may be, many transmutations, the dead husks of that same life. For all at last return to the sea— to Oceanus, the ocean river, like the ever-flowing stream of time, the beginning and the end.

E. F. Schumacher revived the idea of blending spirituality with a political and economic program, in his *Small Is Beautiful,* written in 1973. Coming at the time of the world energy crisis, the book presented an alternative to the culture of consumption, distilled in the maxim, *less is more.* The book inspired the 1970s anti-nuclear, pro-solar movement, reintegrated the spiritual, the personal, and the political, and was the bible for Governor Jerry Brown's reform era in Sacramento.

Schumacher attacked all economic thinking that devalued work and promoted specialization in the name of efficiency. Modern economics, to him, was based on the idea of work as a necessary evil. To an employer it was an "item of cost," which was to be minimized by low wages or eliminated altogether by automation. To the employee, work was considered a "disutility," a sacrifice of time and energy in exchange for money, a means to an end. The definition of success, for orthodox economists, was "simply the total quantity of goods produced during a given period of time."

This attack on the Gross National Product (GNP) as morally deficient was advanced by the work of a professional economist, Herman Daly, who argued for a *steady-state economy* as the alternative to a GNP-based model of infinite growth. He rejected as unscientific the notion of infinite growth, and instead proposed in his essay "A Biblical Economic Principle" that we "consciously face the fundamental limits of creaturehood: finitude, entropy, and ecological dependence." Daly argued that "moral growth" was the real necessity in a steady-state model, a need denied and ignored by economists hiding behind the veil of objectivity. He denied that efficiency is somehow neutral or value-free because the human choice of ends is always involved. Therefore, Daly called for seeking "infinite" moral and spiritual dimensions within the "finite" framework of both our lifespans and material limits, quoting the prophet Isaiah: "Why do you spend your money for that which is not bread, and your labor for that which does not satisfy? . . . Incline your ear and come to me; hear, that your soul may live" (Isaiah, 55:2).

Like Daly's value-oriented economics, Schumacher offered a value-oriented definition of work. In this model, work is the primary mode of creative interaction between the human and the natural worlds, just as ritual is the primary mode of spiritual interaction. Schumacher's "Buddhist Economics" defined work in three ways: the chance to develop one's creative faculties, to overcome ego by joining in collective tasks, and to create goods and services for an improved quality of existence.

To intentionally organize work as noncreative and meaningless, Schumacher believed, represented a "lack of compassion and a soul-destroying degree of attachment to the most primitive side of this worldly existence." Schumacher proposed in a similar vein that consumption be limited to optimal levels, as distinguished from the modern goal of stimulating unlimited craving.

Writers like Schumacher and Daly set the moral framework for an environmental and economic alternative to the status quo. Others like Barry Commoner, Ralph Nader, Hazel Henderson, Amory Lovens, and Paul Hawken have elaborated this vision in concrete detail during the past two decades. In brief, that alternative looks like this:

- A Quality-of-Life Index to replace the Gross National Product, so that qualitative growth in employment, education, health, environment, and race relations can be monitored instead of simply the levels of profit and investment.

- A crash program of resource conservation, energy efficiency, and transition to renewable resources instead of greater dependency on nuclear power and oil. This program would include development of nonpolluting alternatives to the internal combustion engine as one of its highest priorities.

- A priority on pollution prevention at the source rather than top-down managerial regulation in all spheres of industry, agriculture, and health care. A prevention strategy would combine everything from the maximum feasible phaseout of toxic chemicals and pesticides to the positive promotion of health and wellness.

- A foreign policy based on environmental sustainability and protection, focusing on finding solutions for nations like China and India where the population and ecological crises are most acute. This foreign policy would start at home with reduction of our own irrational consumption levels, the urgent development of alternative energy technologies for export, and a global "green corps" modeled on the Peace Corps.

- A maximum decentralization of citizen decision making to the neighborhood and bioregional levels, and the extension of constitutional protections to vital ecosystems including old-growth forests and major watersheds. Private property rights would be ensured as a protection of personal freedom, but in the context of assuring a healthy, sustainable ecosystem as a public trust. This would mean, for example, new incentives for family farms and organic agriculture but strong disincentives against cattle grazing and destructive mining on public lands.

In short, since Earth Day 1970 environmentalists have steadily developed the substance of an alternative: a transition to a sustainable democratic society dedicated to improving the quality of life, in which the protection of nature is both a habit of the heart and a constitutional consensus. What remains is to arouse the spiritual energies of society into a movement strong enough to overcome the powerful inertia of bureaucracies locked into the status quo.

Small Is Beautiful in Sacramento

Such visionary politics briefly took root during the era of Jerry Brown as California governor from 1974 to 1982. It was a time of change: the Middle East oil shortages of the early 1970s created a mandate for alternatives to our dependence on foreign oil; the Watergate Crisis fueled public outcry against political corruption in Washington. To his immense credit, Governor Brown turned California's energy future away from the electrical utility agenda of building forty nuclear plants, toward his agenda of conservation, efficiency, and renewable resources, creating thousands of jobs and saving consumers billions of dollars. Moved by the appeal of Chumash elders and environmentalists, he stopped a liquified natural gas (LNG) terminal being planned for Indian sacred land at Point Conception. In addition, he introduced Schumacher's "small is beautiful" rhetoric into the national political culture.

But Brown's very dissent from cultural and political orthodoxy contributed to his demise as a candidate for the U.S. Senate and presidency in the 1980s. He was elected governor with less than a public mandate for his visionary policies; "an uncertain trumpet," he called it. The public in the early 1970s was disgusted with business-as-usual politics after Watergate, but at the same time held fond memories of Brown's father, former Governor Edmund G. (Pat) Brown, who had promoted a massive growth agenda. (As Pat Brown once said of the California Aqueduct, "I wanted this to be a monument to *me*.")

Jerry Brown was elected governor with his father's name but not his father's agenda. The public wanted change, but a new public consensus on the environmental limits of growth was just emerging. From the beginning Jerry Brown was plagued by the lack of an organized lobby for his visionary politics of the future. There was, for example, no preexisting base of solar energy businesses to support the new governor's plans. But there was a massive lobby for the status quo, composed of builders, developers, nuclear power and oil companies, pesticide manufacturers, and the like. They pilloried Brown as "Governor Moonbeam" and poured millions into the campaign coffers of his enemies.

Brown suffered most grievously when he bravely refused to authorize the helicopter spraying of malathion (a nerve gas derivative that had never been fully studied for its health effects) on urban populations, a demand of agribusiness interests who wanted to contain the infestation of their crops by the Mediterranean fruit fly. Brown pointed out in vain that there were alternatives to spraying of population centers with malathion. If the authorities were telling the public, particularly pregnant women and children, to stay indoors during spraying, Brown questioned how safe the chemical could be. The legislature panicked and overrode Brown. The media portrayed him as a quirky leader who could not make the tough decisions required for economic growth. He never recovered politically, though history has never disproved his judgment on malathion spraying.

Economic Recession and Environmental Crisis, 1973–1994

In response to the first Earth Day, the Nixon administration approved major environmental laws in the early 1970s. With the Vietnam War over and Watergate illustrating the need for political reform, the prospects for significant change seemed to be at hand. But those possibilities began to wane as the economy stagnated. Despite Watergate, the Machiavellian special interest character of the government was preserved. Despite the energy crisis and the faltering of the nation's nuclear power program, the fossil fuel lobbies remained dominant. And despite the welcome passage of the environmental laws, the machinery of the bureaucratic managerial system grew heavier; the federal courts alone addressed an unprecedented 4,000 environmental cases between 1971 and 1988, siphoning environmentalist resources out of neighborhoods into courtrooms.

These seemed to be years of continuing success, however, for the environmental movement. In addition to its grass-roots activism, the movement grew into a more organized and sophisticated lobby of lawyers and policy experts working to influence the system from the inside. The movement gained access to the corridors of power. Contributions from foundations and concerned citizens kept flowing to the tax-deductible accounts of major organizations, who had an estimated collective annual budget of over $2.5 billion by the 1990s. The top ten environmental groups grew from a collective $10 million budget in 1965 to $514 million in 1990. The spiritual and more radical underpinnings of environmentalism slipped into the background in the giddy new climate of greater acceptance.

But then the gears of political economy went into reverse. With few pundits noticing, the growth mechanisms of the economy began eroding. The environmental and energy crises, the fall of the dollar, the emergence of industrial competitors, and the coming of a global marketplace—all resulted in economic stagnation for most Americans. More families were forced to work longer hours at lower wages simply to maintain their standard of living.

Although this economic slowdown had everything to do with myopic anti-environmental policies, it was soon blamed on alleged environmental extremists with their costly agendas. In fact, the actual causes of the economic downturn included an irrational American investment in capital-intensive energy strategies based on fossil fuels and nuclear power. At the same time, America's leading competitors in Japan and Germany applied energy conservation techniques that achieved a dollar's worth of production at half the energy costs of American firms.

In addition, America's Cold War role as military gendarme tied up trillions of dollars in the capital-intensive and polluting military technologies that "defended" the more efficient civilian economies of Japan and Europe. Excessive exposure to toxic chemicals in the workplace, air, water, and food, combined with a national culture of bingeing on fast-food diets, helped make cancer and heart disease the top killers of Americans, and sent inflationary health-care costs soaring out of control. America's energy and environmental policies became an economic albatross that was hard to shed because of the stranglehold of the oil, nuclear, chemical, agricultural, and automobile and highway lobbies over national politics.

But it was the environmentalists who became the convenient scapegoat for an orchestrated backlash in the early 1990s. Americans were told over and over by the likes of Rush Limbaugh that expensive environmental regulations were to blame for their stagnant standard of living. Those regulations came under severe attack in the name of "streamlining." Politicians who had been fair-weather friends of environmentalism now ran for cover under special-interest pressure. The apple-pie popularity of environmentalism came under siege. For example, a $22 million business blitz in 1992 successfully defeated Big Green, an environmental initiative in California, which proposed to phase out cancer-causing chemicals and elect a state environmental commissioner. At first, surveys showed that Big Green's provisions enjoyed more than 60 percent support among voters. But a propaganda campaign financed by major polluters around the world concentrated on a simple phrase: "goes too far, costs too much." As California sank into a recession, the citizens voted against Big Green, an event that fueled the business backlash nationally.

The major environmental organizations were not prepared for this 1990 turn of events. The whole notion of environmental progress had rested on a fragile and false assumption of economic growth. The nation's environmental laws had been passed before the economic contractions of the early 1970s. Environmental cleanup was expected to be financed out of the growth dividend, not from corporate profits, closure of special interest tax loopholes, or a redistribution of wealth. That would have required the environmental movement to become populist on economic issues, a choice it had not made.

The assumption of the major environmental groups was that only a growing economic pie would make possible a green slice. They acquiesced to the market philosophy of growth, and based their strategy on the assumption that the growth dividend would continue. Why not? Unlike the civil rights, labor, and peace movements—which had gone through many years of confrontation, even bloodshed, to become mainstream—the environmental movement of the 1970s was developed with bipartisan blessings and respectability. To challenge the market system and the doctrine of growth was to become marginalized. The leading environmental organizations chose the mainstream instead.

Their unified vision was embodied in *An Environmental Agenda for the Future,* a 1985 book by leaders of the Natural Resources Defense Council, the National Wildlife Federation, the Environmental Defense Fund, the Sierra Club, the National Audubon Society, the Environmental Policy Institute, the Izaak Walton League, the National Parks and Conservation Association, the Wilderness Society, and Friends of the Earth. "Continued economic growth is essential," the environmental leaders declared in the introduction. "Past environmental gains will be maintained and new ones made more easily in a healthy economy than in a stagnant one . . ." There was no hint that stagnation itself was caused by corporate and bureaucratic investment in an economy based on fossil fuels and consumption ethics, or that radical restructuring and changed values might be essential to achieving a sustainable economy as well as environment. Instead the leadership chose the soothing message that environmental restoration, far from being a threat, was exactly what American corporations and government needed.

But corporate America was not buying the message. Why would corporations become green, the bottom-line thinkers of the Reagan-Bush era asked, when the pro-growth lobbies were contributing fifty times more in campaign contributions to Congress than all the public interest groups combined? More was being spent on public relations campaigns to downplay global warming alone than environmentalists were spending on lobbying on all environmental fronts. It was much easier for an oil company to buy television advertisements featuring happy seals than to invest in real alternatives to offshore oil drilling.

CONFRONTING BACKLASH

With economic stagnation a long-term reality and with special interests in the saddle from Washington, D.C., to Sacramento, modern environmentalism reached a turning point in the 1990s. There seemed to be only two narrow possibilities: (1) to fight a defensive holding action against the backlash and, if successful, (2) to return to the limited role of working within a system of moderate environmental management at a time when budgets for government environmental programs were being cut.

The backlash represented a return to the harshest interpretation of the Genesis mandate, expressed by the Contract with America and the likes of Patrick Buchanan and Rush Limbaugh. Their approach in an era of economic stagnation was to scapegoat the environmentalists and return to a militant ransacking of the resources of the earth under the mandate of God. Instead of Earth First!, their message was America First! in the scramble for the earth's resources. Speaker Newt Gingrich once imagined himself as a new Columbus planning the conquest of the moon—"an enormous natural resource, possessed of more than enough minerals and materials to provide everything a self-replicating system needs." He would even combat crime with space mirrors to eliminate darkness as a refuge for criminals, a new twist on the Genesis words, "Let there be light." Gingrich was not alone in seeking to colonize the cosmos when the continents were depleted. Still others rhapsodized about planting a new Jamestown on the moon by the twenty-first century, then employing nuclear explosions to create oxygen and hydrogen from lunar soil before moving out to conquer the asteroid belt and on to "terra-forming" Mars by melting its frozen surface with perhaps those same mirrors. The destruction of the environment was not a worry since the earth itself was disposable.

By 1996, however, partisans of the Republican Contract with America were finding that the American public did not agree that the answer to their economic worries lay in rolling back the environmental laws of the past twenty-five years. The environmental agenda had become too much a part of the American national consensus to be erased. The environmental lobby successfully counterattacked the Gingrich agenda and, with help from the Clinton administration, prevented the dismantling of the Clean Water Act, the Clean Air Act, and other environmental legislation. For the first time, the environmental cause enlisted the support of evangelical Christians in defense of the endangered species laws—a notable and successful response to the most serious threat to environmental laws in many years.

Assuming the environmental lobby continues to succeed in thwarting the backlash on federal and state levels, however, it will succeed only in defending a status quo that is woefully inadequate to achieve the necessary environmental restoration. The status quo can be described, at best, as a stewardship approach to resource management. Its hidden premise is that nothing can be accomplished without consensus from the largest polluters themselves. For example, the Clinton administration created a Council on Sustainable Development in 1993 which included Dow Chemical, Chevron, Exxon, Georgia Pacific, and Ciba Geigy (the pharmaceutical giant), as well as environmental representatives. There is nothing wrong with engaging in the search for common ground between adversaries. What is problematic is the assumption of the consensus approach that reforms are limited to what is acceptable to those corporate interests mainly responsible for degrading the environment in the first place.

In these traditional approaches, economic policy is still based on the stimulation of demand, consumption, and growth, on obtaining more resources from the environment. Even the most enlightened economic thinkers of this administration fail to publicly consider any alternative to this growth formula. Labor Secretary Robert Reich eloquently defines American workers as an undervalued resource, but treats the environment as an economic externality. In his new frontier of knowledge-workers, Reich predicts that the "work community" will replace the "geographic community" as the most important setting for Americans. But work and economics cannot be separated from the natural environment. For Reich the new frontier seems to be a de-natured office full of computer terminals. But as *PC* magazine has pointed out, "The irony is that we're using more paper than ever" for these offices of the future. Corporate America consumes forests of paper: 775 billion pages annually, or 50,000 square miles of former trees. The Environmental Protection Agency (EPA) estimates personal computers and their peripherals waste $2 billion of electricity annually, and cause as much carbon dioxide as 5 million automobiles. Perhaps this waste can be abated, but not without a significant change in the value paradigm of the so-called "information highway."

Thinkers like Reich speak glowingly of the need to enrich human capital, the upgrading of knowledge and skills, but don't seem to consider the expense for environmental capital—the degrading of natural systems on which economies ultimately depend. At best this perspective considers the environmental crisis not as a crisis of values—much less a spiritual crisis—but a problem that can be regulated, mitigated, and lessened by greater efficiencies. The flaws of this approach are, first, the basic hubris of believing that nature can be molded to our economic will; and second, the ignoring of evidence that twenty-five years of environmental managerialism has failed to reverse the continuing depletion of our resources. As the original Earth Day founder, Denis Hayes, described the situation in 1990, "By any number of criteria you can apply to the sustainability of the planet, we are in vastly worse shape than we were in 1970, despite twenty years of effort."

Another example of high-technology mysticism is that of Ken Kelly, an editor of the high-tech magazine *Wired*. Kelly envisions that the new machines should fold back into the Garden, not trample it. Industry should be designed to imitate nature, Kelly argues. As in nature, for example, nothing used by industry should be wasted. Kelly's test would become the ease of product repair instead of production. In a closed-loop system, everything becomes a resource and waste theoretically disappears. Kelly cites a German law that mandates cars be designed for dismantling into recyclable parts. But the problem with this elegant theory is that nature cannot be rearranged so easily. A car's parts can be recycled, but who will restore ancient forests, mountains that have been strip-mined, or rivers that have been dammed? Secondly, the consumerist economy is based on waste, on making products that do not last, the multiplying of new versions of the same products, all backed by advertising machinery that relentlessly stimulates consumer craving. Kelly's promising high-technology agenda cannot reverse this process. Only a spiritual change can.

For most environmentalists, defending the Clintonites against Newt Gingrich is an easy choice. The tougher challenge is how to transcend the traps of managerialism and the delusions of high technology. If this seems utopian today, it is preferable to the dystopia of what candidate Bill Clinton in 1992 called the brain-dead politics of both parties.

A New Politics of Spirit and Nature

A new sustainable environmental politics is needed and can only be accomplished by attaching a spiritual worth to a natural world that is considered disposable today.

A possible alternative to both backlash and managerialism shined forth in the publication of *Earth in the Balance*, written by then-Senator Al Gore in 1992. Gore's book broke with prevailing thought, offering this basic conclusion:

> The place to start with is faith. . . . Perhaps because I have ended up searching simultaneously for a better understanding of my own life and of what can be done to rescue the global environment, I have come to believe in a kind of *inner ecology* that relies on the same principles of balance and holism that characterize a healthy environment.

But I have a suspicion that Gore's book has remained on the shelf in the White House. A cool green pragmatism has prevailed over any spiritual imperative. The environmental crisis is a secondary emphasis in the Clinton agenda.

The administration's top priority, opening new markets for corporate expansion, resulted in a North American Free Trade Agreement that left strong environmental safeguards in limbo, subject to a secretive "dispute resolution" bureaucracy composed of NAFTA trade proponents. The environmental organizations suffered crippling divisions over NAFTA and how to work with the Clinton administration.

The administration has followed a mostly voluntaristic, incentive-based approach to such crises as global warming, which environmentalists would have condemned during the Bush presidency. In California, the administration championed a "cooperative" Bay-Delta agreement with the lords of water export, a compromise that threatened the extinction of spring-run salmon so that Delta water could irrigate crops and recreation in the desert. They have backpedaled from early talk of mandatory fuel efficiency, increased grazing fees, and protection of old-growth forests.

To his credit, the President appointed highly competent environmental advocates to key positions at the EPA, Interior, and even the State Department. And they have fought hard to preserve the Clean Air, Clean Water, and Superfund laws. In comparison with the Gingrich Republicans, of course, the Clintonites look quite green. But so does the color blue when blended with yellow.

Gore himself stated the central issue when he wrote, "The maximum that is politically feasible still falls short of the minimum that is truly effective." How then can the vision of Gore's book be translated into reality? Only by a paradigm shift toward both the environment and politics. The mystical embrace of "growth" by the political culture, combined with the system of fund-raising for elections, dictates that environmentalism will be secondary to special-interest growth agendas. Even with its good intentions, the administration will tend to disappoint its most committed environmental supporters while trying to lessen the opposition of its anti-environmental enemies.

Gore's book, though eloquent in proposing new models of environmental economics and security, is silent on the need for a new model of politics that will support his agenda. In a candid admission, the vice president writes that "I have become very impatient with my own tendency to put a finger to the political winds and proceed cautiously." While the need for more courage and less caution is always welcome, the greater need is for reform of the *system* that cultivates such expediency in the first place.

But a political system that arose from Machiavelli's world view and was imposed on an abundant frontier needs to be changed as well. There is little chance of successfully promoting an alternative spiritual and environmental vision in the foul bowels of a system that rewards the expedient pursuit of reckless growth. Gore's wonderful book proposes that we change our thinking about everything except politics itself; while it gives great hope of joining spirituality and environmentalism in main-stream discourse, the task remains of transforming the present boundaries and incentives of politics to let nature and spirit in.

Václav Havel and the
Politics of the Spirit

Another major political spokesperson for a transformation of our politics has been Václav Havel, the playwright, former political prisoner, and current president of a free Czechoslovak Republic. Like the Dalai Lama, Havel has helped awaken a worldwide interest in synthesizing the issues of spirituality, environment, and statecraft.

Under his Communist oppressors, Havel experienced very painfully the effects of a state dedicated to de-sanctifying both nature and life itself, a state that claimed as its basis an omnipotent knowledge of objective truth. But Communism is only one variant of the system of amoral administration that Havel defines as global.

The administrative machine, which claims an objective knowledge of policy truths, attempts to *master* the ultimate nature of what Havel calls Being, or the spiritual nature of the universe. The administrative state abhors and wars against the *mystery* of this underlying Being. Since Machiavelli, Havel writes, politics has become only a "rational technology of power," a depersonalized and anonymous apparatus of control. "States grow ever more machine-like, men are transformed into statistical choruses of voters, producers, consumers, patients, tourists or soldiers." Modern man, "his natural world properly conquered by science and technology," only objects to smokestacks fouling the sky "if the stench enters his apartment."

For Havel this is the key failure of the utilitarian approach, that it takes action only when pollution disturbs voters' breathing or damages their property. For Havel, on the other hand, the smokestack also "soils the heavens." It assaults the integrity of the natural world by an arrogant assertion of human mastery. It is not enough, in this perspective, to oppose air pollution only because it leads to medical bills and lost productivity. Pollution in Havel's perspective is a sin against the natural order with serious consequences over time.

The bureaucratic utilitarian state therefore violates what he calls the "eternal ground of being" at the sacred heart of things. Havel derides all arrogant administrators for their idolatrous attempt to reorder the universe.

> The term "environment" tacitly implies that whatever is not human merely "environs" or surrounds us and is therefore inferior to us, something we need care for only if it is in our interest to do so.
>
> The world is not divided into two types of Being, one superior and the other merely surrounding it. . . . we are not the masters of Being, but only a part thereof.
>
> Having recognized that we are but a tiny speck in the grand *physical* design of things, we must eventually recognize that we are but a speck in the *metaphysical* structure of things as well.

For Havel, politics is about more than the next election. We are related "to the world as a whole and to eternity" as well. Having dreamt of being "masters of space and time," the Communists brought ruin to the Czech environment with an arrogance that should be a "warning to all contemporary civilization."

The Lost Gospel in Politics

Approved deliberately as an environment latent with possi-
bilities for freedom and democracy rather than for wealth and
empire, the unredeemed desert West might be an unrealized
national resource. It might be valued as a place of inspiration
and training for a different kind of life. Relieved from some
of the burdens of growing crops, earning foreign exchange, and
supporting immense cities, it might encourage an incipient
America of simplicity, discipline and spiritual exploration
[where people] would irrigate their spirit more than their ego.

DONALD WORSTER, *Rivers of Empire:*
Water, Aridity, and the Growth of the American West

The lost gospel is ecumenical and universal. It is a challenge to Christianity, Judaism, Islam, Buddhism, and Hinduism to expand their definitions of the sacred to include the natural world. It is a challenge to nonbelievers, too, to return to a spiritual path whatever their tradition. It demands that ancient nature wisdom be taken as seriously as any chapter of the Bible, Torah, or Koran. It is a connecting thread between the traditions, a common ground of reverence.

The relationship between the human community and the natural world cannot be healed by a single, particular faith, but only by a profound understanding that all faiths should revere a single earth. If it is to succeed, it cannot be as a rival or alternative faith to the major ones, but a spiritual resource to all of them. Therefore, it is not a "new religion" that is needed but a new sanctification of nature in all our religions.

The lost gospel means a change of consciousness and practice. It begins to set forth ethical guidelines (or perhaps natural laws) for the age of ecological crisis. These ethics will eventually transform our daily behavior, which may at first feel like duties but ultimately become satisfying tasks. (Many of our children, for example, don't view the task of recycling as a chore.) As we shed the artificial need for conspicuous and wasteful consumption, for example, we will lessen the stress in our lives and find more time for enhancing life's quality.

As we change, our political and economic institutions will change. Environmentalism already has become a permanent factor in elections and market decisions. As it becomes a deeper matter of values, the pressure on institutions to change will grow in the future.

The lost gospel must be asserted in serious action, not simply filed in our consciousness. The lost gospel is *lost*, after all, not because it was misplaced, but because its vision and visionaries perished and were suppressed. The enemies of the lost gospel, the hard-line zealots still espousing God-given entitlement over the earth, remain entrenched in all spheres of society. The lost gospel must challenge, at times confront, and ultimately change the assumptions of those who justify their war on nature on religious grounds.

This means that more environmentalists need to embrace a spiritual dimension to our struggle. Many, if not most, environmentalists already carry a sense of the lost gospel in their value system. But many do not. Many see ecology as an emerging objective science, and want to convince the elites and the public on empirical grounds that we need to change our behavior. Some of the same environmentalists define their politics as a matter of rational and enlightened planning. They are uncomfortable, even hostile, to talk of spiritual matters. Many of them, understandably, have been wounded by organized religion on levels they can barely articulate. They have deep reservations about mysticism, which they tend to equate with a fanatic denial of rational exchange.

BEYOND SCIENCE

No doubt a science-based approach has made a major contribution to environmentalism. Thinkers like Thomas Berry and Fritjof Capra believe that the new physics is actually a kind of spiritual revelation, proving the fallacy of dualism between human beings and the earth. Barry Commoner has shown that ecological science proves the basic relatedness of all living things. But science is clearly not all we need in order to engage the environmental crisis. Science cannot answer every mystery of nature, and it lacks the motivating force to nourish vital qualities like courage and compassion. We are deficient today not so much in our scientific capacity but our spiritual and ethical resources for approaching the environmental crisis.

I have noticed a broad pattern of defensiveness about spirituality, a tendency to hide our spiritual motives behind a facade of being practical and hard-headed. Many environmentalists seem to fear that they will be scorned or laughed at if they reveal their genuine feelings. But it is unhealthy and self-defeating in politics as well as life to closet one's feelings. It is impossible to challenge the anti-environmental values of our time without expressing an alternate set of values. We cannot splice nature back into our religious and political discourse as if through some technical error it was edited out several thousand years ago. We cannot change other deeply held attitudes without a period of confrontation. If we repress our own feelings about nature and spirituality, we lessen our ability to communicate passionately with others and we become confused about who we are. The danger is becoming only kinder, gentler managers of a declining natural world. There is no way to make environmentalism in the truest sense safe for the status quo. It is the other way around; we need a status quo that is sustainable and safe for species and their habitat.

The lost gospel is an important spiritual anchor against the tendencies to expediency and compromise. As a state senator, I am constantly aware of the temptations of settling only for access, the pressures to go along, the ever-present concern about contributions being gained or lost depending on one's decision. So are most environmentalists I know. The question is how to succeed without succumbing to success.

Sophisticated public relations firms representing the polluting interests are working around the clock to promote the co-optation of the environmental movement. For example, a public relations specialist speaking to the National Cattlemen's Association in 1991 described a strategy to divide and defeat environmentalists as follows: First, isolate the radicals to prevent a deeper critique of the system from permeating the environmental movement and public consciousness. Second, cultivate the idealists into becoming pragmatic realists. Third, give these realists the highest priority by offering trade-offs if they join the system. Finally, look for opportunists who want "visibility, power, followers and . . . employment," and offer them partial victories. "If your industry can successfully bring about these relationships," the PR master concluded, "the credibility of the radicals will be lost and opportunists can be counted on to share in the final policy solution."

This manipulation is a major threat to the integrity and power of environmentalism. It is inherent in the very nature of politics in a pluralistic society. There is no way to withdraw from the arena, at least without accomplishing the very isolation that the bureaucratic manipulators desire. The only answer to seduction and co-optation lies in cultivating strong spiritual values and remaining accountable to the grass-roots activists who are the backbone of the environmental movement and have nothing to gain from access to the corridors of power. I am not arguing for the rigid purity that can arise from the fear that any success within the system is inherently corrupting. I am arguing for what Havel calls a "metaphysical anchor," one that helps us ride in the currents of the mainstream without being blown off course by the winds of opportunism.

SUPPORT FOR A SPIRITUAL APPROACH

Environmentalists (and certainly the pundits) might be surprised at the depth of public support for positions that are often described as controversial. A 1995 volume published by the Massachusetts Institute of Technology provides impressive proof that Americans already are convinced of a message of spiritual environmentalism, especially if it is populist and not elitist.

The authors of *Environmental Values in American Culture* assembled existing survey data as well as doing their own polling and interviews. They broke down their sample into a spectrum of opinion ranging from Earth First! members to Sierra Club members, the general public, and to employees of dry cleaners and sawmills. This was their conclusion:

> Our analysis of American values suggested that environmental advocates are missing an opportunity by basing their argument primarily on utilitarian grounds. . . .
>
> The only utilitarian value we found with real emotional force was that the earth should be preserved for our children. . . .
>
> [Two key American values that] are not now addressed by environmental activists [are] traditional religious teachings and biocentrism.

The survey percentages reveal an underlying consensus supportive of the themes of this book, and of spiritual environmentalism in general.

These results are consistent with other research data that show that majorities of Americans support environmental issues ranging from more spending on toxic cleanup to philosophical identification with animal rights.* All of which reveals the lost

---

* Nearly half of Americans agreed with the statement that animals "are just like humans in all important ways" in a *Los Angeles Times* national poll (Dec. 25, 1993). Forty-seven percent agreed while 51 percent did not. Seventy-six percent supported either the present laws concerning humane treatment or a strengthening of them, while only 17 percent felt they went too far. Fifty percent

Earth First! members	Sierra Club members	The public	Dry cleaning workers	Sawmill workers
"Because God created the natural world, it is wrong to abuse it."				
76	79	78	69	78
"Plants and animals are there to serve humans. They don't have any rights in themselves."				
0	7	23	10	31
"The Creator intended that nature be used by humans, not worshipped by them."				
0	30	35	52	59
"If people only think of making a profit, they won't really see the beauty that nature has to offer."				
100	78	86	87	69
"The present relationship between humans and nature is one of domination rather than partnership. We look at most living organisms as extractable commodities."				
100	82	90	87	81
"Capitalism may be the best system we know of today, but a fundamental problem with it is that it doesn't give any value of things you can't buy and sell, like the environment."				
80	82	90	83	63
"Before Columbus came to this continent, the Indians were completely in balance with their environment. They depended on it, respected it, and didn't alter it."				
58	78	77	80	69
"Global climate change would disturb the whole chain of life."				
100	85	93	90	81

William Kempton, James Boster, Jennifer Hartley, *Environmental Values in American Culture* (MIT 1995).

gospel as a populist credo, in the tradition of the early prophets, St. Francis, and Chief Seattle. While the lost gospel must be analyzed and debated like any question of moral philosophy, it arises from an intuitive kinship with nature and there it will always belong. It must be consistently populist, always aiming to awaken consciousness from the bottom up. Because of its distrust of hierarchies imposed on nature, the lost gospel is implicitly opposed to hierarchies based on race, class, or gender as well.

The lost gospel cannot be proclaimed from only outside institutions; it must surface everywhere the spirit awakens. Perhaps an environmental Martin Luther should nail a Green Spiritual Manifesto on the vaulted doors of the powerful. But we also need an environmental clergy leader like Martin Luther King to march through those doors proclaiming the revelation that nature is sacred. We need an environmental equivalent of Jesse Jackson to preach and mobilize for elective offices at all levels from school boards to the national government. We need the resurrection of the spirit of Cesar Chavez, who combined Catholicism, nonviolence, and labor organizing with a spiritual attachment to the land.

The lost gospel has to be carried into the den of politics because the defensive institutions of the status quo will only

---

opposed the wearing of clothes made of animal fur, while 35 percent did not. Fifty-four percent opposed the hunting of animals for sport. The data from more than a thousand respondents showed that while the animal rights agenda remains very divisive, a very large number of Americans have rejected dominance and anthropocentrism.

react in painfully inadequate, token, and gradual ways to a threat from the environmentalists outside. The institutions themselves—their hierarchies, their addiction to wasting resources, their detachment from the damage they do, their rotting organizational cultures—need to be transformed from within by a living change of values. Simply put, an environmental code of ethics has to pervade our organizational settings where today the environment is at best an afterthought, like a plea to recycle posted by the office copier.

Reflecting the Popular Will

The survey I have cited shows a crisis in our democratic political system that requires profound change: the system still thwarts the majority will. While public opinion certainly has an effect on the system, it cannot be said that our elected government reflects the pro-environmental sentiment expressed in the polls. The electoral system is corrupted by special interests dependent on stealing environmental resources from future generations, while externalizing the cost from themselves to those same generations. The administrative leviathan is based on exploiting those same resources while suffocating public participation in the decision-making process.

Both the electoral system and the bureaucracy are designed to thwart the majority will where it might interfere with access to natural resources. Even where the environmental interest prevails, say in a judicial decision, it is at the cost of tremendous effort, resources, and time by determined environmental advocates. All environmental progress is slow, incremental, and focused on specific, hot issues, while in the meantime the overall system of environmental exploitation is subsidized and preserved.

What better example could there be than the continued grazing subsidies for cattle-owning absentee corporations that represent a tiny fraction of a percent of the citizens of America? Or the trillions being spent in subsidies for nuclear power plants that would collapse overnight if exposed to competition from renewable resources and democratic review by the public? The politicians' opportunistic complaints about rising welfare costs apply only to poor women, never to well-connected polluting corporations living off the taxpayers and consumers.

The Machiavellian special-interest state is the demonic enemy of the spirit of nature. The Machiavellian state is based on the use and disposability of nature, but also on the domination, use, and disposability of human beings, as well. Whatever is done to the web of life, Chief Seattle warned, is done to ourselves. In degrading nature, the human community cannot be exempt. The special interest state perpetuates itself by turning both humans and nature into raw material for its organizational needs. That is why the environment cannot be restored without also restoring government to democratic ends and ridding it of the corruption of Machiavellian special-interest groups.

The Necessity of Spirituality

When a system like the Machiavellian state smothers our souls, we have no choice but to respond spiritually. We need a spiritual base to sustain ourselves as human beings. I have come to the conclusion that being spiritual is not a choice on a menu of selections, but a matter of understanding that we *are* spiritual. It is part of being human to be connected to eternity and its cycles, to a living creation, something larger than ourselves.

Those who accept a spirit in nature actually are gaining access to a powerful resource that lies within our grasp. To think otherwise is to perpetuate the illusion and denial that we are separate from nature, or that our minds can understand and control its force. But how can we still claim to conquer, control, and manage a creation larger and greater than ourselves? The modern state and its adherents may attempt to dominate and transcend nature, but the effort is finally in vain. No state is greater than the state of nature. No government can usurp the governance of nature's laws of life and death. No executive can be the chairman of the corporate earth. No planner can comprehend what is larger than mind.

Machiavellian statecraft is idolatry. In trying to conquer nature to build empires, we have left ourselves weakened. We have forgotten another possibility, of being modern villagers in the country of nature, souls participating in creation itself. It is never too late to remember the lost gospel of our origins.

Afterword

by Rabbi Daniel Swartz

Visionaries are so often labeled "prophets" that the term has taken on aspects of a cliché, and so calling what you have just read prophetic means less than it should. But it means less than it should for a more fundamental reason than its clichéd overuse: most people no longer understand what the Hebrew Scriptures meant by the word prophet. These "seers" were noted less for seeing the future than for seeing the truth, for understanding the deeper meaning, the holistic view, the spiritual message of the present moment. Shedding unblinking light on the pain and injustice of the present, the prophet calls, *Sh'ma*—"hear," but also more deeply "understand," and, deepest of all and intrinsically linking action to understanding, "heed." It is in this sense of true vision and a call to respond that *The Lost Gospel* is prophetic. What then are the key lessons of this work that we should hear, understand, and heed? Five of Tom's themes particularly struck me.

The first, which underlies all others, is the need for a renewed breadth to our envisioning of God. Rabbi Lew Barth has said that idolatry is not worshiping the wrong god, but rather worshiping only one part of the greater reality and calling that god.

My faith connects me neither to a rivergod nor a skygod, but to God of both river and sky, forest and city, soil and air—God not only of humans but of the universe, God not only of the past, but present in the present. God's omnipresence can be felt as the root of all relatedness, the source of all kinship. For these reasons, my tradition calls God *Nishmat Kol Chai*, the Soul-breath of all life, and *Tzur Y'ladicha*, the Rock that birthed you, and *Yotzer Or*, the Potter who fashions light, and countless other names, knowing that none can completely capture the all-pervasiveness of the Divine. Jewish blessings refer to God "Who creates" in the present tense—not who created once and since has sat back uninvolved, in some separate spiritual realm. Creation should be an ongoing miracle to all, spilling over the dikes that divide—as Tom has noted—our psyches from the world. Only thus can we overcome generations of denial and establish just and true relationships with our world.

Once we reestablish our contact with the perfect wholeness, the *shlemut*, of the Divine, we can begin our second task—to reevaluate the position of humans in the cosmos. Tom has forcefully argued that we are a part of, not apart from, our environment. Our role in the biosphere is neither as cancer nor as king, but as part of creation's greater chorus. To deny our deep kinship with the rest of our planetary home is both arrogant and foolish: self-destructive self-deception.

Yet it remains important, I believe, to confront part of the uniqueness of humanity that remains, to reinterpret it in terms of "chosenness." My people have sometimes been criticized for the doctrine of the "chosen people," accused of using it to elevate ourselves over others, to deny the worth of others even as we arrogantly claim our own—and, unfortunately, this doctrine has been thus abused. A more humane, and I believe both more common and more authentic, view of chosenness focuses on the Jewish people's special responsibilities as bearers of a tradition that calls for justice and morality. All human beings have capabilities that differ both quantitatively and qualitatively from our fellow living beings on this planet, qualities that need to be constructively addressed, rather than denied or exalted. Most plants and animals modify their surroundings to some extent, but we humans have the capability to change our environment more radically and more rapidly than any other creature. We also have the spiritual capability to choose whether or not to use such technologies. We can look the Darwinian imperative—pass on your genes to as many as possible—in the eye and choose not to expand simply because we are able to. Tom quoted Aldo Leopold as saying that now humanity's "evolution is self-directed." Now more than ever, we have the choice laid out in Deuteronomy: the good and the blessing or the evil and the curse. How do we move toward blessing?

The third theme that resounds through Tom's book, justice, takes us far along our journey. For too long, the secular environmental community ignored the fundamental link between the environment and justice that Tom intuitively understood from the beginning. It is a link strong in both consequence and cause. The consequences of degradation of the natural environment fall disproportionately upon the poor, upon minorities, upon disenfranchised populations. And that is no coincidence, for our violence against ecosystems stems from the same causes as our violence against other humans, as the Bible and those who have heeded its call, such as St. Francis or Nachman of Bratslav, have realized. In our greed and our arrogance, we place ourselves at the center of the universe, strut like the Bible's Pharaoh, proclaiming ourselves to be little godlings, enslaving others to fulfill our oversized appetites. We will never learn to live in balance with the biosphere until we value human justice—and we will never achieve human justice until we realize that we cannot sublimate our exploitative urges onto the environment. When we see the world, or other people, only as useful tools, we enter into exploitative I-it relationships, spiritually crippling both victim and victimizer. Exploitation is one of the worst forms of idolatry and self-worship; kinship with creation, a humble acknowledgment of God's ownership of and sovereignty over all, is one of the highest forms of prayer.

Fourth, to establish a system of environmental justice, pervasive in economy and ecology, we need to recognize the importance of community. Currents of rabid individualism swirl throughout our culture, fed in no small part by some who call themselves religious. In the name of faith, these people would destroy our ability to build communities of faith, communities blessed with the knowledge of each person's indebtedness to and responsibility for all. Rabbi Hillel taught, "Do not separate yourself from the community." This was both prescription and description—do not separate yourself because you are not separate. The deepest lessons of both faith and environmental science are that we are bound up together in the bond of life, a sacred web woven through countless millennia. To build sustainable communities, however, we will need more than faith and science combined.

Finally, we also need a sense of history—history that does not shirk from the worst of our past misdeeds, but that at the same time focuses our energies on possibilities for a future better than any past. Our search is not for some ecological original sin, but to help us stop sinning against our origins. No culture is completely blameless throughout its history and we all have "native" wisdom to contribute to the building of a reharmonized world. If we study Tom's message closely, it is a source of great hope that we may yet create a sustainable community that will last *l'dor va-dor,* from generation to generation.

In my work through the National Religious Partnership for the Environment, I have been privileged to witness green sprouts beginning to flourish in congregations across our country, even across our globe. Religious schools are once again studying the long-ignored ecological wisdom of our various religious traditions. Clergy and lay leaders alike are not only preaching about the environment, not only "greening" their own institutions, but increasingly becoming key players in building the spiritual and physical ecologies of our society. As we come to the end of this century, an ecological consciousness is becoming more and more a basic component of what it means to be religious.

Tom has called for a "letter from the rainforest" to take us farther down the road to a just biosphere like "a letter from the Birmingham jail" set us upon the path toward civil rights for all.

But here in Tom's work, we already have a "letter from the Santa Monica Bay," one that calls us to realize both the transcendent and immanent aspects of the Divine, to set our species in the context of life as a whole, to integrate human and ecological justice, to strengthen our communities, to learn from our history. If we can hear, understand, and heed this call, we can move from the poverty of utilitarianism to the rich possibilities of a politics of the spirit.

Rabbi Daniel Swartz
Associate Director
National Religious Partnership
for the Environment

Notes

PREFACE

The articles on declining salmon runs were in the *New York Times* (March 7, 1994) and the Associated Press (July 27, 1995).

The history and condition of California salmon, including the story of Rev. Pesonen, is told in Alan Lufkin, ed., *California's Salmon and Steelhead: The Struggle to Restore an Imperiled Resource* (Berkeley: University of California Press, 1991). See also Peter Moyle, "Saving California's Salmon: The Legacy of Ishi," in *Trout* (Summer 1993) and "Past and Present Status of Central Valley Chinook Salmon," in *Conservation Biology* 8, no. 3 (Sept. 1994). See also transcripts of the California Senate Committee on Natural Resources and Wildlife hearing (Feb. 14, 1995).

CHAPTER I. THE LOST GOSPEL

The observations of Aldo Leopold appear in his masterful essay "The Land Ethic," in *A Sand County Almanac* (New York: Oxford University Press, 1987, 209–10). For Sisyphus, see Edith Hamilton, *Mythology* (Boston: Little, Brown, 1942, 439–40).

The controversy over "life" is detailed in Robert Augros and George Staniciu, *The New Biology* (Boston: Shambhala, 1987, 19). The pioneers of the Gaia hypothesis are James Lovelock, in *Healing Gaia* (New York: Crown Publishing Group, 1991), and Lynn Margulis and Dorion

Sagan, in *Microcosmos* (New York: Simon & Shuster, 1986). Monod's view can be found in a transcript from the BBC interview (July 1970).

For global warming, see the *New York Times* (July 23, 1995); *San Francisco Chronicle* (July 29, 1995); Ross Gelbspan, "The Heat Is On," *Harpers* (December 1995); also the Associated Press article "Panel Accepts Fossil Fuel Tie to Global Heat" (Sept. 10, 1995). "New data have determined that the ozone layer protecting the Earth from harmful solar radiation has continued to shrink at an unabated and unacceptable pace, government scientists reported." From "Earth's Ozone Layer Still Shrinking, Scientists Find," *Los Angeles Times* (Apr. 25, 1996).

In early 1996 British and U.S. scientists reported that the North Pole is melting: "A layer of water under the ice is warming very fast and the temperature has jumped one degree centigrade in just five years." *Irish Independent* (Apr. 8, 1996).

For figures on population, poverty rates, topsoil and rainforest loss, chemicals and cancer rates, and the increase of infectious diseases, see: Paul Kennedy, *Preparing for the Twenty-First Century* (New York: Vintage, 1993, 95–121); Lester Brown, "The Battle for the Planet: A Status Report," in *Environment in Peril* (Washington, D.C.: Smithsonian, 1991, 165); the *State of the World* reports (Washington, D.C.: Worldwatch Institute, issued annually); Laurie Garrett, *The Coming Plague* (New York: Farrar Straus Giroux, 1994); Sheryl Stolberg, "Afflictions Expected to Kill Four Million Annually by 2010," *Los Angeles Times*, (Mar. 30, 1993); and *Rachel's Environmental and Health Weekly*, #472, *Loss of Biodiversity* (Dec. 14, 1995). In June 1996, the World Health Organization declared a "global crisis" in which "no country is safe" from infectious diseases that cause one out of three premature deaths (Los Angeles *Times*, May 26, 1996).

The article about the scientist weeping was in the *Irish Times* (Jan. 23, 1995).

Robert Bellah's "habits of the heart" is explained in his book by the same name (Berkeley: University of California Press, 1985).

To understand the dismissal of environmentalism by scientific defenders of growth, see Ronald Bailey, ed., *The True Fate of the Planet* (New York: Free Press, 1995). They agree that world population has doubled since 1950, that energy consumption has increased 50 percent since 1970, that fishing harvests have plummeted by similar margins, yet they believe contraceptives, pesticides, aquaculture, nuclear power, and other technical fixes are the solutions to avert an eco-catastrophe (while denying that we already are entering a period of preventable mass suffering).

For more detail on Leonardo Boff's exploration of the natural world as sacred within the context of liberation theology, see pages 86 and 155 of his *Ecology and Liberation* (Mary Knoll, NY: Orbis Books, 1995).

CHAPTER 2. OVERCOMING THE DIVIDE
OF SOUL FROM NATURE

The chapter epigraph is quoted in Robert Sayre, *Thoreau and the American Indians* (Princeton, NJ: Princeton University Press, 1987, 93).

The sea as "beginning and end" is explained in Rachel Carson's beautiful *The Sea Around Us* (New York: Oxford, 1972).

The Marge Piercy poem, "The Common Living Dirt," is from her volume of poetry *Stone, Paper, Knife*, which appears in the anthology edited by Lorraine Anderson, *Sisters of the Earth* (New York: Vintage, 1991, 340–42).

The dissenting opinion by William O. Douglas can be found in *Sierra Club v. U.S. Secretary of the Interior Rogers P.B. Morton* 70–34 U.S. (April 19, 1972).

The quotes from John Muir throughout this book are from his collected philosophical writings in Edwin Way Teale, ed., *The Wilderness World of John Muir* (Boston: Houghton Mifflin, 1954).

The Milky Way quote is from Thomas Berry and Brian Swimme, *The Universe Story* (San Francisco: HarperSan Francisco, 1994, 44–45).

The Martin Buber observations are in his *I and Thou* (New York: Charles Scribner, 1987, 8).

The description of the musk-ox is from Barry Lopez, *Arctic Dreams: Imagination and Desire in a Northern Landscape* (New York: Bantam, 1987, 48–55).

Joanna Macy's wonderful essay, "The Greening of the Self," appears in Allan Hunt Badiner, ed., *Dharma Gaia* (Berkeley: Parallax Press, 1990).

The textbook on psychology is by Spencer A. Rathus, *Psychology* (New York: Holt Rinehart, 1990, 664–71).

The insights of Theodore Roszak are from his *The Voice of the Earth* (New York: Simon & Schuster, 1992, 14); Sigmund Freud's comments on nature are from his *Future of an Illusion* (New York: Norton, 1989, 16) and *Civilization and Its Discontents* (New York: Norton, 1961, 11, 15, 16, and 27). Carl Jung's essay "Archaic Man," is in his *Modern Man in Search of a Soul* (New York: Harcourt Brace, 1933, 145); Abraham Maslow's comments are in his preface to his *Toward a Psychology of Being* (Princeton, NJ: Van Nostrand Reinhold, 1968).

The story about the Alaskan resource official was told to me by conservation officials during a visit to that state; the timber consultant on "self-centered" old-growth forests is in David Kelly and Gary Brasch, *Secrets of the Old Growth Forest* (Salt Lake City, Peregrine Smith Books, 1988, 35–38).

Rachel Carson on a child's imagination is in her *Sense of Wonder* (Berkeley: The Nature Company, 1990).

The overview of environmental neglect in textbooks is by C. A. Bowers, in *Education, Cultural Myths, and the Ecological Crisis* (Albany: SUNY Press, 1993, 131–32); Bowers cites John Dewey on page 93; the neoconservative views of William Bennett are in his *Book of Virtues* (New York: Simon & Schuster, 1993) and *Index of Leading Cultural Indicators* (New York: Touchstone/Simon & Schuster, 1994, 85); also see E. D. Hirsch, *Cultural Literacy* (New York: Vintage, 1988).

Notes

The best monitor of the media's environmental failures is the organization Fairness and Accuracy in Media (FAIR); see its newsletter, 3, no. 4 (April–May 1992): 14.

The story of Shabecoff and the *New York Times* is told in the *Washington Post* (May 6, 1991); for the Keith Schneider articles, see the *New York Times* (Mar. 21–25, 1993). The changes at the *Los Angeles Times* were told to me by *Times* editors and reporters.

CHAPTER 3. THE DEFAULT OF
ORGANIZED RELIGION

Pat Buchanan's attack on environmentalists, in the *Los Angeles Times* (Aug. 13, 1995) is a real "stump speech" from someone wishing to cut down as many trees as possible.

The testimony of James Watt is in David Helvarg's *The War Against the Greens* (San Francisco: Sierra Club Books, 1994, 69), an excellent overview of the rising threats of violence against local environmentalists.

"Dominion theology" is described in Harvey Cox, "The Warring Visions of the Religious Right," *The Atlantic Monthly* (November 1995): 59–69; and in Gary DeMar, "Are Christians Supposed to Take Dominion? A Reconstructionist Reply," *Christian Research Journal* (Winter/Spring 1989): 30. Pat Robertson's thinking is revealed in *The New World Order* (Dallas: Word Publishing, 1991, see pages 227 ("God of Jacob"), 223 ("worshippers"), and 227 ("Satan"); Rushdoony is cited in the Cox article, op cit., 68.

Pope John Paul on goddess worship, in *New York Times* (July 3, 1993); on politics and birth control in Poland, in *New York Times* (November 26, 1995).

My friend Dennis Praeger's attack on evil environmentalists is on a taped "lecture to Germans and Jews," personally received; for similar comments, see his *Think a Second Time* (New York: HarperCollins, 1995, 203).

The anti-environmental theology articles can be found in the *Wall Street Journal* editorial (Apr. 2, 1993) and in *Forbes* (Oct. 29, 1990); Watt's "cartridge box" remark is cited by Helvarg, *The War Against the Greens*, 358; Oliver North was cited in the *San Francisco Chronicle* (October 1, 1992); Rush Limbaugh fulminates in *The Way Things Ought to Be* (New York: Pocket Star, 1992, 153–69); the Wise Use people on paganism is in *E* magazine (Sept. 10, 1992): 34; the "spiritual war" and Helen Chenoweth is detailed in Sidney Blumenthal, "Her Own Private Idaho," *The New Yorker* (July 10, 1995): 31–32; Putting People First quote, in People for the American Way's *Right-Wing Watch* (Mar. 1995): 2; the chronology of attacks on environmentalists, including the "60 Minutes" reference, is in Helvarg, op. cit., 411.

For an example of the lack of consideration of the modern environmental dilemma in religious texts, see Huston Smith, *The Illustrated World's Religions: A Guide to Our Wisdom Traditions* (San Francisco: HarperCollins, 1991, 6).

The 1980s Catholic catechism is that of John Hardon, ed., *The Catholic Catechism* (New York: Doubleday, 1981, 70); "Redemptor Hominus" was in *L'Osservatore Romano* (Mar. 29, 1982); the current *Catechism of the Catholic Church* (New York: Doubleday/Image, 1995) references "perfection" and "goodness" on page 98; "domination" on page 106; "exist" on page 102.

Other source books include: Andrew Greeley, *The Catholic Myth: The Behavior and Beliefs of American Catholics* (New York: Macmillan/ Collier, 1980, 289–309); John McManners, *The Oxford Illustrated History of Christianity* (New York: Oxford University Press, 1990, 629); and Arthur Hertzberg, *Judaism* (New York: Simon & Schuster/ Touchstone, 1991, 11).

The reference to the first Buddhist environmental texts is in Sulak Sivaraska, "True Development," in Allan Hunt Badiner, ed., *Dharma Gaia* (Berkeley: Parallax Press, 1990, 175); on the first Islamic environmental texts, see Fazlun Khalid and Joanne O'Brien, *Islam and Ecology*

(London: Cassell, 1992, x, 12, 14). See also Marshall Hodgson, *The Venture of Islam* (Chicago: University of Chicago, 1974); Kenneth Cragg, *The Event of the Qur'an: Islam in Its Scripture* (Oxford: Oneworld, 1994); and J. Baird Callicott, "Hinduism," in his *Earth's Insights* (manuscript, 1993, 90–130). The references to Hinduism, including cutting down the forests of Krishna, are in Ranchor Prime, *Hinduism and Ecology* (London: Cassell, 1992, 108).

Thomas Aquinas condemned "dumb plants and animals" in "Whether It Is Unlawful to Kill Any Living Things," and "Whether Irrational Creatures Also Ought to Be Loved Out of Charity," in *Summa Theologica II*, question 25, article 3; both are cited in the excellent survey by Lewis Regenstein, *Replenish the Earth* (New York: Crossroad, 1991, 72–73).

For Sir Francis Bacon's views on our relationship to the environment see the essays "The Great Insaturation," "Novum Organum," and "The Masculine Birth of Time," in James Spedding, Robert Leslie Ellis, and Douglas Devon Heath, eds., *Works* (London: Longman's Green, 1870). See also the excellent analysis by Carolyn Merchant, *Radical Ecology* (London: Routledge, 1992, 46).

My extracts of René Descartes, *Discourse on Method*, can be found in E. S. Haldane and G. R. T. Ross, eds., *Philosophical Works of Descartes* (New York: Dover, 1955, 119); see Regenstein, *Replenish the Earth*, 79; Immanuel Kant, *Preface to the Critique of Pure Reason*, 2nd edition, Norman Kemp Smith, trans. (New York: St. Martin's Press, 1965, 20).

Stephen Hawking's thought is in his *A Brief History of Time: From the Big Bang to Black Holes* (New York: Bantam, 1988).

Alexis de Tocqueville's commentary is in Lee Clark Mitchell, *Witnesses to a Vanishing America: The Nineteenth Century Response* (Princeton, NJ: Princeton, 1981, 1).

Fredric Jameson on the postmodern is in Fintan O'Toole, *Black Hole, Green Card: The Disappearance of Ireland* (Dublin: New Island, 1994, 39).

The Port Huron Statement is discussed in my book *Reunion* (New York: Random House, 1988).

The United Nations quote is in "Science and Technology for Development," *Report of the United Nations Conference on the Application of Science and Technology for the Benefit of Less Developed Areas* 2 (New York: Natural Resources, 1963): 18; the Solow quote is in Narendra Singh, "Robert Solow's Growth Hickonomics," *Economic and Political Weekly* 22, no. 45 (Nov. 7, 1987). I am indebted to Vandana Shiva for these citations, in "Resources," *The Dictionary of Development* (London: Zed, 1992, 217).

The California environmental codes can be obtained from my office, Room 2080, State Senate, State Capitol, Sacramento, California, 95814.

The California Department of Conservation's mission is officially explained in the *Governor's Budget 1996–97*, R28.

Limbaugh's prediction of violent revolution was on Feb. 21, 1995, according to the transcript printed in Brian Keliher's gadfly publication, *The Flush Rush Quarterly* (summer 1995). Also see *New York Times*, "Bomb Echoes Extremists' Tactics" (Apr. 26, 1995): A14; and David Helvarg's "The Anti-Enviro Connection," in *The Nation* (May 22, 1995): 722–24.

Theodore Roosevelt is quoted in Robert Gottlieb's excellent *Forcing the Spring: The Transformation of the American Environmental Movement* (Washington, D.C.: Island Press, 1993, 23).

The Earl Warren proclamation on water is in Alan Lufkin, ed., *California's Salmon and Steelhead: The Struggle to Restore an Imperiled Resource* (Berkeley: University of California Press, 1991).

Groundwater cases and Mono Lake are described in Norris Hundley, *The Great Thirst: Californians and Water, 1770s–1990s* (Berkeley: University of California Press, 1992, 338, 389).

Resource wars are projected in Thomas F. Homer-Dixon, Jeffrey

Boutwell, and George W. Rathjens, "Environmental Change and Violent Conflict," *Scientific American* (Feb. 1993): 38.

The day of reckoning quote is from *Forbes* (June 22, 1992).

Carl Jung on religion in "Psychological Types" in *Collected Works*, 6; in Anne Baring and Jules Cashford, *The Myth of the Goddess: Evolution of an Image* (New York: Viking, 1991, 447). I strongly recommend the Baring-Cashford book as one of the finest on women and religion.

The scientists' statement, "preserving and cherishing the Earth," was drafted by Carl Sagan, in Regenstein, *Replenish the Earth*, 167. Father Rossi's statement appears in the same work, page 158.

Background on the National Religious Partnership for the Environment appears in their winter 1993 grant proposal (1047 Amsterdam Avenue, New York, NY 10025). I am indebted to my old friend Paul Gorman, the director of the Partnership, for his insights and leadership.

Fritjof Capra, *The Tao of Physics* (New York: Bantam 1988); Thomas Berry, *The Dream of the Earth* (San Francisco: Sierra Club Books, 1988); Matthew Fox, *Creation Spirituality* (New York: HarperCollins, 1991); and Charlene Spretnak, *The Spiritual Dimension of Green Politics*, (Santa Fe, NM: Bear & Co., 1986) have deeply influenced the development of my thinking on religion and the environment. Al Gore's great work *Earth in the Balance* (Boston: Houghton Mifflin, 1992, 345), helped me see the links with politics and policy.

Martin Luther King's famous, "Letter from Birmingham City Jail," is in Diane Ravitch, ed., *The American Reader: Words That Moved a Nation* (New York: Harper Collins, 1990, 325–29).

The Bruce Babbitt references are by Cal Thomas, "God as an Endangered Species," *Los Angeles Times* (Feb. 16, 1996).

The story of the religious coalition to save the Endangered Species Act, an offshoot of the Religious Partnership, is in the *Los Angeles Times* (Feb. 1, 1996).

Joseph Campbell is quoted in Baring and Cashford, *The Myth of the Goddess*, 660.

Matthew Fox describes mysticism in *The Coming of the Cosmic Christ* (HarperSan Francisco, 1988, 38).

The D. H. Lawrence quote is from "Last Poems," in *The Complete Poems of D. H. Lawrence*, 1 (New York, Penguin, 1977, 17); once again I am indebted to Baring and Cashford, *The Myth of the Goddess*, 664.

Wisdom literature is explained in detail in Roland Murphy, *The Tree of Life* (New York: Anchor, 1990, 1–3).

The "green fundamentalist" position is well stated in Calvin DeWitt, ed., *The Environment and the Christian* (Grand Rapids, MI: Baker Book House, 1991).

Hildegard von Bingen, *Illuminations*, with commentary by Matthew Fox (Santa Fe, NM: Bear and Co., 1985, 30–33); see also Fox, ed., Hildegard von Bingen's *Book of Divine Works* (Santa Fe, NM: Bear and Co., 1987); and Barbara Lachman, *The Journal of Hildegard of Bingen* (New York: Bell Tower, 1993).

Nachmanides, Maimonides (Moses ben Maimon), Nachman of Bratslav, and other Jewish nature writings are collected and analyzed excellently in *To Till and to Tend: A Guide to Jewish Environmental Study and Action*, by the Coalition on the Environment and Jewish Life. See especially "Jews and the Natural World," by Rabbi Dan Swartz (1–12). Rabbi Swartz was an early guide in my research, gave lectures in my classes, and is an extraordinary resource of environmental and religious knowledge. The excerpt quoting *The Guide of the Perplexed* by Maimonides is from Clive Ponting, *A Green History of the World: The Environment and the Collapse of Great Civilizations* (New York: St. Martin's Press, 1991, 145).

The "Voice in the Whirlwind" is in Stephen Mitchell, trans., *Book of Job* (San Francisco: North Point Press, 1987, 79, 88); his introduction is extraordinary.

Christian and Jewish scholars who reveal the environmental limits of their traditions are Susan Power Bratton, "Christian Eco-Theology and the Old Testment," in Eugene Hargrove, ed., *Religion and Environmental Crisis* (Athens: University of Georgia Press, 1986, 69) and Rabbi Saul Berman, *To Till and Tend*, 17.

On the struggles to secure the holy lands, see Richard Cartwright Aust, *Hope for the Land: Nature in the Bible* (Atlanta: John Knox Press, 1988); Mary Condren, *The Serpent and the Goddess: Women, Religion, and Power in Celtic Ireland* (San Francisco: HarperSan Francisco, 1989); Carol Robb and Carl Casebolt, *Covenant for a New Creation: Ethics, Religion, and Public Policy* (Mary Knoll, NY: Orbis, 1991, 1–23); and Daniel Jeremy Silver, *A History of Judaism* (New York: Basic Books, 1974).

The excerpt from Francis Parkman's *The Conspiracy of Pontiac and the Indian War after the Conquest of Canada* (New York: Charles Scribner's, 1915, vol. 1, ix, 48) is cited in David Stannard, *American Holocaust* (New York: Oxford University Press, 1992, 22).

Christopher Columbus on the "terrestrial paradise" appears in the letters from his third voyage, in Samuel Eliot Morison, ed., *Journals and Other Documents on the Life and Voyages of Christopher Columbus* (New York: Heritage Press, 1963, 286–87). The biblical rationale for subduing the continent is in Basil Mitchell, "The Christian Conscience" in John McManners, ed., *The Oxford Illustrated History of Christianity*, 618.

The quotes from Bradford, Winthrop, Cotton Mather, and John Quincy Adams are from Carolyn Merchant, *Radical Ecology: The Search for a Liveable World* (New York: Routledge, 1992, 66) and Merchant, "The New England Forest in the Seventeenth Century," (manuscript provided to author).

The survey of early textbooks is in Ruth Miller Elson, *Guardians of Tradition* (Lincoln, NE: University of Nebraska Press, 1964, 17–19).

The revolt of Francisco Roldan is narrated in Giani Granzotto, *Christopher Columbus: The Dream and the Obsession* (New York: Doubleday, 1985, 237–38). The diaries of Bartolome de Las Casas are in Merma Briffault, trans., *The Devastation of the West Indies* (Baltimore: Johns Hopkins Press, 1992). See also Kirkpatrick Sale, *Conquest of Paradise* (New York: Knopf, 1990, 154).

The history of the first counter-culture in America, including those who "went Croatan," danced around the maypole, and formed utopian communities is contained in Ron Sakolsky and James Koehnline, *Gone to Croatan: Origins of North American Dropout Culture* (Brooklyn: Autonomedia, 1993).

Richard Nixon on Genesis is excerpted from E. F. Schumacher, "The Age of Plenty: A Christian View," in Herman Daley and Kenneth Townsend, eds., *Valuing the Earth* (Boston: MIT Press, 1993, 160).

The criticism of Genesis by John Muir is in *The Wilderness World of John Muir*, 317; the criticism by Lynn White is in "The Historical Roots of Our Ecological Crisis," *Science* (Mar. 10, 1967): 1203–07; the opinion surveys on Genesis are from George Gallup, Jr. and Robert Bezilla, Princeton Religion Research Center, reported in *Los Angeles Times* (June 26, 1993).

Everett Fox, *Genesis and Exodus* (New York: Schocken Books, 1990, 15); in citing the biblical texts, I have used Bruce Metzger and Roland Murphy, eds., *The New Oxford Annotated Bible* (New York: Oxford University Press, 1991) and F. E. Peters, ed., *Judaism, Christianity, and Islam*, 1 (Princeton, NJ: Princeton University Press, 1990); J. Baird Callicott, "Genesis and John Muir" in Robb and Casebolt, *Covenant for a New Creation*, 107–37.

For the concept of "viceroy" in Islam, see Iqtidar Zaidi, "On the Ethics of Man's Interaction with the Environment, an Islamic Approach," in Hargrove, *Religion and Environmental Crisis*, 113.

For the meaning of "rada" and "kabas," see Bratton article in Hargrove, *Religion and Environmental Crisis*, 65. I rely also on personal consultation with Rabbi Daniel Swartz.

The *New Oxford Annotated Bible* interpretation of "dominion" is from page 3n.

For King David and the bedouins, see Robb and Casebolt, *Covenant for a New Creation*, 12; "nature primeval," in Callicott article, ibid, 121; see also John Gardner and John Maier, *Gilgamesh* (New York: Vintage, 1985).

Nathaniel Altman, *Sacred Trees* (San Francisco: Sierra Club Books, 1994, 26–29).

For more on the Iroquois white pine, see Bruce Johansen, *Forgotten Founders: How the American Indian Helped Shape Democracy* (Cambridge: Harvard Common Press, 1982); also Paul Wallace, *The Iroquois Book of Life: White Roots of Peace* (Santa Fe: Clear Light, 1994).

Black Elk is cited in Roderick Nash, *American Environmentalism* (New York: McGraw Hill, 1990, 14).

Anthropocentrism is attacked in the Callicott article, Robb and Casebolt, *Covenant for a New Creation*, 123.

There is an immense and growing literature on women, spirituality, and nature to draw on. These modern feminist scholars seek to "bring to the fore and make audible again the subjugated voices and suppressed traditions that have left traces in ancient writings," like the tradition of Sophia (or wisdom), writes Elizabeth Schussler Fiorenza in *Searching the Scriptures: A Feminist Commentary* (New York: Crossroad Publishing, 1994). See Sherry Ruth Anderson and Patricia Hopkins for *The Feminine Face of God: The Unfolding of the Sacred in Women* (New York: Bantam, 1991); Elaine Pagels, *Adam, Eve, and the Serpent* (New York: Vintage, 1988) and *The Origin of Satan* (New York: Random House, 1995); Gilda Lerner, *The Creation of Patriarchy* (New York: Oxford University Press, 1986); and Anne Baring and Jules Cashford, *The Myth of the Goddess.* I am indebted, as well, to Rebecca Bridges for her thesis paper, "By Man Defined: Images of the Wilderness in Seventeenth-Century Puritan New England," May 1991, received from the author. The story of Patricia Ireland's textbook protest was in the *New York Times Magazine* (Mar. 1, 1992): 38.

The Simone de Beauvoir quote is from Alan S. Miller, *Gaia Connections* (Savage, MD: Rowman & Littlefield, 1991, 21). Also see Simone de Beauvoir, *The Second Sex* (New York: Vintage, 1952, 157, 177, and 281).

Henry David Thoreau, *Faith in a Seed* (Washington, D.C.: Island Press, xvii).

CHAPTER 5. THE LOST GOSPEL
IN OUR NATIVE HISTORY

The Cherokee term *eloheh* is defined in Gerard Reed, "A Native American Environmental Ethic," in Hargrove, ed., *Religion and Environmental Crisis*, 33.

The article on the conflict between sweetgrass and development was in the *New York Times* (June 5, 1995). For the cover story on lost tribal wisdom, see "Lost Tribes, Lost Knowledge," *Time* (Sept. 23, 1991). The loss of languages is noted in Wolfgang Sachs, ed., "One World," *The Development Dictionary* (London, Zed, 1992, 102).

The comparison of Irish and other native people, including famine and emigration, is developed in a forthcoming work I have edited with Irish and Irish-American writers, *Irish Hunger* (Niwot, CO: Roberts Rinehart, 1997).

A massive literature exists on ancient Irish history and on the Famine of 1845–51. For an introduction to the early Irish, see John Sharkey, *Celtic Mysticism: The Ancient Religion* (London: Thames and Hudson, 1975); Tim O'Brian, *Light Years Ago: A Study on the Cairns of Newgrange and Cairn T. Loughcrew, Co. Meath* (Dublin: Black Cat, 1992); and N. L. Thomas, *Irish Symbols of 3500 B.C.E.* (London: Mercier, 1988).

On the Great Famine, a selection of important material includes:

Cecil Woodham-Smith, *The Great Hunger, Ireland 1845–49* (New York: Penguin, 1992); Christine Kinealy, *This Great Calamity: The Irish Famine, 1845–52* (Dublin: Gill and Macmillan, 1994); Robert Scally, *The End of Hidden Ireland: Rebellion, Famine, and Emigration* (New York: Oxford University Press, 1995); Kerby Miller, *Emigrants and Exiles: Ireland and the Irish Exodus to North America* (Oxford University Press, 1985); and Oscar Handlin's classic, *The Uprooted* (New York: Little, Brown, 1951). Famine novels include Sean Kenny, *The Hungry Earth* (Dublin: Wolfhound, 1995) and Liam Flaherty, *Famine* (Dublin: Wolfhound, 1984). Personal anecdotes are in Cathal Poirtier, *Famine Echoes* (Minneapolis: Gill and Macmillan, 1995). The quote from the *London Times* is in Poirtier, ed., *The Great Irish Famine* (London: Mercier, 1995); see especially the essay by Kevin Whelan, "Pre- and Post-Famine Landscape Change," 19–33. The reference to Irish skull size is from Peter Quinn, "Closets of Bones," *Irish-America* magazine, February 18, 1995.

For more on the connection between Irish language and the land, see Tim Robinson, "Listening to the Landscape," *The Irish Review* (Belfast: Institute of Irish Studies, summer 1993): 21–32.

Ireland as an "apprenticeship" for the British conquest of America is in Frederick Turner, *Beyond Geography: The Western Spirit Against the Wilderness* (New Brunswick, NJ: Rutgers University Press, 1983, 179). Fintan O'Toole on Celtic spirituality is in "Mixed Blessings: The End of the Irish Church," from his *Black Hole, Green Card*, 126–33. John Waters's essay comes from the *Irish Times*; also in Hayden, ed., *Irish Hunger*.

For the native histories of Michigan and Wisconsin, see: Charles Cleland, *Rites of Conquest: The History and Culture of Michigan's Native Americans* (Ann Arbor, MI: University of Michigan, 1992, 59); Helen Hornbeck Tanner, ed., *Atlas of Great Lakes Indian History* (Oklahoma City: University of Oklahoma Press, 1987); Simon Otto, *Walk in Peace: Legends and Stories of the Michigan Indians* (Grand Rapids, MI: Michigan Indian Press, 1990); James Clifton, George Cornell, and James McClurken, *People of the Three Fires: The Ottawa, Potawatomi, and Ojibway of Michigan* (Grand Rapids: Michigan Indian Press, 1992); Betty Sodders, *Michigan Prehistory Mysteries* (Au Train, MI: Avery Color Studios, 1990); and the excellent work by the former director of the U.S. Park Service, Roger G. Kennedy, *Hidden Cities: The Discovery and Loss of Ancient North American Civilization* (New York: The Free Press, 1994).

The Los Angeles environment, energy waste, and poverty are de-scribed in C. Douglas Lummis, "Equality," *The Dictionary of Devel-opment* (London: Zed, 1992, 46); "One hundred and five miles of poverty" is from Dr. Rick Brown, UCLA; Mary Nichols and Stanley Young, *The Amazing LA Environment* (Venice, CA: Natural Resources Defense Council, Living Plane Press, 1991).

The MCA quote about City-Walk in Los Angeles is from Philip L. Fradkin, *The Seven States of California: A Natural and Human History* (New York: John MacRae/Henry Holt, 1995, 355–56).

The complete story of the effect of cattle on California trout can be found in the *Los Angeles Times* (Mar. 3, 1996).

The quote about the Wintu people's inability to express "personal domination and coercion" is from Stannard, *American Holocaust*, 22.

For native people generally, including the California experience, see David Stannard, *American Holocaust* and Vine DeLoria, *God Is Red: A Native View of Religion*, Fulcrum/Boulder, 1994. The quote from Fr. Ascensíon is from Stannard, 135.

California Indians as "accomplished botanists" is in Robert Heizen and Albert Elsasser, *The Natural World of California Indians* (Berkeley: University of California Press, 1980, 59–60); also see Thomas Black-burn and Kat Anderson, *Before the Wilderness: Environmental Man-agement by Native Californians* (Menlo Park, CA: Ballena Press, 1993).

Tomols and Hutash legends are described in Lynne McCall and Rosalind Perry, *California's Chumash Indians* (Santa Barbara: Santa

Barbara Museum of Natural History, 1986, 30, 50, 61–62); for more on the Chumash, see Thomas Blackburn, *December's Child: A Child of Chumash Oral Narratives* (Berkeley: University of California Press, 1975).

The story of Major Savage and Teneiya in Yosemite was first told in Lafayette Houghton Bunnell's *Discovery of the Yosemite, and the Indian War of 1851 Which Led to that Event,* published in 1880, thirty years after the events that Bunnell witnessed. The book is available from the Yosemite Association: Yosemite National Park, 1990. See pp. 156–57.

The myth of California as terrestrial paradise is from the 1510 novel *Las Sergas de Esplandian,* by Garcia Rodriguez Ordonez de Montalvo, cited in T. H. Watkins, *California: An Illustrated History* (Palo Alto, CA: American West, 1973, 1); also see Warren Beck and Ynez Haase, *Historical Atlas of California* (Oklahoma City: University of Oklahoma, 1974). The *Los Angeles Times* on "utopia" is in Watkins, op. cit., 249; for an example, see Irving Stone, *Men to Match My Mountains* (New York: Berkely Books, 1956).

California's ancient and present environment is described in *Life on the Edge: A Guide to California's Endangered Natural Resources* (Santa Cruz/Berkeley; Biosystems Books/Heyday Books, 1994).

The study of the Sierra Nevada's collapse was reported in the *Los Angeles Times,* June 2 and 8, 1996.

See James Rawls, *Indians of California: The Changing Image* (Oklahoma City: University of Oklahoma Press, 1984, 6), for racism and oppression; on the Maidu, see Malcolm Margolin, "Among Kin," in *California Indians and the Environment,* in *News from Native California* (spring 1992): 2; Darryl Wilson, "Mis Misa," *California Indians and the Environment,* op. cit., 30–34; Rawls, op. cit., comparison to monkeys, 26, "four footed," 46, like "brutes," 49; "diggers" in Kat Anderson, "At Home in the Wilderness," *California Indians and Environment,* op. cit., 20; Marsh quotes, in Rawls, op. cit., 77; the governor endorsing extermination, in Stannard, *American Holocaust*, 144; Mission experience is in Rawls, op. cit., 14–21; death rates also in Stannard, op. cit., 137; caloric intake, 138; two-by-seven-foot rooms, 138; population decline between 1769–1834, 142, 145. See also Sanders, *Lost Tribes and Promised Lands: The Origins of American Racism* (New York: HarperCollins, 1978, 98–99) and Kirkpatrick Sale, *The Conquest of Paradise*, 99, 103, 199; Peter Matthiessen, *Indian Country* (New York: Penguin, 1979, 3); for more on the Arawak, see Frederick Turner, *Beyond Geography*, 96, 129; "giving their hearts," in Stannard, op. cit., 124; Peter Martyr quote in Sale, op. cit., 199.

The Tom Paine quotes are in Donald A. Grinde and Bruce E. Johansen, *Exemplar of Liberty: Native America and the Evolution of Democracy* (Los Angeles: University of California Press, 1991, 152, 154).

Indians "ready to be given orders and put to work" quote is in Granzotto, *Christopher Columbus*, 62; "no religion" in Sale, *Conquest of Paradise*, 96–97; "a desert," in Sale, op. cit., 166; Cortés quote in Turner, *Beyond Geography*, 170; "Satan himself" in Stannard, op. cit., 64; see also Alfred Crosby, *Ecological Imperialism: The Biological Expansion of Europe 900–1900* (Melbourne: Cambridge University Press, 1986). The de Crèvecoeur quote is in Crosby, *Ecological Imperialism*, 300.

The reference to the Cortés quote, "exhaust them, destroy them, leave them," is from Frederick Turner, *Beyond Geography*, 170. The Cotton Mather quote is on page 227.

Indian terms for spirit, including Black Elk, are in Hargrove, *Religion and Environmental Crisis*, 26–27, 34. Chief Seattle's speech explicated in Timothy Egan, "Chief's 1854 Warning Tied to 1971 Ecological Script," *New York Times* (Apr. 20, 1992); also see Donald Grinde, Bruce Johansen, *Ecocide of Native America* (Santa Fe, NM: Clear Light, 1995, 24) who write that "regardless of the exact wording of S'ealth's speech, it *did* contain environmental themes." For Indians as ecologists, see Sale, *Conquest of Paradise*, 317–24.

On "dreaming," see Thomas Berry, *Dream of the Earth*, 186, 190,

193; and Berry, interview with author and in "Religion in the Ecozoic Era," unpublished address to the American Academy of Religion (Nov. 22, 1993) in Washington, D.C. Also see: Donald Grinde, Bruce Johansen, *Ecocide of Native America*, 13; Barry Lopez, "The Country of the Mind," in his *Arctic Dreams* (New York: Bantam, 1987, 266); Dreamtime sources are in Robert Lawlor, *Voices of the First Day* (Rochester, VT: Inner Traditions, 1991). The ancestors "retired into the earth, the sky, the clouds, and the creatures to *reverberate like a potency* within all they created." Susan Griffin, *A Chorus of Stones: The Private Life of War* (New York: Doubleday, 1992, 9).

CHAPTER 6. THE LOST GOSPEL IN BUDDHISM

I am indebted to Joanna Macy, Joan Halifax, Stephen Mitchell, Allen Ginsberg, and Charlene Spretnak for their personal contributions to my understanding. The writings of Alan Watts, Gary Snyder, Rick Fields, and Thich Nhat Hanh have guided me as well.

Joanna Macy, Joan Halifax, and Rick Fields gave helpful criticism of the original draft of this chapter. The remaining defects are mine. I was pleased that Joanna wrote "thanks for your boldness in saying Buddhism has missed the boat as much as any other major religion when it comes to Earth (His Holiness the DL [Dalai Lama] agrees with that, too)."

Thich Nhat Hanh's writings include *For a Future to Be Possible* (Berkeley: Parallax Press, 1993, 134, 272); also see his *Love in Action* (Berkeley: Parallax Press, 1993) and *The Sun in My Heart* (Berkeley: Parallax Press, 1988).

Gary Snyder's recent work is *A Place in Space* (Washington, D.C.: Counterpoint, 1995).

My excerpts for Hermann Hesse were taken from *Siddhartha* (New York: Bantam, 1981, 71).

On Hinduism, see: Vandana Shiva, *Staying Alive: Women, Ecology and Development* (London: Zed, 1989); Charlene Spretnak, *States of*

Grace (New York: Harper Collins, 1991); Ranchor Prime, *Hinduism and Ecology* (London: Cassell, 1992); and Catherine Ingram, *In the Footsteps of Gandhi* (Berkeley: Parallax Press, 1990). The neglect of ecology is referenced in Prime, op. cit., 112.

The story of the Buddha is well told by Spretnak, *States of Grace*.

The Korean concept of *Cheong* was presented in a 1995 speech by Dr. O. Young Lee at the Korean American Museum dinner in Los Angeles.

The Sanskrit word *buddha* means to awaken. A buddha is an enlightened one. On the "buddha nature" of all things, see Thich Nhat Hanh, in *For a Future*, 209. He quotes the Buddha from a fourth-century translation of the *Upasakra Sutra*, no. 128, to "practice love and compassion, and protect all living beings, even the smallest insects."

The Jewel Net of Indra is analyzed by Francis Cook in *Nature in Asian Traditions of Thought*, an excellent collection edited by J. Baird Callicott and Roger Ames (Albany, NY: SUNY Press, 1989, 213–29). In the same collection see: for the sixth-century "particle of dust" reference, William LaFleur, "Saigyo and the Buddhist Value of Nature," 184–85; for *wu-yu*, David Hill, "On Seeking a Change of Environment," 109–10.

Alan Watts on the empty mind is in *Nature, Man and Woman* (New York: Vintage, 1991, 77); also his *Watercourse Way* (New York: Pantheon, 1975, 22). Fritjof Capra's *Tao of Physics* (New York: Bantam, 1984, 84) explains the mystical and the analytic.

Thich Nhat's Hanh's statement on *tiep hien*, or inter-being, is in his *Love in Action*, 133.

The eleventh-century quote is from Liu I-Ming, in the *Taoist I Ching*, Thomas Cleary, trans. (Boston: Shambhala, 1986, 19).

The story of Thai monk Prajak Kuttajitto appeared in the *Sacramento Bee* (Nov. 30, 1992).

The Dalai Lama on Tibet as a free refuge was in his Nobel Prize lecture, printed in Martin Batchelor and Kerry Brown, eds., *Buddhism and Ecology* (Washington, D.C.: World Wildlife Fund, 1992, 112).

See Rick Fields's history, *How the Swans Came to the Lake: A Narrative History of Buddhism in America* (Boston: Shambhala, 1992, xiii, 55, 62–63, 256, 307). Thoreau's translation of the *Lotus Sutra* is in *Tricycle* (winter 1992): 8.

Watts's critique of Asian religion is in *Nature, Man and Woman*, 152.

Dharma Gaia was published on Earth Day 1990 (Berkeley: Parallax Press). The critique of Buddhism is on page 182.

The "bundles of sense perceptions" is in Robert Aitken, *Taking the Path of Zen* (San Francisco: North Point Press, 1982, 41).

For more information on Japanese Shinto traditions, see Hori Ichiro, et al., eds., *Japanese Religion* (Tokyo: Kodomsha International, 1990); also see Sokyo Ono, *Shinto: The Kami Way* (Tokyo: Charles Tuttle, 1976, 1–23).

See "Japan's Whale Hunt: A Case of Ecological Piracy," by Richard Mott of the World Wildlife Fund in the *Los Angeles Times* (Feb. 12, 1996); for the Monju breeder reactor, see the *New York Times* (Feb. 23, 1996).

On the *koan*, see Thomas Merton, *Mystics and Zen Masters* (New York: Noonday, 1989, 249).

CHAPTER 7. THE LOST GOSPEL, ENVIRONMENTALISM, AND POLITICS

The classics influencing Western political economy have included: Saint Augustine, *The Confessions* (New York,: Image Doubleday, 1960); Dino Bigongiari, ed., *The Political Ideas of St. Thomas Aquinas* (New York: Hafner, 1952); Matthew Fox, *Sheer Joy: Eight Conversations with Thomas Aquinas on Creation Spirituality* (San Francisco: Harper Collins, 1992); Sebastian de Grazia, *Machiavelli in Hell* (New York: Vintage, 1994); Niccolo Machiavelli, *The Discourses* (New York: Pelican, 1970); Thomas Hobbes, *Leviathan: Or the Matter, Forme and Power of a Commonwealth Ecclesiastical and Civil* (New York: Collier, 1962); and Lucius Annæus Seneca, *Letters from a Stoic* (New York: Penguin, 1969).

For the balance of powers, see James Madison, *The Federalist Papers*, nos. 14 and 51.

The Henry Commager quote is in Bruce Johansen, *Forgotten Founders: How the American Indian Helped Shape Democracy* (Boston: Harvard Common Press, 1982, 115). His work, along with that of Donald Grinde, is a pathbreaking effort to recover the role of native Americans on the idea of democracy.

The passages from Jean-Jacques Rousseau are from *The Social Contract* (New York: Penguin, 1968). See introduction by Maurice Cranstron (ibid., 28–29).

On power as "medicine": see the essay on the Anishnabeg by John Grim and D. P. St. John, "The Northeast Woodlands," in L. E. Sullivan, *Native American Religions: North America* (New York: Macmillan, 1989, 118); and also Cleland, *Rites of Conquest*, 67. The reference to Iroquois pine tree chiefs is in Johansen, *Forgotten Founders*, 28.

The reflections of Thomas Jefferson on Native Americans, including passages of *Notes on Virginia*, as well as the quotes by Franklin and Paine, are from Johansen, *Forgotten Founders*, 87 and 116; also see Donald Grinde and Johansen, *Exemplar of Liberty*, 179; on Delaware chief Tammany and Tammany Hall, 170–71.

For more on Jefferson's view of nature, see Charles A. Miller, *Jefferson and Nature: An Interpretation* (Baltimore: Johns Hopkins University Press, 1988, 200). Jefferson wrote in 1811 that "no occupation is so delightful to me as the culture of the earth, and no culture comparable to the garden." Nevertheless the garden had to be domesticated and cultivated for its value. Emerson on nature as "made to serve" and furrowed by the plow, is in Carolyn Merchant, *Earth Care, Women, and the Environment* (New York: Routledge, 1995, 38). See also Charles B. Sanford, *The Religious Life of Thomas Jefferson* (Richmond, VA: University of Virginia Press, 1984).

The small-scale republic is discussed in Montesquieu (David Wallace Carrithers, ed.), *The Spirit of the Laws*, (Berkeley: University of California Press, 1977). The statement that "it is natural to a republic to have only a small territory; otherwise it cannot long subsist," is from book VIII, chapter 15, 176. The views of Adam Smith are set forth in *The Wealth of Nations* (New York: Knopf, 1991).

For the Romantics versus the Hamiltonians, and the writings of Thomas Carlyle on machinery, see Leo Marx, *The Machine in the Garden: Technology and the Pastoral Ideal in America* (Oxford: Oxford University Press, 1964).

"I wish to speak a word on Nature" is from Henry David Thoreau, *Walking*, the edition that combines Thoreau's essay with Emerson's *Nature* (Boston: Beacon Press, 1991).

Emerson as a racist is in Luke Gibbons, "Post Colonialism and Irish Identity," in Trish Ziff, ed., *Distant Relations* (CITY: Smart Art Press, 1996).

On Transcendentalism, see Frederick Turner, *Rediscovering America: John Muir in His Time and Ours* (San Francisco, Sierra Club Books, 1985); Perry Miller, *The Transcendentalists: An Anthology* (Cambridge: Harvard University Press, 1950); Robert Richardson, *Henry Thoreau: A Life in the Mind* (Berkeley: University of California Press, 1986); and Lee Clark Mitchell, *Witnesses to a Vanishing America: The Nineteenth Century Response* (Princeton, NJ: Princeton University Press, 1981). The de Tocqueville quote on American culture appears on page 2 of Mitchell's work. See also the history by Roderick Frazier Nash, *The Rights of Nature: A History of Environmental Ethics* (Madison, WI: University of Wisconsin Press, 1989); also Nash, *Wilderness and the American Mind* (New Haven, CT: Yale University Press, 1967); and Clarence Glacken, *Traces on the Rhodean Shore: Nature and Culture in Western Thought in Ancient Times to the End of the Eighteenth Century* (Berkeley: University of California Press, 1967).

The Thoreau reference to America as Eden is in *Walking*, 93. His reference to politics as the "cigar smoke of man" is also in *Walking*, 81. See also Thoreau, *Walden and Civil Disobedience* (New York: Penguin, 1983) especially the essay "When I Lived," 125–43.

Robert Gottlieb's excellent history is *Forcing the Spring: The Trans-*

formation of the American Environmental Movement (Washington, D.C.: Island Press, 1993).

Aldo Leopold's essay "The River of the Mother of God" (1924) was found in his desk after his death. It was considered the "most poignant of Leopold's wilderness essays" by Susan Flader and J. Baird Callicott, who gave the same title to their edited collection of Leopold's essays (Madison, WI: University of Wisconsin Press, 1991, 123–27). In this essay, Leopold makes his observation that humans are the first creatures to create their environment "in a spiritual sense," in contrast to the quantitative impact of the "Gigantosaurus."

Rachel Carson's lyrical ode to the sea is in *The Sea Around Us*.

"Buddhist economics" is explained by E. F. Schumacher in *Small Is Beautiful: Economics as if People Mattered* (New York: Harper and Row, 1973).

Herman Daly on moral growth and biblical economics is found in "A Biblical Economic Principle and the Steady-State Economy," in Carol Robb and Carl Casebolt, *Covenant for a New Creation*, op. cit. (New York: Orbis, 1991, pp. 47–60). For the Isaiah quote, also see Daly, "On Biophysical Equilibrium and Moral Growth," in Daly, *Steady State Economics*, 2nd edition (Washington, D.C.: Island Press, 1991, pp. 168–77).

Governor Pat Brown's quote on the Water Project as a monument to himself is in Norris Hundley, *The Great Thirst* (Berkeley: University of California Press, 1992, 279). The statement that the Mono Lake decision was "radical" is on page 338.

The joint agenda of the "top ten" environmental groups is in *An Environmental Agenda for the Future* (Washington, D.C.: Island Press, 1985, 6, 7).

Newt Gingrich's proposals to mine the moon and place mirrors in space to fight crime on earth can be found in his book, *A Window of Opportunity: A Blueprint for the Future* (New York: St. Martin's Press, 1984).

Robert Reich's economic philosophy is spelled out in his *The Next American Frontier* (New York: Times Books, 1983) and *Work of Nations* (New York: Knopf, 1991).

The conclusion that the computer world is using more paper than ever is from *PC* magazine (May 25, 1993): 112.

Denis Hayes, cited in Mark Dowie, *Losing Ground: American Environmentalism at the Close of the Twentieth Century* (Boston: M.I.T. Press, 1995, 26).

Al Gore on faith and inner ecology is in *Earth in the Balance.*

The writings of Václav Havel, including his excellent "Politics of Hope," are in *Disturbing the Peace* (New York: Knopf, 1990, 165–206). His environmental remarks were made in the Tanner Lecture at the University of California, Los Angeles (Oct. 25, 1991).

The call for irrigating the spirit instead of the ego is in Donald Worster, *Rivers of Empire: Water, Aridity, and the Growth of the American West* (London: Oxford University Press, 1985, 335).

The effort by public relations strategists to manipulate the environmental movement is from John Stauber and Sheldon Rampton, *Toxic Sludge Is Good for You: Lies, Damn Lies, and the Public Relations Industry* (Monroe, ME: Common Courage Press, The Center for Media and Democracy, 1995, 66–67).

Polling on environmental values is from Willett Kempton, James Boster, Jennifer Hartley, *Environmental Values in American Culture* (Boston: M.I.T. Press, 1995) and the *Los Angeles Times* (Dec. 12, 1993).

Index

Index

Index

Grinde, Donald, 147*n*
Guide of the Perplexed (Maimonides), 77–78

Halifax, Joan, vii–viii, 175
Hamilton, Alexander, 194
Handlin, Oscar, 112, 113–14
Havel, Václav, 226–27, 232
Hawken, Paul, 210
Hawking, Stephen, 53–54, 79
Hawthorne, Nathaniel, 88
Hayes, Denis, 222
Heaney, Seamus, 107
Hebrew Scriptures
    nature mysticism in, 72–73, 74–75
    prophet in, 239
    rebellion against monotheism, 83
Helvarg, David, 65
Henderson, Hazel, 210
Hertzberg, Arthur, 47
Hesse, Hermann, 160–63
Hetch Hetchy Valley Dam, 205
Hildegard of Bingen, 5, 77
Hinduism and Ecology (Prime), 163–64*n*
Hinduism, environmental ethic and, 48, 49, 163–64*n*
Hirsch, E. D., 40, 41
Hobbes, Thomas, 188

I and Thou (Buber), 28
Index of Leading Cultural Indicators, The (Bennett), 40–41
Indigenous cultures. *See also* Native Americans
    earth-based spirituality, 5
    nature mysticism, 74, 103–5

relation to sun, 27
    vanishing, 105
Infertility, chemical exposure and, 8
Intergovernmental Panel on Climate Change, 6
Ireland
    Celtic spirituality, 106–8
    clachan and *rundale* agricultural system, 108, 110
    early Christian spirituality, 108–9
    emigration from, 112–14, 115–17
    Great Hunger of 1840s, 110–11
    Irish language, 106, 110
Iroquois Confederacy, 145, 189, 190
Iroquois League, 192
Islam, environmental ethic, 48
Islam and Ecology (Khalid), 48

Jameson, Frederic, 55
Japan
    energy conservation techniques, 215
    environmental policies, 179–80
    nuclear program, 180–81
    religion and state, 178–81
Jefferson, Thomas, 190, 193, 195
Jewel Net of Indra, 168
Jewish Guide to Environmental Studies, 81
Job, Book of, 101
    eco-consciousness in, 78–81
John Paul I, Pope, 61–62
Judaism
    chosenness, 240–41
    environmental ethic, 47–48, 62
Judeo-Christian religions. *See also* Nature mysticism

Index

Naropa Institute, 175

National Partnership on Religion and the Environment, 14–15, 68, 70, 78, 243

funding, 69

Native Americans

California history, 125–36

ecological contributions, 144–47

genocide and ecocide, 141–42, 147–48

land relatedness, xiii–xiv

Michigan history, 117–21

slavery, 135–36

view of power, 189–92

war of extermination, 135–36

Natural Resources Defense Council, 123, 217

Nature

domination of, 36

within ourselves, 11

as resource, 55–60, 186–87

treatment of in participatory democracies, 203–4

Nature (Emerson), 197, 200

Nature mysticism

Celtic cultures, 106–14

decline of, 108–14

in Hebrew scriptures, 72–73, 74–76

in indigenous cultures, 103–5

vs. monotheism, 73

recovering, 87–89

separation from mainstream Christian religion, 81–82

Nature-based religion, 165–66

in Buddhism, 181–83

New Biology, The (Augros, Stanciu), 3–4*n*

New World Order, The (Robertson), 61

Newton, Isaac, 53, 188–89

Nixon, Richard, 89

Nixon administration's environmental laws, 214

Notes on Virginia (Jefferson), 190

Nuclear power plants, subsidies for, 236

On Princely Rule (St. Thomas Aquinas), 187

"On the Pulse of Morning" (Angelou), 184–86

Origin of Species (Darwin), 200

O'Toole, Fintan, 108, 109

Overgrazing, 7

Oxford Illustrated History of Christianity, 47, 86

Padmasmambhava, 174*n*

Pagan worship, 83–85

Paine, Thomas, 139, 190

Parker, Theodore, 197

Parkman, Francis, 137

Participatory democracy, treatment of nature in, 203–4

Passenger pigeon, extinction of, 118, 141

Persian Gulf War, environmental dimensions, 42–43

Pesonen, Everett, xxiii, xxiv

Pinchot, Gifford, 205

Politics

American political vision, 192–95

as machine, 188–89, 193

Index